John Haydon
1700-1774
(74)

|

Joseph Kelland Down
(d.1801)
= Elizabeth Eltingham
1757-1830 (73)

John Haydon
1726-1788 (62)
= Jane Langdon
1744-1806 (62)

Sarah
1769-1845 (76)
= Peter Duthoit

Joseph Almond Down
1783-1848 (65)

=

Hannah Haydon
1785-1870 (85)

Jane Elizabeth Down
1809-1890 (81)

Sarah
1820-1901 (81)
= Philip Crellin

John Langdon Haydon Down
1828-1896 (68)
= Mary Crellin (in 1860)

Laura
1839-1873
(34)

Emiline
1841-1875
(34)
= John Lilley
Anthony

Palmer
1842-1913
(71)
= Harriet Hall
1855-1947 (92)

Clara
1844-1874
(30)

Gerard
1849-1934
(85)
= Elizabeth
Cliff

Charles Ford
1887-1974 (87)

Walter Langdon
1870-1946 (76)
= i Frances Pressland
(d.1931)
ii Freda Hurry (d.1949)

John Harold
1873-1957 (84)
= Ellen Carse Easdale
1878-1958 (80)

Everard Kenneth
1879-1958 (79)

Muriel Eleanor Haydon Lloyd
1893-1939 (46)

John Neville Brown
1904-
= i Ursula Dimsdale
1892-1977 (85)
ii Elske Nalder
iii Ann Skevens

Helen Easdale
1907-1977 (70)
= Wilfrid Dimsdale
1906-1981 (75)

DISSENTING
FORBEARS

John Maynard Keynes in 1940.

DISSENTING FORBEARS

The Maternal Ancestors of
J.M.KEYNES

Neville Brown

Phillimore

1988

Published by
PHILLIMORE & CO. LTD.
Shopwyke Hall, Chichester, Sussex

© Neville Brown, 1988

ISBN 0 85033 670 8

Printed and bound in Great Britain by
RICHARD CLAY LTD.
Bungay, Suffolk

Contents

List of Illustrations

Frontispiece: John Maynard Keynes in 1940

The author is grateful to the following people and institutions for permission to reproduce illustrations: Guildhall Library, London, no. 4; Ordnance Survey nos. 12, 19-22, 37, 68; Laidlaw Thompson Ltd., no. 36; John Rylands Library, Manchester (Kenneth Brown Collection), no. 45; University of Liverpool, no. 49; Faber & Faber, no. 54; Press Association, no. 69; Photo Source Ltd., nos. 84, 85 and 86.

Acknowledgements

One can compile a history of a family in earlier centuries from the writings of its members, from those around them and from public records, but when one reaches the present century contemporary assistance is necessary.

I am particularly indebted to Professor Sir Austin Robinson, C.M.G., F.B.A., not only for the Foreword he has been kind enough to contribute but also for much helpful comment. As pupil, colleague, biographer of Maynard Keynes, as editor of his writings and as one who gave much of his life to working with Keynes, no one is better qualified.

Family assistance is vital and I have been fortunate in having had much. Richard and Anne Keynes were so warmly approving of a draft of the earlier chapters that I felt encouraged to proceed, but I think that I might still have failed to continue had it not been for Milo Keynes. I knew him already to have a number of literary works to his credit and I have found him to be a most helpful and skilful adviser: indeed, I owe the title, *Dissenting Forbears*, to him. Further, he contributed the important part of the record of our uncle, Sir Walter Langdon-Brown. David Hill has contributed a sketch of his mother, Margaret (born Keynes). Polly Hill and Simon Keynes, both authors of experience, knew the labours which I was taking upon myself and helped, not least, by letting me draw on their fine collection of family photographs. John and Janet Humphrey (born Hill) supplied photographs and much encouragement. Philippa Hill, Maurice's widow, thought that the extraordinary contribution to the public good made by Florence Keynes (born Brown) needed emphasising and gave me much valuable material. My nephew, Nicholas Dimsdale, compiled a table of the Retail Price Index over the last two centuries to which I have referred throughout. There is little that Suzanne Rendell, who was at my Aunt Florence's side from 1942 till the end, does not know about us and no one with a kinder judgement as to what to disclose and what not. I am much indebted to her.

I have thus had warm support when writing as a matter of family piety (though, of course, this does not imply agreement when I express personal opinions) and am deeply grateful.

The Principal of Newnham College, Miss Sheila Browne, the Bursar, Mrs. D. Hahn and the Librarian, Miss Ann Phillips, could not have been more helpful in giving details of Jessie Lloyd's (born Brown) benefaction for the building of the Principal's Lodge in memory of her daughter, Muriel, nor the Master of Christ's College, Professor Sir Hans Kornberg, F.R.S., for telling of her husband, Albert Lloyd's association with that college.

The family has been strong in Medicine ever since Dr. John Langdon Down (who first described the congenital defect now known as 'Down's Syndrome'), and, with the help of Milo, I have drawn fully on obituaries which appeared in *The Lancet*, *The British Medical Journal*, *Munk's Roll*, publications of the Royal College of Surgeons and others. Miss Jean Ferguson of the Royal College of Physicians, Edinburgh, threw light on Dr. Alice Brown and, in the case of my sister, Dr. Helen Dimsdale, I have had invaluable help from her colleagues, Dame Frances Gardener, Dame Josephine Barnes, Dr. Edith Gilchrist, Dr. A. M. Ramsay and Dr. Joan Harman.

Suffolk friends have helped too. Perenel Guild of Aspall Old Rectory has told me of her versatile great-great-grandfather, the Rev. John Chevallier, M.D., who officiated, not as a divine, but as a surgeon, at the birth of David Everard Ford at Long Melford in 1797. Muriel Kilvert, great-niece of the diarist, helped me in my examination of the Ford Diaries, whilst Mary Levy enlightened me on the points at issue in the politico-religious battles David Everard Ford fought, and Laurence Griffiths assessed the hymn tunes he wrote.

The wealth of knowledge and information housed in public and private libraries is accessible by reason of the devotion of librarians and archivists who never seem to become bored by tedious questions and go to great lengths to find what one wants. Miss Patricia Bell of the North Bedfordshire County Council Record Office and A. S. Frankland of the Salford Local History Library produced, not only material for which I asked, but material of great interest of which I did not know. I got much help from the staff of the Guildhall Library, the British Library Map Library, the Law Society, John Rylands Library, Manchester, the Westminster Central Library, the Holborn Libraries, University Archives, Liverpool, the Royal College of Veterinary Surgeons' Wellcome Library, as well as from public bodies such as the Metropolitan Borough of Stockport and the County Councils of Cambridge, Cornwall, Essex, Suffolk and the Lymington and Pennington Town Council. Other bodies to whom I am indebted include Yale University, Lloyds of London, the Manchester Ship Canal Company, the National Council of Women of Great Britain and the Police Federation of England and Wales. Nonconformist associations have helped, including the United Reformed Church History Society and the Baptist Union of Great Britain and Northern Ireland.

Friends and individuals who have given valuable information include David R. Wightman and A. P. Goodwin of Turner Kenneth Brown, Edward Weston of St Brelade, Jersey, Paul A. G. Dixey, Alan Circket of the Bunyan Meeting, George Abel of Salisbury and Bill Williams on the subject of Manchester Jewry. Laidlaw Thompson gave me the free run and photographs of Park Chapel, Manchester. Thos. Agnew & Sons Ltd. confirmed the original ownership of Richmond Hill, Salford. R. W. Alcock, when proprietor of Buttermarket Studio, Ipswich, got more out of faded old photographs than one would have thought possible.

And, but for Virginia Milne of our nearby village of Easton, I should never have completed this history. Her patience and skill in reading my writing, typing and retyping and, finally, in indexing, have been outstanding.

NEVILLE BROWN

Kettleburgh
Woodbridge
Suffolk
1987

Foreword

by

SIR AUSTIN ROBINSON

Emeritus Professor of Economics, Cambridge University

This book is by design, and most successful performance, a family history, written by the eldest member of the family for the benefit of grandchildren, great-grandchildren and others in the family of a similar generation. Neville Brown possesses an amazing stock of family records and has unearthed more, and I am certain that the young members of the family will be fascinated in what he has been able to discover and record.

But for those like myself who cannot claim the privilege of being part of the family, this book has a quite different and equally fascinating interest. Neville Brown, whom I first knew 65 years ago when he was an undergraduate studying economics in Cambridge and I was a young fledgling teacher learning how to teach economics, is a nephew of Florence Brown who married Neville Keynes and mothered those three remarkable children, Maynard Keynes, the greatest economist of the 20th century, Geoffrey Keynes, one of the very great surgeons and equally distinguished as literary editor and bibliographer, and Margaret, who married the great physiologist, A. V. Hill, and who, like her mother before her, was a great innovator in active social welfare.

Thus I cannot help reading this book – and the author does everything to help and encourage me – as the pedigree of a genius. Where did the amalgam of qualities that made up Maynard Keynes come from? Neville Brown has his views about some of the contributors. I have mine. We do not, I think, always agree. But here, so far as it can be provided, is the evidence on which one can speculate.

I say 'speculate' deliberately. Despite all the remarkable work of the past century, no serious scientist would, I think, claim that it is an exact study, or that the results of breedings are at all precisely predictable in individual cases. One has only to look at the difference between brothers and sisters to be aware of the uncertainties. For some two hundred years race-horse owners have been trying with no certain success to solve the problem of how to breed a Derby winner. We do not know how to breed a genius. But Derby winners do not come by pure chance from accidental matings of horses with no claim to past distinction. It is not wholly profitless to study the ancestry of such a person as was Maynard Keynes and to look in his ancestors for qualities that were predominant in him. And curiously this had always interested Maynard himself. What we know of the Keynes family as distinct from the Brown family largely comes from work that he, himself, did as a schoolboy at Eton.

In reading the manuscript with this in mind, I realised that the qualities for which I was looking were not always the same as those for which Neville Brown was looking. This brought home the difficulties of being certain what one was looking for. Maynard Keynes had an immense variety of facets and a wide variety of groups of people in which he exercised his gifts. Most of us (I certainly) knew him in only a few of his facets and did not know him over the full range. Thus it was very easy for any one person to see in him certain qualities that he possessed in abundance and which one valued and wished that one possessed oneself.

Neville Brown, born in Manchester, seeing him mostly in the 1920s, himself a good Manchester Liberal, sees Maynard as the perfect Manchester Liberal, occasionally in later life when exhausted, falling into error. I, myself, closest to Maynard Keynes in the last years of his life when he was maturing the thinking that went into the *General Theory* and convincing himself and most economists that the economic system was not self-righting, feel convinced that Keynes changed and matured between 1920 and 1936. By 1936 he was, as I see him, no longer the simple uncritical liberal, though he certainly was never the woolly uncritical socialist that some of his disciples would have us believe. But my point is that I find myself possibly looking for somewhat different characteristics in his ancestry than Neville Brown is seeking, and in particular for capacity to seek truth at whatever cost and to change one's thinking when pursuit of the truth required it.

That apart, what are the qualities for which one is looking. I would say, above all else, a penetrating quickness of mind, an intuitive grasp of what must be the solution of a problem which led him to see the answer first and then use his immense analytical powers to justify and corroborate his conclusions. I always remember that it was his niece, Polly Hill, who lived with Maynard and Lydia at Gordon Square during the War and thus saw much of them, who told me that he had a feminine mind.

Where then did Maynard Keynes's outstanding characteristics come from? In the obituary I wrote for the *Economic Journal* immediately after his death in 1946 from which Neville Brown quotes, I, perhaps rashly, attributed his administrative precision and concern with getting the detail right to the Keynes element in his make-up. I attributed his quick intuitions to his mother and the Browns. Neville Brown agrees with me and, with much more evidence, I have not changed my mind.

I knew both his father and his mother, the father only slightly, the mother rather better. In the Cambridge of the 1920s, much smaller and more intimate than today, one could not escape knowing about the great university administrator who controlled all the activities of us minor beings. One had the impression of great capacity to handle detail and to solve problems. But he was very much more than a good civil servant. As an economist he was the only Cambridge critic that the great Alfred Marshall consulted and respected. His books on philosophy and on the scope and method of economics were fine pieces of thorough scholarship and clear thinking. But while he passed on many of these qualities to his son, I do not believe that the Keynes contribution to his make-up accounts for the qualities in Maynard that made him so exceptional.

In the case of his mother it was a very different thing. Throughout his life he was very close to his mother. In the crises of his life – during his agonies over the Versailles Conference for example – it was to his mother that he wrote. And she was much more than just a devoted mother. She had been one of the first Newnham students, with a first-rate mind and great practical judgement in whom Maynard found an intellectual equal. And she, in addition to all her own activities, lived his life also. The big memorial edition that we have published of the *Collected Writings of John Maynard Keynes* could hardly have been produced if she had not laboriously pasted daily into scrapbooks the press cuttings of all his more ephemeral writings and speeches. Neville Brown records her many activities and achievements.

Thus far I had myself known something of the story. It is when one comes to the make-up of Florence Keynes that the book takes one into a world of which I knew little or nothing. Florence Brown, as she was born, was a daughter of a great Congregationalist minister, himself a fine scholar, biographer and custodian of Bunyan and his chapel, of whom I have learned a lot from this book. She undoubtedly inherited much from him. But, again, it is her mother that I, following Neville Brown, find most remarkable.

Ann Haydon Brown, born in 1837, was a forceful and dominating but at the same time caring and affectionate character. Under her mother she had first learned how to teach and run a small school. In the days before state schools and while church schools required adherence to the church, there were frequently demands from Congregationalist parents for local schools for their daughters. After marriage to John Brown and their move from Manchester to Bedford, she had started a school there which she ran successfully for many years. Florence Keynes was taught by her before becoming one of the early women students at Cambridge.

It is when one tries to account for the make-up of Ada Haydon Brown that I begin to have views of my own. She had been born Ada Haydon Ford, one of five daughters and three sons born to two remarkable parents, David Everard Ford and Jane Elizabeth (born Down).

David Everard Ford was unquestionably a great man and a strong personality. Neville Brown possesses many documents descending from him and seems to have acquired an admiration of him. Born in 1797, the son of a Congregationalist minister he too, after a few unhappy years in business, was ordained to be Congregationalist minister at Lymington in Hampshire and while there married. But after some seven years of ministry, he and his congregation fell out of sympathy, and for some years he earned what he could as a supply preacher, serving for a few weeks at a time all over the country. Thereafter, he was appointed minister of a newly-established chapel in Manchester. There he remained for nine years, apparently happy. The congregation were largely well-to-do middle-class merchants. But he and the deacons of the chapel began to find themselves at loggerheads over his preaching and, after nine years of ministry, he was in effect dismissed and for the rest of his life depended on the much lower earnings of an itinerant preacher, on the sales of books of devotion that he wrote, and on his wife's earnings from two schools that she organised.

I do not doubt that he was a remarkable man, of strong personality. But I find it difficult to identify in him contributions to the make-up of Maynard Keynes. Indeed in many respects I find him the antithesis of Maynard – temperamental, mercurial, easily depressed, where Maynard was eternally buoyant, able to face unpleasant facts, to play Cassandra, but to come up with a plan to overcome them; lacking in self-confidence and defeatist where Maynard was always full of self-confidence and the courage to fight back, as he did when things went wrong at Versailles; verbose in literary style where Maynard had an incomparable gift of compression and tight writing. The quality that Neville Brown finds in the two of them is a tendency to dramatise. I do not deny its occasional appearance in the great-grandson, but I think it was only conversational and momentary and did not cloud his thinking.

But I think my own doubts about the contribution of the great-grandfather derive largely from admiration for the great-grandmother, Jane Elizabeth Down. She, when David Everard Ford persuaded her – I had almost written bullied her – into marrying him, was already running a school of her own in Plymouth. She continued through most of the rest of her life to set up and run small schools for the education of the daughters of her Dissenter friends, first in Lymington, while bearing the earlier of her eight children, and later, first one school in Manchester and then a second, when her elder daughters were old enough to take charge. It was she who provided the backbone of the family, the security of its income, the power of self-criticism. It was she also, I suspect to Neville Brown's irritation, who destroyed parts of her husband's private diary, kept secret from her, or wrote in it pungent comments of disagreement. I suspect that she was usually right and that David Everard Ford used his diary, as many military commanders and top politicians have done, as a safety-valve for the tribulations of the day rather than as a balanced appraisal for posterity. I wish we had more of her serious judgements and depended less on her irritated comments on her husband's exaggerations.

She, in her turn, was mothered by Hannah Haydon, daughter of John Haydon, born in 1700, schoolmaster, mathematician, contributor to the 18th-century research on the problems of navigation inspired by Pepys's navy, and Jane Langdon. Haydon, himself, almost certainly comes from a great and talented Devonshire family. But here history runs out.

Fascinated by the female line, I have almost certainly exaggerated its importance. I have paid far too little attention to the Keyneses, tracing back to Normandy, to the Fords and the Everards, all of whom made their contributions. All of this, so far as documentation exists, is here for a reader to explore and interpret for himself. There is far too little literature seeking to explain the descent and make-up of the geniuses of the world. Whether or not one always agrees with him, many who are interested generally as well as all those who are more particularly interested, as I am, in Maynard Keynes, will be deeply indebted to Neville Brown and all the work he has put into this most enthralling of family histories.

Cambridge, July 1987   AUSTIN ROBINSON

Introduction

I cannot remember when I first began to look at the Ford diaries seriously, though I had held them since 1958. Then, at the Keynes Centenary Celebrations in 1983, my cousin, Janet Humphrey, said to me, 'You ought to write a family history. When my children ask me about it, I don't know what to tell them'.

It was as the last surviving grandchild of John and Ada Brown (born Ford) that the famly records passed to me. They comprise books, diaries, sermon registers, autobiographies and letters stretching over two centuries. They throw much light on the social history of the times as well as the progress of the family.

In my generation we also knew much which had come down to us verbally, and this I have tried to preserve. In writing, there is Florence Keynes's *Gathering up the Threads*, published by Heffer of Cambridge in 1950 when she was eighty. It is a little masterpiece. Sir Walter Langdon-Brown's *Thus we are Men*, collected essays and papers, published by Kegan Paul in 1938, show a man of vision ranging far beyond the profession in which he was eminent. The Royal Economic Society published *The Collected Writings of John Maynard Keynes* (29 vols. 1971-83). And there is Sir Geoffrey Keynes's distinguished autobiography, *The Gates of Memory*, published by the Clarendon Press in 1981, when he was ninety-four. It covers a vast field, far wider than the family.

Like very many families we can, with certainty, trace our descent back to the early 18th century, but beyond there are only traditions which cannot be verified. In the 17th century the English had revolted, not only against absolute rule, but also against religious intolerance and would not allow William and Mary to accede to the throne unless they would agree the Act of Toleration of 1689, by which Protestant Dissenters gained freedom to worship and to preach and to teach. It was as preachers and teachers that most of our ancestors emerged. John Everard (1730-1806) was a successful merchant and a Freeman of the City of London, but he was also a Baptist deacon and the smuggler's son, David Ford (1763-1836), became an Independent, that is to say, a Congregational minister, as did his son, David Everard Ford. These two Fords together preached 14,658 sermons between 1791 and 1875, and we know from their sermon register exactly where and when they preached, and can check mutilated and incomplete diaries. Dr. John Brown's sermon register began in 1850 and continued until 1917, and his handwriting is as firm and clear at the last entry as at the first. It is held by the County Records Office in Bedford, while I have his autobiography.

Thus, the framework within which the earlier generations of the family lived and worked was Nonconformity, and this is also true of the Keyneses, for Richard Keynes, Maynard's great-great-uncle, was a Congregational minister in Blandford in 1825. As we shall see, the paths of his grandfather, John Keynes, and his mother's grandfather, David Everard Ford, almost certainly crossed in a Salisbury chapel in 1832.

English Nonconformity began as a Puritan movement within the Church of England. It sought to bring ritual and organisation nearer to Lutheran and Calvinist forms, abolishing bishops and the clerical hierarchy but wished to remain within the Church. Parish clergy were to be elected presbyters (elders) and the wider organisation would be presbyteries, hence the Presbyterians of Cromwell's times. But some wanted to be independent of the Church of England and held that the only organisation should be the local congregation, hence the Independents and the Congregationalists. These the Church of England persecuted, under Elizabeth I's Act of Uniformity of 1559, and there were flights of refugees to Amsterdam and Leyden in the late 16th century. The Pilgrim Fathers who sailed in the *Mayflower* in 1620 were Congregationalists. The Baptists of 1611 were Independents; the Quakers appeared in 1647. Methodists and Unitarians did not appear until the 18th century. In 1972 the Congregationalists and the Presbyterian Church of England (but not of Scotland) joined together to become *The United Reformed Church in the United Kingdom*.

Though Nonconformity faded in importance after the 1914-18 War – even earlier – it had been a most powerful formative force in English history. Dr. David M. Thompson in his *Nonconformity in the Nineteenth Century*[1] cites four main contributions which he considers Nonconformity made and which I quote because they so clearly indicate what inspired some of the lives we shall be studying.

1. Nonconformity was largely responsible for the freedom of religion and the freedom of thought enjoyed in nineteenth century Britain. This established a tradition in which political liberty itself flourished.

2. Nonconformity provided the means, in an age before mass education, for many humble folk to improve themselves and find a sense of social identity.

3. Nonconformity saved England from anti-clericalism such as that which developed in the rest of Europe.

4. The religion of commitment and action associated with Nonconformity has played an important part in national and religious life. For some this meant social action; for others it meant political action. In this way Nonconformity has been the source of much of the idealism in British public life, and has contributed to both the Liberal and the Labour parties.

If one looks carefully in any English town or village, which has not been too greatly transformed by developers, one is struck by the great number of small unobtrusive chapels. They provided healthier meeting places for the young than discos and greater consolation for the old than bingo halls. Whilst the Church of England tended to be largely of the gentry, the Nonconformists reached the ordinary people and played no small part in establishing a standard of honesty and behaviour which at one time was the envy of the world.

The children of the Rev. Dr. John and Ada Brown all ceased to be chapel-goers, but none of them became church-goers and none of them came to regard their Nonconformist roots and tradition with other than affection and respect. They simply slipped painlessly into the agnosticism of their time. When I come to write of them, the scene ceases to be that of pastorates. The world of Florence Keynes, Sir Walter Langdon-Brown, Kenneth Brown, Lord Keynes and Sir Geoffrey Keynes was far wider, but in their approach to its problems there was much of the old Independents.

Some of the diaries and other family records, particularly those of David Everard Ford, mention sums of money. For these to have relevance we have to have some idea of their present equivalent. I have, therefore, inserted in parentheses after each figure quoted, the 1986 equivalent drawn from the table Nicholas Dimsdale has compiled. He would insist, however, that such comparisons can only be approximate and are to be treated with reserve.

In drawing up our genealogical tree, I have omitted some members of the very numerous families our forbears produced when they do not contribute to the main story. Nor do I extend the history beyond the grandchildren of John and Ada Brown: I do, however, list the succeeding generations.

I have written a short account of some members of your family, who are mere names to most of you. If I have dealt overmuch with their foibles, it must be remembered also that they belonged to an age which produced many famous men, but which depended largely for its greatness and prosperity on the English middle class. They were sturdy, upright and courageous, those professional men and traders of the Victorian age. They lived honest and decent lives. They seemed to know instinctively the difference between right and wrong, and they brought up their large families simply and in the fear of God.

Malcolm Letts
The Old House, A Generation of Lawyers

Chapter One

JOHN EVERARD
(1730-1806)

Freeman of the City of London

John Everard was a Silk Merchant in Spitalfields and one might be tempted to think that his ancestry was Huguenot, as his name, his trade and his habitat suggest. The main flood of Huguenot refugees reached this country in the 1680s fleeing the dragonnades, and the publications of the Huguenot Society of London give full lists of those who arrived. I have, however, been unable to find an Everard from whom we could be descended: nor have we a family tradition of Huguenot ancestry.

We know that John Everard's father, William, was a weaver in the parish of St Leonard's, Shoreditch, which would suggest that he was of earlier French or Flemish descent, and we know that he and his wife were religiously inclined, since they relished sermons preached by the Rev. George Whitefield, the founder of the Calvinistic Methodists. They also saw to it that their son was regularly apprenticed, in 1745, to a certain William Parker, a frame knitter.

Having served his apprenticeship, John Everard was Admitted and Sworn to the Worshipful Company of Frame Knitters in 1757 and, in 1762, was Admitted into the Livery and Cloathing of that Company. He was elected Master in 1780, clearly a successful man, held in esteem by his fellows. We have his seal and his silver-capped Malacca cane. Admission to his Guild in 1757 entitled him to become a Freeman of the City of London and I reproduce his certificate of admission, together with that of his great-great-granddaughter, Helen Easdale Dimsdale (born Brown). She, a doctor of medicine, was elected to the Apothecaries Guild and, hence, became a Freeman in 1965, 280 years after her ancestor.

Like his parents, he found the teachings of the Rev. George Whitefield of interest, for we have a notebook inscribed 'John Everard' and dated 7 November 1772, the first page of which reads: 'The Texts preached from the young men of Lady Huntingdon's College before their departure to America at the Tabernacle in Moorfields, London, beginning 19 October'.

Selina Hastings, Countess of Huntingdon (1707-91), was left a wealthy widow when she was thirty-nine. She was already a Methodist and, in 1751, appointed the Rev. George Whitefield to be her chaplain. She poured money into his extreme Calvinist branch of the Church of England, setting up chapels, one of which was the Moorfields' Tabernacle. In John Everard's notebook there are notes of some twenty texts and sermons and the name of each young man who preached. They are crudely evangelical in content and, if a fair sample of religious ideas fed into North America in the 18th century, would go far to explain some of the more remarkable versions of the Christian faith to be found there. One of the young men, by the name of William Larwell, took Solomon's Song, Chapter II, 'My beloved is mine and I am His', as his text and through 10 carefully numbered, closely argued paragaphs, explained how this meant that Christ was the Christians' Beloved. This would, no doubt, be an interpretation acceptable to the Countess and her chaplain.

John Everard had not the outlook of a religious extremist and though he went to hear the young Methodists preach and made notes of what they said, he, himself, was a Baptist, being a deacon, first at Redcross Street Chapel (EC1), and then at Devonshire Square Chapel, Spitalfields. He also allowed his daughter, Mary, to attend a Congregational

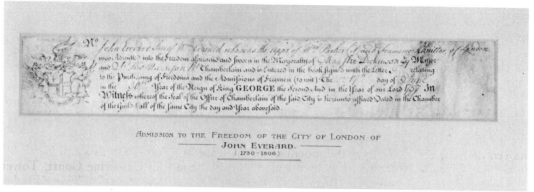

1. Certificate of Admission to the Freedom of the City of London of John Everard (1730-1806).

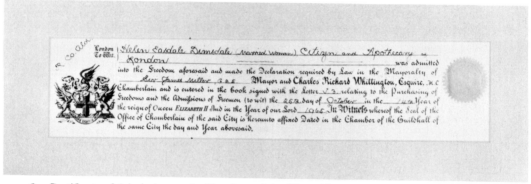

2. Certificate of Admission to the Freedom of the City of London of Helen Easdale Dimsdale (1907-1977).

chapel, where she met her future husband, David Ford. Mary's meeting with David was pleasantly romantic as we shall see when we come to his story. He was a student at the Homerton Academy for young men destined for the Congregational ministry. Their son, David Everard Ford, writes:

> At first Mr. Everard objected and looked very coldly on the prospects of a minister whose only independence was the independence of his principles. In due course he gave his full consent, though often drawing pictures greatly to the disadvantage of his eldest child. The second daughter, Elizabeth, was engaged to his partner in the business, Mr. Hale, and the third, Sarah, to a worthy member of the Stock Exchange, Mr. Duthoit.[1]

> Mr. Everard, my mother's father was a silk manufacturer in Spitalfields. At the time when my father made his acquaintance, he was guilty of what was thought a most wasteful piece of extravagance. In addition to his warehouse in Primrose Street, Bishopsgate, he occupied a country residence in Paradise Fields, Hackney. He used to say he was the second master silk weaver of his neighbourhood who ventured on such an experiment; and many were the predictions of speedy ruin which would result from such a course.[2]

The exodus to the suburbs, or surrounding country, is older than we are apt to think. Whilst Primrose Street is in the heart of the old Spitalfields (it is now the second bridge over the rail tracks leaving Liverpool Street Station, and members of the family should bow when passing under it), Paradise Fields were on the edge of open country. They were on the east of Mare Street in Hackney Village and were not built over till the 1850s. But even so they were not countryfied enough for John Everard because he let his house there in 1804 for 18 guineas a year (about £415) and moved to 9 Astley's Row, Islington. Astley's Row is still there, overlooking a curious narrow path with rocks and trees, now known as New River Walk. All the original houses have been rebuilt and the whole Row and Walk are surrounded with buildings, but it must have been a charming spot when John Everard moved there in 1804. We have the indenture of the lease he granted for his Paradise Fields house in which he is described as 'gentleman' but his tenant of Catherine Court, Tower Hill as 'merchant'. Niceties of this kind are the enduring stock-in-trade of solicitors' clerks.

We have various deeds respecting trust and loans. There is an interest-bearing bond of 1785 drawn in his favour by one, Miles Atkinson, of High Holborn for £200 and another to do with the same transaction for £500. The total, £700, would be about £30,000 in 1986. But, as well as being respected and of substance, he must have been likeable, or his grandson would not have written of him: 'I well remember the dear old man, his annual visit to Long Melford and his generous kindness to his grandchildren.[3] Under his George brown wig I used to fancy all the wisdom of the ancients'.[4]

In 1794, his eldest daughter, Mary, married the impecunious young Congregational pastor, David Ford, who had just been appointed to his first pastorate at Long Melford in Suffolk. After a comfortable family home with her father, mother and two sisters, she must have found the manse at Long Melford cheerless and remote, and one can doubt, in view of her husband's earnest melancholy, whether he was a young man with the gifts to cheer a homesick bride. She apparently wrote sadly to her father, because we have his reply:

> My dear Daughter, By the kindness of Mrs. D.[5] your kind, dutiful and affectionate letter came duly to hand. In reading it I was much affected to find your mind so much agitated at being separated from your friends and should be much more so if I was not persuaded time will in some measure cause an abatement as to the present sensation, but I doubt not but filial, childlike affections will continue as long as life shall endure. You seem to be distressed on account of your having been the occasion of grief to me at any time when you were with me, but I acquit you from any charge of that kind towards me and believe you were never wilfully or intentionally disobliging and do assure you that this is no small pleasure for me to reflect upon. Therefore, I beg you will not indulge any thoughts of that kind.

He ends with a religious discourse, normal to his beliefs and times, but there is no doubt of the strength of the family tie. We find in her husband's diary notes of the frequent and long visits she paid to her family in London throughout their married life. Though her name appears beside that of her husband on the tombstone in Long Melford, her remains were buried in the Everard family vault in Bunhill Fields. But there is no breath of criticism anywhere in her husband's voluminous writings and her sons write of her with much affection.

There was a close connection between the Everards and the Hales, a leading Dissenting family of Colchester. William Hale, already a wealthy young man, went into partnership with John Everard and married his second daughter, Elizabeth. He had an establishment in the semi-country of Homerton. It was described as a beautiful Georgian house with a marble bath and a Greek temple in its large garden. Elizabeth's nephew, David Everard Ford, her sister Mary's son, had happy memories of the Hale hospitality. He was to write: 'The good old English hospitalities of Homerton were my Christmas cheer, long after the

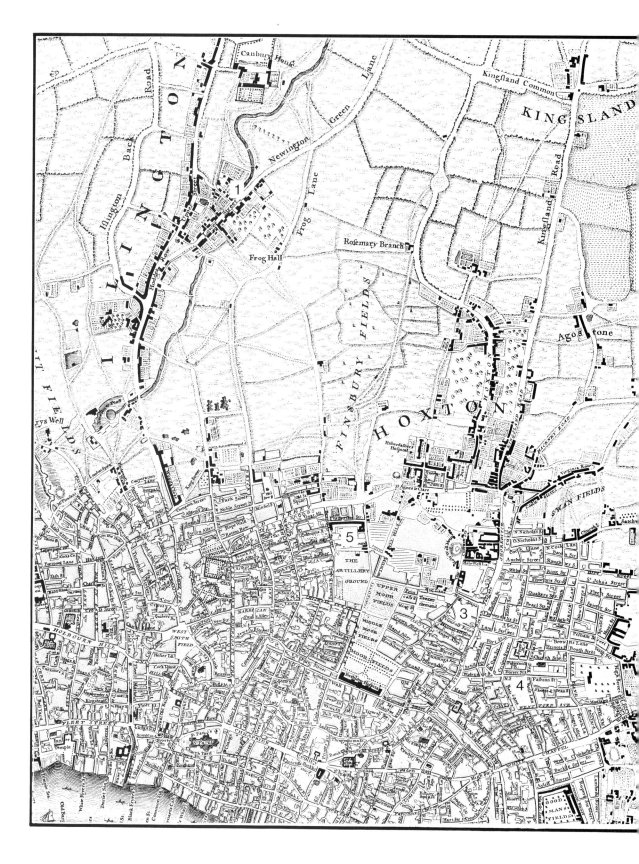

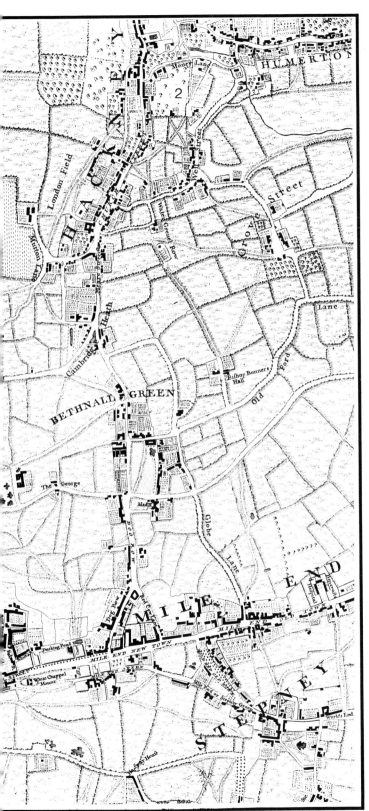

3. The City of London from John Rocque's Map, 1746.

1. Astley's Row
2. Paradise Fields
3. Primrose Street
4. White's Row
5. Bunhill Fields

Lower Street, Islington, is now Essex Road. Homerton is only half a mile north-east of Paradise Fields.

youngest of my cousins had outlived the age of snapdragons. They were happy gatherings. They cheered the dark days of my apprenticeship, and they gladdened my heart in the years of student life'.[6]

William Hale was not only genial and hospitable, he was also active in all manner of business and civic affairs and was described by the Rev. John Campbell of Kingsland as 'a man who has done more for the lessening of human misery in the metropolis than any man with whom I am acquainted'. He impressed upon his fellow manufacturers the futility of forcing down wages in times of depression, quoted Adam Smith at length, and advocated measures of which Maynard Keynes, a descendant of his partner, John Everard, would have approved.

He was also concerned about another notorious London problem, prostitution. He contested the value and wisdom of Female Penitentiaries for the 'abandoned harlots who parade the nocturnal walks of prostitution, the infamous seducers of our youth'. But where he was in power he was able to boast: 'There is not one house of ill-fame in our parish of Christchurch, Spitalfields, nor a prostitute suffered to parade our streets. If a woman of this description were to be seen, the watchman, upon whose walk she was discovered, would receive a severe reprimand for neglect of his duty'. He wrote a series of detailed addresses upon the subject from 1809 till 1812. This involved him in controversy with the *Evangelical Magazine* which advocated penitentiaries and religious tracts for 'poor midnight wanderers for bread', whereas he pointed out that the Overseers of the Poor were in a position to house the really destitute in the workhouse.

His writings were in splendid Johnsonian English published at his own expense, those on prostitution wrapped in unlettered brown paper so that they might not fall easily into the hands of the young.[7]

David Everard Ford's uncle Hale was clearly an acute observer with wide interests and an unusual command of English. He must have contributed much to the atmosphere of the Everards' circle which David frequented during his formative years.

Though we have only one of John Everard's letters, an attractive picture of him builds up. That he was much respected by his peers is clear from his election to Mastership of his Livery Company. He was happy in his relationships with his sons-in-law, one of whom, William Hale, was his partner in business, and he was kindly and much loved by his children and grandchildren.

Chapter Two

DAVID FORD
(1763-1836)

Son of a Smuggler

David Ford was born on 22 October 1763. We have both his own diary and the diary and autobiography of his son, David Everard Ford.

David Ford wrote in his diary that he was born at Broadwater, Sussex, but his son, David Everard Ford, writes, 'prior to my father's birth, as well as afterwards, his parents were residing not at Broadwater, but at Lancing'.[1] The memory of his father may have failed, or a certain degree of vagueness may have been desirable, because David Ford's father and uncle were smugglers. Thomas Ford, David's father, died in 1768 after an affray with Revenue men when out at night landing a cargo with his elder brother Robert. Just as the 'Black Economy' kept our houses habitable until recently, so smugglers kept the cellars of our ancestors stocked. David Everard Ford writes of smuggling, '. . . then the staple trade of the British coast and accounted no more a breach of any law, human or divine, than to catch a rabbit or to shoot a blackbird'.[2] He recounts:

> Passing that way in 1851, I met a very old man who told me Lancing had been his residence for 63 years. 'Then', said I, 'you can tell me something about my kindred'. 'I suppose I can', he said, 'but first you must tell me your father's name'. I did so. His eyes instantly sparkled with the light of other days. 'Ah, indeed', he said. 'I believe I can. Why, your father's brother was my first master. I lived in his service three years: and better it would have been for me now if I had lived with him for thirty. Ah, many a night have I been down on the coast for him with 150 horse at a time'. 'Smuggling, I suppose', said I. 'Yes, to be sure', replied the old man. 'Those were the days for poor folk to get a living! We wanted no Union Workhouse then. Ah, Sir, your uncle was a kind master and he took good care that nobody that served him should ever want'.[3]

This kind Robert Ford, who was unmarried, would surely have looked after his brother's widow and her three infants, the eldest of whom was David, aged four and a half, but he, Robert, also died in 1768. The widow, no doubt, did what she could, but David Everard writes, 'In consequence of some painful occurrence,[4] which he never explained, my father manfully quitted his mother's home when only about 12 years of age and betook himself to London in search of a livelihood'.[5] All that David Ford records in his own diary is, 'In July 1776, I was placed by providence in London with Wm. Harris, in Wood Street, who was a wholesale hosier – with him I continued nearly four years'. His son tells us why his father had to leave: 'One evening, without having asked permission, he carried a box for a servant who was leaving the family: for that very serious offence, he was turned into the streets, at night, without a home and without a friend. A kind providence, however, soon directed his steps to a more comfortable situation. It was to Lombard Street, at the corner of St George's Yard where there resided Mr. Goldfinch, a hatter'.[6]

He had the highest regard for Mr. Goldfinch, a religious man, and stayed with him seven and a half years. He was also much influenced by a pious old watchman whose box stood in St George's Yard. Having had an unsatisfactory home, it is probable that in the vice and squalor of 18th-century London, these two saved him. He began regularly to attend the Congregational Chapel in White's Row, Spitalfields. White's Row is still there, to be approached by Artillery Lane, across Bishopsgate from Liverpool Street Station. The

4. 'The Rev. Mr. Trotman's Meeting, in White's Row, Spittle Fields.'

chapel, then considered 'a noble structure', has gone and in its place are dreary Victorian houses and warehouses, but there is one worthy mansion, rather in the Dutch manner, which gives one some idea of the substantial nature of White's Row in David Ford's time. The minister at the chapel was the Rev. Nathaniel Trotman whose vigorous and dramatic sermons drew a congregation from near and far. There may have been an element of frenzy which attracted, for unfortunately he was to die in an asylum and suicide was rumoured.[7]

Unlike his son's, David Ford's writings are extremely uncommunicative and what account he may have written of his religious conversion is denied us. In his diary, he tells us in one pious page that he became a member of the White Row's chapel in 1784 and was received under the patronage of the King's Head Society.[8] The succeeding pages of his diary have been cut out till it tells of his arrival at Homerton, a Dissenting Academy, in 1787 aged 24, being student number one hundred and forty one.

The members of the King's Head Society were 'dealers in lace, linen, paint, tallow, tea, an upholsterer, a glover, a Spitalfields Silk Weaver, apothecaries, booksellers and stationers',[9] in other words, London tradesmen, the commercial middle class amongst whom so much of the strength and drive of English Dissent lay. To them the Church of England was the great oppressor. Under Elizabeth, James I and Charles I, oppression had involved violence leading to flight overseas, but the exclusive registration by the Church of the things about which people feel deeply, births, deaths and marriages, continued into the 19th century.

Dr. John Brown's pamphlet, *The Revolution of 1688* celebrating the bicentenary of the Act of Toleration, gives an excellent account of the removal, step by step, of the disabilities under which Dissenters and Roman Catholics had laboured. I think that the long struggle in which our ancestors engaged influenced the attitude of our family on many issues.

In distancing themselves from the Church of England and all its works, Dissenters deprived themselves of that miracle of faith, wisdom and beauty, the Book of Common Prayer. Their services were, therefore, dependent upon the personality and gifts of their pastors who had to have the power to lead them in prayer and sustain them in their faith by solid and inspiring discourse. This could not be done by men of little education, however burning their faith. Denied access to universities, Dissenters realised early that they had got to set up their own training colleges, and various groups did so. One of these was the King's Head Society which, in 1768, bought a mansion in High Street, Homerton with that object. Homerton was in the country to the north-east of the City. It was a pleasant village where city merchants, many of them Dissenters, were able to build themselves substantial houses with large gardens. We have seen that John Everard's partner, William Hale, acquired a fine house there.

The Dissenting Academies played an important part in the social history of this country and in the rise of our family. They were marked by high moral earnestness and much theological argument, at times contentious,[10] but they studied the sciences, modern history and philosophy, not studied at Oxford and Cambridge, which slumbered illiberally through the 18th century.

In 1847 when Prince Albert was elected Chancellor of the University of Cambridge and began his great reforms, almost all the fellows of Trinity and St John's Colleges were clergymen.[11] The best of the Dissenting academies, with their wider syllabuses, even in the 18th century attracted men like Harley and Bolingbroke – certainly not destined for the Dissenting ministry – and Defoe,[12] but they could not fill the gap in the higher educational framework of this country. One of the many causes of our failure to hold the technical and industrial lead which we had established in the early 19th century may have been the stranglehold which the Established Church, with its pre-Darwinian hostility to science, had on Oxford and Cambridge. The famous Dr. Jowett of Balliol, whose influence upon Oxford was profound, declared war upon science as late as 1884, writing, as Vice-Chancellor, that we 'have a hard and bitter battle to fight against the physical sciences . . . which will certainly lower the character of knowledge if they are not seriously counteracted'. The clergymen who predominated amongst the Masters and Fellows of their college had no wish to, nor could they, compete with the industrious scientific academics of Berlin and Heidelberg engaged in turning out the men who were to build the modern industrial Germany, and an approach to industry and commerce to which America also turned, rather than to the English rule of thumb. British industry began to fall behind those of Germany and America by the 1880s, but our massive world interests kept us in the top league until 1914-18. The Cambridge of the Cavendish Laboratory and Science Park did not appear in time.

The Homerton Academy had its ups and downs, but under the Congregational Board of Education it served the intentions of its founders all through the 19th century. Homerton, E.9, however, became less and less salubrious. Cholera outbreaks were sustained at times. In 1893, the Congregational Union financed the take-over by the Homerton Academy of the land and buildings of the defunct Cavendish College, Cambridge. Men were no longer admitted and it became the leading Women's Teacher training college. Today, Homerton College is an approved society in the University of Cambridge from which both men and women proceed to degrees in Education. The 18th-century London tradesmen builded better than they knew.

It would not have been possible for David Ford, employed as a hatter's assistant, to sustain himself from 1787, when he entered the Homerton Academy, till 1794, when he was appointed to his first pastorate, but for a legacy from his kind, smuggler uncle Robert.[13] Profits made in one calling were used to fertilise another.

The chapel in White's Row, where the Rev. Nathaniel Trotman was drawing large congregations, was also attended by Mary Everard, eldest daughter of John Everard, the successful silk merchant, then living three-and-a-half miles away in Paradise Fields, Hackney. Mary must have been a girl of some independence because, though her family were keen Baptists, she continued to walk three-and-a-half miles out and three-and-a-half miles back to sit under a Congregational preacher. Perhaps she had noticed the gaze of the shy young man, David Ford, whom she knew to be a student at Homerton and who already knew that she lived in Hackney. A rainy day gave the young man, who had an umbrella, the chance to escort the pretty girl. Their son was to write, 'That single walk was to lead to a happy mutual pilgrimage of nearly 40 years'.[14]

David Ford had entered the Homerton Academy in 1787 at the rather advanced age of twenty-four. We do not know the year he first became acquainted, in the rain, with Mary Everard, but there could be no question of marriage until he obtained Pastoral Office. His sermon register tells us something of his progress because students were encouraged to engage in extra-mural preaching. His first public sermon was preached at Coggeshall in Essex on 24 December 1791, from the text, Corinthians II, Chap. 7 verse 6 'Nevertheless God, that comforteth those who are cast down, comforted us by the coming of Titus'. Our young Titus evidently thought he might be adequate. A year later, 30 December 1792, he preached to a London congregation, a congregation, no less, than that at White's Row, accustomed to Mr. Nathaniel Trotman and it must have been something of an ordeal, all the more so because 'Received only two hours notice, was therefore obliged to preach No. 14' is entered in his diary. Number 14 had been tried, also on rural Coggeshall. But he was doing well, because on 10 June 1793 he preached at the New Broad Street Chapel at what he notes was 'Probationary sermon before ministers, called pass trials'.

In his sermon register there are, at first, three columns headed 'with notes', 'without notes' and 'partly with notes'. In his first year he filled in the totals showing seven, fifteen and seven respectively. From his 30th sermon onwards he nearly always preached 'without notes'. For the next three years, during which he preached 440 sermons, he went on recording in a single column that he had preached without notes. Thereafter, that column disappears so that we can assume that for the succeeding 6,705 sermons he was to preach, he did not use notes.

We know from his sermon register that during 1793 he preached a number of times at Coggeshall and other places in North Essex, such as Little Baddow and Halstead. Long Melford is in South Suffolk and when the pastor there died, the deacons would have soon heard from their brethren in North Essex that young David Ford from London was available as a supply preacher. They invited him to preach on 29 December 1793.

This chapel was built in 1725.[15] It is of substantial and unusually good secular design as compared with the general run of chapels. It is said to have been influenced by the halls of city guilds which were, on occasion, let to Nonconformists for services. The pastorate of Long Melford includes the neighbouring villages of Glemsford and Foxearth and their funds were united, the endowments being conditional upon the minister preaching once a fortnight at Glemsford and also at Foxearth. These endowments invested in three per cent. Consols yielded about £55 (£2,200) annually. In addition to endowment income there would also be pew rents which would rise if the preacher could draw a bigger congregation. David Ford continued to preach at Long Melford and its dependencies and on 25 March 1794 received an invitation from the deacons of Long Melford to become their pastor.

David Ford did not accept the invitation to the pastorate of Long Melford until his prospective father-in-law, John Everard, had made the eight hours' coach journey on 19

A List of Sermons preached, ᵇ D.F— Publickly

Num:	Text	with notes	with: notes	partly with notes	Place	Date
1.	2 Cor: 7: 6		Dᵒ		Coggeshall 1	Deᶜʳ 27 Tues 1791
2	Acts 13.26		Dᵒ		Dᵒ 2	Jany 3 Dᵒ 1792
3	Psal: 31. 23.4			Dᵒ Dᵒ	3	July 15 Sab: Mᵍ
4	Rom: 7: 24	Dᵒ		Dᵒ	4	Dᵒ 15 Dᵒ Aᶠᵗ
5	1 Cor: 3. 11			Dᵒ Dᵒ	5	Dᵒ 17. Tues: Evᵍ
6	Acts 17.31	Dᵒ		Dᵒ	6	Dᵒ 22 Sab: Mᵍ
7	1 Joh: 4: 10	Dᵒ		Dᵒ	7	Dᵒ 22 Dᵒ Evᵍ
8	2 Tim 2.19			Dᵒ Dᵒ	8	Dᵒ 24 Tues Evᵍ
9	Deut: 29:29		Dᵒ		Dᵒ	9	Dᵒ 29. Sab: Mᵍ
10	Acts 17: 31	Dᵒ			Little Baddow 1	Aug: 12 Dᵒ Mᵍ
11.	Acts 14:22		Dᵒ		Dᵒ 2	Dᵒ 12. Dᵒ Aᶠᵗ
12	Heb: 6: 18		Dᵒ		Coggeshall 10	Dᵒ 19 Dᵒ Aᶠᵗ
13	Rom: 6: 14		Dᵒ		Dᵒ 11	Dᵒ 26. Dᵒ Evᵍ
14	2 Cor 12. 9		Dᵒ		Dᵒ 12	Sep: 2 Dᵒ Mᵍ
15	2 Cor: 13:11		Dᵒ		Dᵒ 13	Dᵒ 2 Dᵒ Aᶠᵗ
16	2 Cor 12: 9		Dᵒ		White Row 1	Dᵒ 30. Dᵒ Aᶠᵗ
17.	Rom: 7:24	Dᵒ			Dᵒ 2	Octᵒ 2: Tues Evᵍ
18.	Tit: 1: 2		Dᵒ		Coggeshall 14	Deᶜʳ 23 Sab: Mᵍ
19	Joh: 3: 16			Dᵒ Dᵒ	15	Dᵒ 23 Dᵒ Evᵍ
20	Matth: 28:5:6			Dᵒ Dᵒ	16	Dᵒ 30 Dᵒ Mᵍ
						1793
21	1 Cor 1:23.4			Dᵒ Dᵒ	17	Jany 1: Tues: Evᵍ
22	Psal: 51: 12			Dᵒ Dᵒ	17	Dᵒ 6 Sab: Aᶠᵗ
23	Joh: 15: 16	Dᵒ			White Row 3	Dᵒ 29 Tues: Evᵍ
24	Jer: 23:6		Dᵒ		Dᵒ 4	Feby 3. Sab: Mᵍ
25	Ephes: 4:20	Dᵒ			Dᵒ 5	Dᵒ 5 Tues: Evᵍ
26	Joh: 3: 16		Dᵒ		Dᵒ 6	Dᵒ 26 Dᵒ
27	Rom: 6: 17		Dᵒ		Dᵒ 7	Mar: 31 Sab: Moᵍ
28	Acts 21: 14		Dᵒ		Dᵒ 8	Ap: 30 Tues: Evᵍ
29	2 Cor 7: 6		Dᵒ		Founders Hall 1	May 19 Sab: Moᵍ
		7	15	7		4

5. The Rev. David Ford's Sermon Register, 27 December 1791.

6. Long Melford Independent Chapel.   7. The Manse, Long Melford.

May to see the conditions under which his daughter, Mary, would be living. He may not have been happy with the prospects of his son-in-law, but the house of which his daughter would be mistress was suitable so he could hardly have done other than approve the match, and may have promised an allowance.

Having received his future father-in-law's approval, David Ford wrote his letter of acceptance:

> It having pleased God in his providence, in taking away your late pastor, to leave you in a state of widowhood, as sheep without a shepherd, it must afford peculiar consolation. . . . When I reflect on the manner in which I was brought among you, and what hath taken place since I have been with you, I must acknowledge it appears the will of providence I should continue among you. I do, therefore, though it be with much diffidence, accept the call you have given me, to take on me the solemn office of being your pastor. Conscious of much weakness I beseech your prayers – that the word of God may be succeeded with a divine blessing. . . . For should it please God to settle me with you, I should wish the union might be permanent; and trust it will not be dissolved on my part, while there shall remain a prospect of usefulness and comfort. I pray God his spirit may be poured out upon us, and that the grace of his Son which hath appeared unto you, may diffuse its influence through your souls, and enable you to adorn the doctrine of God our saviour in all things.
>
> I Remain
> Yours faithfully   D. Ford

The union was to be permanent and did not dissolve till his death in 1836.

His induction was a grand affair which took place on 17 July 1794, and we have the document attesting to it. Ten ministers from the small towns and villages of West Suffolk and North Essex officiated. The proceedings are recorded in his diary. We learn from it that Bentley Crathern, Pastor of the Church of Christ, Dedham, gave a discourse on the nature of the Christian Church, that Robert Stevenson, Pastor of the Church of Christ, Castle Hedingham, advised him suitably by preaching a text from 1 Tim. iv.16, 'Take heed unto thyself and unto the doctrine', and that W. Hickman, Pastor of the Independent Church at Lavenham, closed with prayer. But all ten must have been allowed to say their piece so the proceedings went on all day. Some of these worthy pastors would have risen at dawn

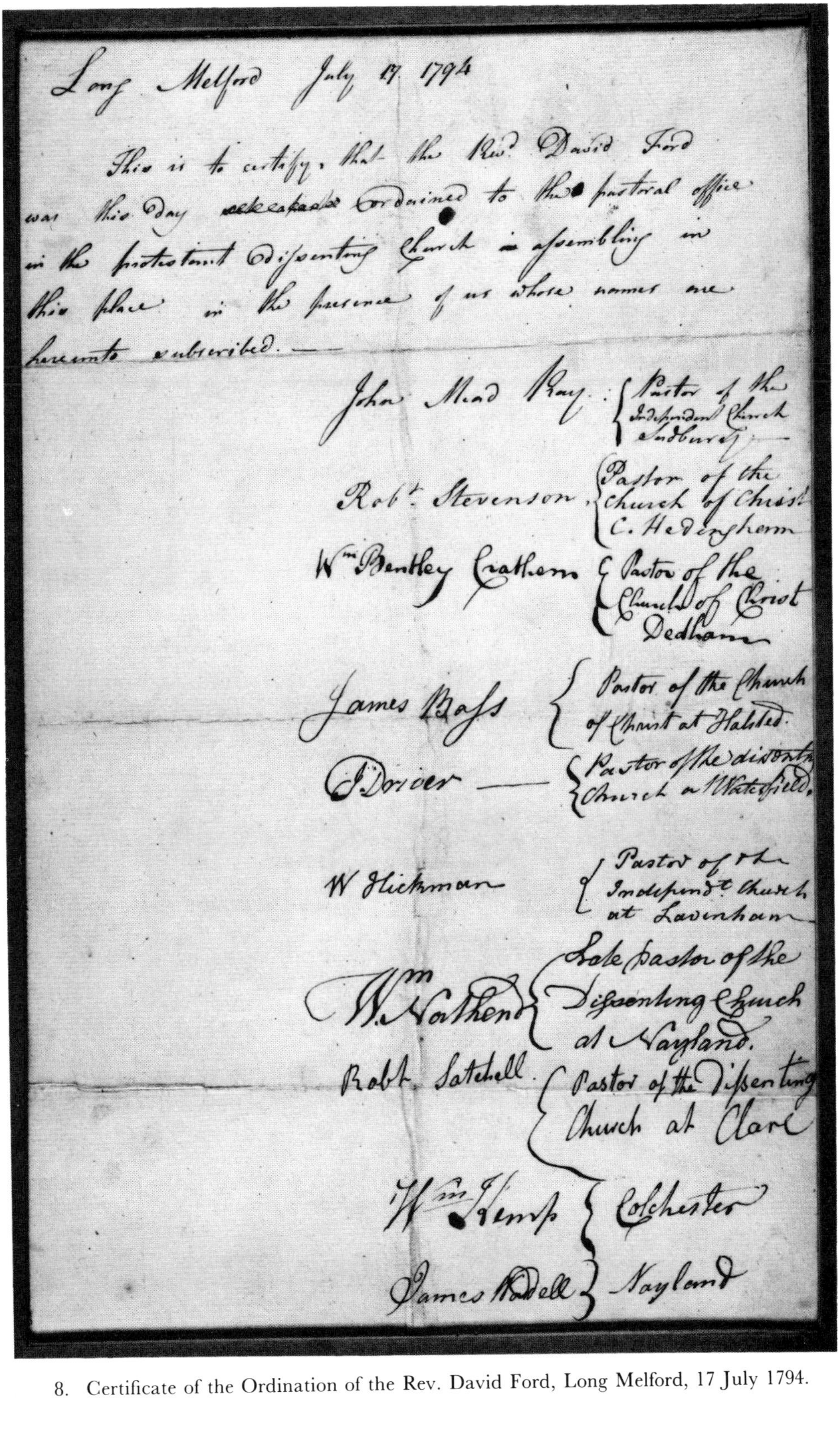

Long Melford July 17. 1794

This is to certify, that the Rev.d David Ford
was this Day ~~celebrated~~ Ordained to the pastoral office
in the protestant Dissenting Church ~~is~~ assembling in
this place in the presence of us whose names are
hereunto subscribed. ———

John Mead Ray { Pastor of the
Independent Church
Sudbury

Rob.t Stevenson { Pastor of the
church of Christ
C. Hedingham

W.m Bentley Grabham { Pastor of the
Church of Christ
Dedham

James Bass { Pastor of the Church
of Christ at Halsted.

P. Dowee ——— { Pastor of the dissenting
Church at Wattisfield.

W. Hickman { Pastor of the
Independ.t Church
at Lavenham

W. Northend { Late pastor of the
Dissenting Church
at Nayland.

Rob.t Satchell { Pastor of the Dissenting
Church at Clare

W.m Hemp { Colchester

James Waddell { Nayland

8. Certificate of the Ordination of the Rev. David Ford, Long Melford, 17 July 1794.

and walked many miles so they would be hungry and thirsty, but one can be sure that the ladies of the congregation would have been active and as good and generous cooks as the countywomen of Suffolk today.

The Everards were a very united family and throughout David Ford's diaries there is a record of frequent visits between London and Long Melford. Mary's married sisters, Mrs. Hale and Mrs. Duthoit, were frequent visitors, sometimes with their husbands, and the Fords were constantly going to London. To be the wife of a Dissenting minister in the country evidently did not involve the isolation one might suppose. The early 19th century, just before the railways were built, was the golden age of the stage-coach. McAdam had introduced his method of 'metalling' roads and on turnpike and other main roads the hundreds of coaches which plied them averaged about eight miles per hour. The 56 miles from London to Sudbury were thus covered in seven hours. The diary often refers to the Sudbury coach which left the *Green Dragon*, Bishopsgate, every morning at 9 o'clock and on three days a week there was the Bury St Edmunds coach leaving at noon which passed through Long Melford and did not involve a change at Sudbury.[16]

When Mary was pregnant, she was taken to London to see her parents.

9. The Norwich Mail Coach passing *The Eagle* at Snaresbrook and about to enter Epping Forest. After a painting by James Pollard, engraved by R. G. Reeve and published by T. Helme in 1832.

2 June.   Left London and my dear Mary, whom God preserve.
27 July.   Mrs. F. this day much indisposed.
30 July.   Mrs. F. this day exceedingly ill.
13 Sept.   This morning, O God, I thank thee for all the kindness to my dear Mary in the
            safe delivery of a son at half-past nine this morning after 36 hours illness – to
            thee O God, I devote this child.

One can hardly regard 36 hours labour as a kindness but then he believed what he had been told in the Bible, that it was the lot of women to bring forth children through pain. In the next century when the use of anaesthetics in childbirth began, religious *men* protested that the practice was contrary to the Will of God.

Dissenters were then not allowed to register the baptism of their children at their parish church and there was no civil registration till 1837. The Fords, therefore, took the precaution of having their son, David Everard's birth certified by the surgeon, midwife and her assistant, and he writes of this:

> Such a document as that to which these three names are appended may seem to have been written in burlesque. But it was no joke then. In those days, and for some years afterwards, Dissenters had not, as now, the means of civil registration for their children and their baptismal records, though respected by some lawyers and judges, by sundry others were held in contempt and treated as nullities. Many a valuable appointment was lost and not a small amount of property fell into wrong hands because the expectant or claimant could find no document to supply in place of a parish register.[17]

The document with which David Everard Ford was provided read,

> This is to certify all whom it may concern that we whose names are hereunto affixed were present at the birth of David Everard Ford, who was born on Wednesday morning, 13 September 1797 about half-past nine o'clock at Long Melford in the county of Suffolk as witness our hands.
>   Signed: John Chevallier, Surgeon
>   Eliz. Bartlett, Nurse
>   Lettice Codlin.

Those of us who live in Suffolk are at once interested by the name Chevallier, that of an old and respected family in these parts. Why was a Chevallier acting as a surgeon, not in those days a particularly highly regarded calling? In his autobiography, David Everard Ford merely writes: 'John Chevallier afterwards became an M.D., and then exchanged the care of health for the care of souls. A family living falling vacant, he went into holy orders and took for the text of his first sermon Luke V, verse 31, "They that are whole need not a physician, but they that are sick". My impression is that he was better fitted for medical practice than for pastoral duties'.

The Chevalliers originally came from the Channel Islands and have held the Manor of Aspall in Suffolk, since 1702. I am indebted to Mrs. Perenel M. Guild of Aspall for telling me of her great-great-grandfather, this remarkable Dr. John Chevallier. He was the youngest son of the Rev. Temple Chevallier of Aspall Hall and had studied Medicine in Edinburgh. His youngest sister, Sophie, had married Dr. Cream of Long Melford. As David Everard Ford writes, he was subsequently ordained and succeeded his father as incumbent of Aspall and occupier of Aspall Hall, but remained deeply interested in Medicine, for in 1833 he applied for a licence to house six insane persons in Aspall Hall believing that conditions better than those at Bedlam could produce better results. He was also an agricultural pioneer of some note and was praised by Arthur Young. He became famous, in particular, as the originator of Chevallier barley and he also greatly improved the production of cyder which art the family brought with them from the Channel Islands and which they still practise in Aspall today. He was, in short, an example of the versatility and originality

10.   John Chevallier, M.D. (1774-1846).

which so often sprang up, as did Parson Malthus, in unexpected places in this country. He married three times and had children by all three marriages. One of his daughters was the mother of Lord Kitchener of Khartoum and Aspall.

I have digressed, but not entirely, for if John Chevallier had been less skilful our family would not have been here in its present mix.

We might have expected that David Ford, now a father, and in pleasant pastorate and married into an affectionate family, could have looked forward to a happy life. But he could not, because he was cursed with depressions, an inborn melancholia he apparently passed on to some of his descendants. 'Ford Depressions', as we call them, have hit some of us and missed others. A psychologist, reading his diaries could, I am sure, have diagnosed his case and, with modern drugs, have given him great, if not permanent, relief. What he had instead was the worst possible treatment for his complaint – crude Calvinism.

Through hundreds and hundreds of pages of his diaries, decade after decade, there is little of interest but only anguished gloom and self-reproach interspersed with brief periods of relief.

Thus we get: '1 December 1793. The past week has been truly distressing: every day hath witnessed strong cries and tears: painful sensations and hasty conclusions have attended me. The Lord appears to have passed me by and to have given me up the prey to Satan'. And the day after: 'I have this day been shaken over hell, surely legions of Devils are let loose on me'. 25 March 1794. He had just been offered the pastoral office of Long Melford, but: 'It is not always the portion of the believer to enjoy peace and tranquility of soul. Unbelief is too strong for me and I call into question the goodness of God'.

A contemporary depressive of his, the poet Shelley, wrote: 'Many a green island needs must be – In the deep sea of misery'. And so it was with David Ford for, on 8 May 1794, we find: 'At this time I enjoyed much of the divine presence – how happy is it for the children of God that there are some seasons in which the blessed God does revive his people with his presence'. But then back again: '6 December 1804. A fiery furnace is by no means pleasant to flesh and blood, yet this is often the portion of my soul'.

We see from a notebook of his that he dabbled in mathematics, rudimentary science and also the study of gems and fossils. Florence Keynes suggests in *Gathering up the Threads* that his study of fossils may have increased his plaguing religious doubts. This could be so, though one conventionally attributes the raising of such doubts to Charles Darwin's *Origin of Species*, which appeared in 1859. Charles Lyell, however, in his *Principles of Geology* of

1830 suggested that evidence drawn from fossils pointed to the evolution of the world through long ages. This he might possibly have read.

Though David Ford suffered greatly, there is no suggestion that he was ever crippled for long, as were some of his descendants, nor is there ever any note of suicidal despair. He was a diligent pastor. We find at the back of volume 1 of his diary a register of the people he baptised from 1793 to 1821. They number two hundred and nineteen. There is then a note, 'For the rest see New Register Book', which we have not got. There is also the register of 62 people buried at Long Melford Meeting House during the same period, followed by the same note. In rural areas, Dissenters had to provide their own burial grounds until 1880, and that of the chapel at Long Melford is there today, well kept, though part of it is the chapel's nursery school playground.

David Ford was much less tied down by his calling than one would have expected. He paid many and lengthy visits to London and the southern counties, preaching as he went. There is a full record in his sermon register.

Though his diary is largely a record of the state of his soul, there is much of family movements and, occasionally, an item of general interest. For example, we read on 7 August 1796: 'This morning received a letter from Mrs. Hale giving an account of Mr. Wm. Everard being shipwrecked with £800 (£24,800) worth of goods belonging to her father'. This is further evidence that John Everard was in a good way of business, but he does not tell us whether his brother, William Everard, survived, but remarks: 'The Lord giveth, the Lord taketh away'. This could merely mean that the goods were not insured, though Lloyds was active by that date.

I became a little curious as to the happiness, or otherwise, of David and Mary's married life when I noticed that she would leave him for long periods, which grew longer, to stay with her family in London. He often joined her, but absences of six weeks or two months raise doubt, particularly when they became routine at Christmas. He never complained by word or implication. They had only three children which was unusually few for those days, but it may have been his glooms which compelled her to escape to her jolly parental home whilst still loving him – as did his sons. Depressives are reputed to have nice natures, as I think he had.

We get the spirit of the man in almost the last letter he wrote to his son, David Everard Ford, rather than the moody introspective thoughts he committed to his private diary. He wrote this on 23 September 1835 when his sight was failing badly. He was then seventy-two. Pencil lines had been ruled on the paper to help the old man to write.

> My dearly beloved D—,
>   It would have given me great pleasure if it had been in my power to have solved the problem as to your change of residence: and it would have been promptly given. But as I have felt conscious insufficiency in myself, I followed your own example and laid the case before a gracious God whose promise is that he will not fail to direct your steps.
>   We rejoice with you in your safe return from Plymouth and though you have left a large flock and resumed your accustomed labour in a smaller sphere of action, yet remember *Home*, sweet home is best. It should also be recollected that we are not at our own disposal and the great and good shepherd will acknowledge a faithful discharge of duty with a few sheep as well as if our sphere of action had been on a larger scale. Well done, good and faithful servant will express his approval at the close of service.

He then lapsed into what might have been one of his sermons about what Joshua did when he was in Shiloh, but emerges to continue with:

> Your dear little Mary must now be entertaining and growing solicitude will increase and many prayers will be filed for her in heaven long before her little lips will be able to lisp one petition for herself. May your fondest wishes on this point be fully realised for

your comfort. I must for the present omit any reply to her very dutiful epistle, however I do not forget her. Dearly beloved Jane and yourself must be careful lest you make an idol of what is only lent for a season. Our supreme affections are meant for God and he has first and highest claim. It is good to hold our mercies in our hand, ready to obey the will of our heavenly Father – and this is the surest measure of enjoyment.

John Holman's son, Henry, went on an adventure to Hobart about eighteen months since. Information has been received of his death – he was murdered by some convicts. This is all I know and I did not pursue this subject further. That is one *Momento*: now for the second. On September . . . Fisk and Lord Cad . . ., near relations and both keen sportsmen, were in pursuit of game – one on one side of a hedge and one on the other, each stooping down. The birds rose, Fisk fired and C. rose up just in time to receive F.'s charge in his face. One eye is gone and the other much injured. *Momento 3rd*. Mrs. Blunden, a widow of Melford, lost three grown-up daughters (all her females) by typhus in six weeks. Two of them got over in vain hope's ferry boat[18] but the third, who was married, in great distress of mind. She wished to see me; her husband would not permit it, but sent the curate and him she would not see: thus cruelly was she treated.

When I was in town, a gentleman was speaking of age. I told him I was nearly 72. 'Then', said he, 'your leave is out'. To which I replied, 'I once heard Mr. Wilkes make the same remark of himself but said I, it was an improper expression for I never had a leave. I have always been a tenant at will. I have had many warnings to get out and only remain on sufferance. But I have a house not made with hands nearly ready for me whither I am bound'.

As respects my sight, I have two eyes: for distinction one is called Alexander and the other Stevenson. The latter the operation has certainly improved but not so much as I expected. The former has, I suppose, by sympathy, gained strength.

We join in our love to dear Jane, little Mary and yourself.
        Yours   affectionately,   D.   Ford.

The joke about the names of his eyes had to do with the names of the two surgeons who operated on him for cataract. It was the second, Stevenson, who caused his death in 1836, when he was seventy-three. At the end of volume 2 of his diary, his son added a morbid account of his unnecessary death at his hands when he undertook an operation he had no right to perform.

David Ford appears as a sad, gentle figure, cursed by his depressions but not without a sense of humour. He was clearly loved by his family and his flock, whose pastor he remained for over forty years. He had preached 7,282 sermons between 1791 and 1835, recording the texts in his sermon register. He was interred in the chapel at Long Melford where the carving on the tombstone in the south aisle has been sadly worn. It also records the death of his wife in 1842. She was on a visit to London and was buried in her family vault in Bunhill Fields, City Road, just above Finsbury Square. It is still there.

Bunhill Fields Burial Ground

The history of the Bunhill Fields Burial Ground is of some interest. As we have seen, Dissenters might not be buried in churchyards. The Dissenters of London, therefore, with the concurrence of the Corporation of the City of London and the Church of England, to whom the land belonged, took to burying their dead in Bunhill Fields outside the City walls. This was about the middle of the 18th century. The land was due to revert to the church in 1867 and negotiations as to the future of the burial ground were opened in 1865. The Ecclesiastical Commissioners regarded it as ripe for development. They felt that they were trustees for the pious benefactors to whom the church owed its lands and it was their duty to maximise the financial return obtainable from them. After all, the graves there, albeit 120,000 of them, were only those of Dissenters and, therefore, did not appear to them important, nor did the fact that many were those of famous men such as Bunyan, Defoe and

Blake. To the suggestion, therefore, that the Bunhill Fields Burial Ground should be held sacred forever, the Commissioners replied that they were entitled to the land absolutely and that it was thought to be worth at least £100,000 but that they were willing, under the circumstances, to accept £10,000.

This attitude caused great indignation and on 16 November 1865 the Court of Common Council of the Corporation of the City of London met and, with 153 members present, unanimously passed a Resolution in very strong terms deploring the fact that the Commissioners would only concur in preservation upon terms of sale and purchase and

> in consideration of the historical interest attaching to Bunhill Fields Ground and in consequence of the interment of so many distinguished and honoured men of all creeds and parties, this Court is willing to accept the care and preservation of the ground on behalf of the public . . . the final resting place of so many thousands of their fellow citizens.

The Resolution ended – 'Ordered, that a copy of the foregoing Resolution be transmitted to the Ecclesiastical Commissioners'. It was clearly thought proper that the Commissioners should be left in no doubt as to the contempt in which they were held by the City of London and in the end it was felt that only an Act of Parliament could protect Bunhill Fields Burial Ground forever from desecration by the Commissioners or their assigns, and such was passed in 1867.

Chapter Three

HAYDONS AND DOWNS

11. Cadhay House.

In *Gathering up the Threads*, Florence Keynes writes of a John de Haydon, a reputed follower of William the Conqueror and his descendant, John de Haydon, a Judge in 1272. From him were descended the Haydons of Cadhay House, near Ottery St Mary, Devonshire. They are said to have ruined themselves by extravagances at the court of Charles II, but they struggled on, till 1736 when, hopelessly in debt, Cadhay House had to be sold and those Haydons disappeared.

We are unquestionably descended from John Haydon (1700-74) of Braunton near Barnstaple, whose son, John Haydon (1726-88) was the master of the Free School of Braunton. These Haydons claimed that they were descended from the Haydons of Cadhay House and, indeed, used their crest. The second John Haydon had wide interests for a village schoolmaster, being a student of one of the most important practical applications of mathematics and astronomy of his time – navigation, the fixing of a position of a ship at sea. That art was so uncertain but so important that, in 1713, an Act of Parliament was

20

passed offering prizes of £10,000, £15,000 and £20,000 for anyone who could devise a method of fixing a ship's position within 60, 40 and 30 miles. These were enormous limits and enormous sums of money. Twenty-thousand pounds in 1713 would be over one million in 1986. It was a certain Yorkshire clockmaker, John Harrison, who devised a sea-going chronometer and a technique still used alongside radio beacons and satellites, but he had to spend his life extracting only a proportion of the prize money from the Admiralty by 1773. Meanwhile, John Haydon may have had a happier life continuing in the tenour of his way and begetting a large family which included a remarkable daughter, Hannah, from whom we are descended.

Florence Keynes writes at some length on the Haydons of Braunton and her sister, Jessie Lloyd, did much research in trying to establish the connection. In 1915 her husband, Albert, a very thorough man, went down to Ottery St Mary and Exeter and worked on baptismal and probate records but in the end he had to write, 'We must be content to regard Cadhay, and through it, Woodbury, as probable without being able to display the chain'.

John Haydon (1726-1788) married Jane Langdon (1744-1806). The Langdons were a noted Cornish family but one of their daughter's connections by marriage, Henry Down, was not impressed. We have a letter in which he wrote, 'The Langdons were schemers but the Haydons were workers'.[1] He was certainly right about the Haydons, because with John's daughter, Hannah, we get the emergence of a strong family characteristic – remarkable women. Hannah Haydon (1785-1870) married John Joseph Almond Down in St George's, Hanover Square. He was the son of a London merchant but was, himself, unsuccessful in London as an apothecary and equally unsuccessful when he moved to Bideford in Devon. Finally, he bought some small shops at Torpoint. Torpoint is on a promontory of the Cornish side of the River Tamar, opposite Devonport and, being the only hard ground in the mud of the Hamoaze, has for centuries been a ferry terminal linking Plymouth and South Devon with Cornwall. It must have been of greater importance before the bridges were built at Saltash, but can never have offered much scope.

The shops in Fore Street had interconnecting doors and sold drapery, ironmongery, groceries and one was a chemist and stationers combined. It was the usual small family business, with wife and children assisting. Henry Down wrote of his uncle Joseph: 'He, or rather his brave little wife, commenced a business and for 80 years the Down family resided at Torpoint. Depend upon it that her family owed all to her and very little to Mr. Down'.

Henry Down was not the only person to appreciate the qualities of Hannah Down. We have a letter of her grandson's, H. Langdon Down, to Jessie Lloyd, written in 1948, in which he tells her how a certain Captain Pope, formerly of the East India Company, had settled in Torpoint and much admired the character and reputation for shrewdness of Mrs. Hannah Haydon Down. One day, he said to her, 'Haven't you got a sister like yourself who would make me a good wife?' Hannah sent for her eldest unmarried sister, Mary, whom Captain Pope then took as his third wife, and they lived happily ever after, or so one would hope. But, there are doubts, because in a letter of David Everard Ford's of 25 August 1835 to his wife (Mary's niece) he says 'I do not think that your feeling towards your aunt Pope is quite scriptural. You know that her infirmity is an unhappy temper'. And, of course, her husband, a former captain in the East India Company, was likely to have been peppery.

Joseph Almond Down died in 1848 and, in the census of 1851, Richard, the eldest son, was returned as Head of Family. Their trade was entered as Grocers, etc. Perhaps the 'etc' included the pharmacy, because it is likely that John Langdon Haydon Down, the youngest, acquired his interest in medicine, not only from his father, but also from day-to-day contact with customers obviously in need of more than the pills and plasters he could hand across the counter. In 1853, he left Torpoint and entered the London Hospital as a student. The London Hospital had a strong tradition in neurology started by James Parkinson, who was

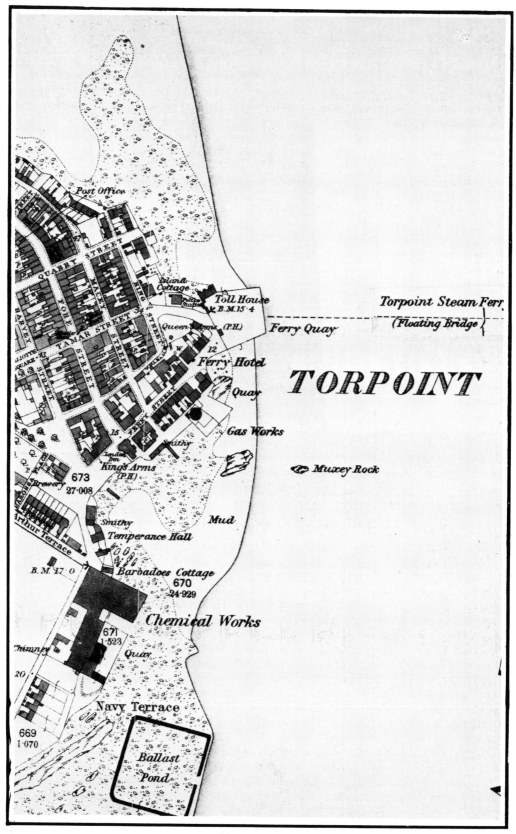

12. Torpoint.

COUNTY RECORD OFFICE
COUNTY HALL
TRURO TR1 1AY
CORNWALL. UK.

DATE: 3/4/1985. REF: CRO 50/PL/7/BS

DATE OF CENSUS:	31st MARCH 1851. CRO Ref.:	1851/ Reel S. PUBLIC RECORD OFFICE REF: HO 107/1900 /34 /35

PLACE/STREET: 2M 28 FORE ST. TORPOINT   PARISH/BOROUGH: ANTONY

NAME and Surname of each Person	RELATION to Head of Family	CON-DITION as to Marriage	AGE last Birthday of Males	Females	Rank, Profession, or OCCUPATION	WHERE BORN	1 Deaf-&-Dumb 2 Blind 3 Imbecile or Idiot 4 Lunatic
Richard M. Down	Head	M.	40		Grocer &c	Devon LANDCROR	
John L. M. Down	Brother	U.	22		"	Cornwall ANTONY	
Susanna Down	Wife	M		42	Wife		
Hannah Down	Mother	M.		66	Mother		
Elizabeth A. Down	Daur			6	Scholar		
Mary M. Down	do.			4	do.		
Ellen D. Down	do.			2	At home		
Mary E. Ford	Visitor			16	Minister's Daughter		
Mary G. Stephens	do.			14	Grocer's Daughter		
Mary A. Colenso	Assistant			22	do. L Assistant		
Emma M. Gregory	Apprentice			16	do.		
James Adams	Assistant		17		Grocer's Assistant		
Mary A. Boutons	Servant	U.		20	House Servant	Cornwall ST GERMANS	
Matilda Jackson	do.	U.		15	Do.	Cornwall ANTONY	

Census 31 March 1851

Joseph Almond Down, the husband of Hannah, had died in 1848.

John Langdon Haydon Down had not yet returned to London to study medicine.

Mary Ford had arrived safely to stay with her aunt not withstanding her father's fears.

(See page 58.)

13. Census of 31 March 1851, Torpoint.

14. Dr. John Langdon Down, M.D., F.R.C.P.

made famous by his *Essay on the Shaking Palsy* (1817), and John Langdon Down's best known contribution to medicine was to be his recognition and description of the variety of mental deficiency which he called 'mongolism' in his paper on *Ethnic Classification of Idiots* in 1866. In post-Hitler days his idea that some types of mental deficiencies exhibited the characteristics of certain races of mankind was labelled as 'racist' and the deficiency he identified is now known as Down's Syndrome. (In fact, Langdon Down was liberal in his views and was keenly on the anti-slavery side in the American Civil War.) As a student he worked with John Faraday, and was elected Fellow of the Royal College of Physicians in 1869. Milo Keynes thinks it is possible that Walter Langdon-Brown (Chapter Eighteen) may have been influenced by his uncle Down's achievements, particularly his book on *Mental Afflictions of Childhood and Youth* (1887).

We are not direct descendants of Dr. Langdon Down, but of his eldest sister, Jane Elizabeth. She was a capable young woman who branched out from Torpoint to Plymouth, where she established, or took over, a flourishing school in Frankfort Street in the centre of the town (swept away in the reconstruction following the air raids of 1939-45). By the time she was 25, she had become a successful young career woman in the only profession open to serious women in her day — teaching. She was to show, through the years, that she was exceedingly clear-headed, decisive and of great fortitude, hard on herself and on others. However, at the house of Captain and Mrs. Pope in Tavistock Place, Plymouth,[2] she met David Everard Ford and, giving up her independence, married him, probably against her better judgement.

Chapter Four

DAVID EVERARD FORD
(1797-1875)

Long Melford to Lymington 1797-1836

David Everard Ford is the most colourful of our ancestors. His flair, his vigour and his versatility were undoubted. So, unfortunately, was his flamboyance and his eccentricity which infuriated his wife and which led, in the end, to his eclipse. His father was a gentle depressive; his mother, though with a will of her own, retiring and happiest with her own relations, so his vitality and physique, as well as his sense of fun, must have come from earlier generations – perhaps the smugglers.

Always full of ideas, he was a compulsive writer of vivid English as we shall see from extracts of his diary. His autobiography ended unfinished in 1868, and his diary is also incomplete, though for another reason. I think that he intended his autobiography to be published, for it is full of stories about odd personalities and unusual happenings and was intended to show him in a good light. He disposes of his wife and his marriage in a couple of lines and does not mention the profitable schools she established which made so much difference to their financial situation and about which he worried and fussed, to her great annoyance.

His wife did not know that he kept a diary and, when, on his death in 1875, she first came upon it, she was deeply pained and infuriated. She destroyed the first volume which covered his early years and courtship. This is an irreparable loss to his biographers. She cut important pages out of the succeeding seven volumes and wrote grieved and indignant comments across many of its other pages. 'Diaries, what an evil', she wrote.

We also have his sermon register which ran from 1816, before he had entered Wymondley College, till 1875. It logs 8,395 sermons, giving, like his father's, a serial number, the text, the place from which he preached, and the number of times he preached there. It is an invaluable supplement to his diary, in which there are many gaps, because it tells where he was on any particular Sunday, and often weekday, through 59 years. We also have copies of his religious and other publications such as hymns and hymn tunes, many letters and various records of some of his contentious doings. He has a place in the *Dictionary of National Biography*[1] and we have a book of press cuttings of the eulogies he received in appropriate journals.

David Everard Ford was born at the Manse, Long Melford, Suffolk, on 13 September 1797. He never went to school but was at first taught by a Miss Mary Palmer, a maiden lady, the only child of a deceased pastor. She taught him to read, she taught him Latin and much else besides, and she loved him which must have counted for much when his mother was away on her frequent visits to her parents in London. He was much distressed in 1807 when she died. He was then 10 and his father took over and completed his schooling.

He claims to have had a happy boyhood but, to use his own words, he 'had not undergone that change which is introductory to all truly religious life'. It happened that Miss Palmer, as well as having folios of John Bunyan's works and Fox's *Book of Martyrs*, had a copy of Dr. Dodderidge's *Life of Colonel James Gardiner* published in 1747. We have her copy which was the eighth edition of 1798. It is indeed a remarkable work combining some military adventure with much extreme piety. Gardiner was wounded at Ramillies, serving under

Marlborough in 1706, and was killed at the Battle of Prestonpans in the 'forty-five' rebellion. One hundred and sixty pages of his adventures, and Dr. Dodderidge's reflections upon them, separate these events.

The passage which led to David Everard Ford's religious awakening in 1812, when he was 15, relates how Gardiner had spent the evening in some gay company, and had an assignation with a married woman whom he was to attend at exactly twelve. The company broke up about eleven. On retiring to his chamber to wait, he picked up a religious book, which his good mother or aunt had, without his knowledge, slipped into his portmanteau. It was called, *The Christian Soldier or Heaven taken by Storm.* Dr. Dodderidge goes on to relate that, though Gardiner did not go to sleep,

> He thought he saw an unusual blaze of light fall on the book whilst he was reading, but on lifting up his eyes he apprehended that there was before him a visible representation of Jesus Christ upon the cross . . . and a voice, or something equivalent to a voice, came to him 'Oh sinner did I suffer this for thee, and are these the returns?'

David Everard Ford recalls 'The sentence which was so powerfully impressed upon the mind of Colonel Gardiner was engraved on my heart in letters of fire'. . . . He goes out of his way to remark 'I was then, be it remembered in my 15th year and a child at home, unconscious of vice, ignorant of temptation and as pure of mind as might be expected under the most favoured circumstances'. Pages and pages of his diary are then given up to the need the youth felt to make reparation to an offended Saviour and of remorse and mental agony which, he says, altered his conduct, his appearance and his health. It would seem as if the account of Gardiner's intentions had triggered off some adolescent sexual problem. It speaks well for the relationship which he had with his father that he 'resolved to tell my honoured father the secret of my wound'. His father's 'language breathed thankfulness and hope'. But whatever he said, the therapy of a kindly listener worked.

When at 16, the time came for him to seek work, he went to London where he had uncles and aunts on his mother's side. The eldest daughter of John Everard, Mary, was his mother; the second, Elizabeth, was married to William Hale, her father's partner, and the third, Sarah, to Peter Duthoit of the Stock Exchange. Unlike his father, who arrived in London at the age of 13, knowing no one, he had kindly and hospitable houses open to him. In particular: 'Uncle Hale, then in full vigour kept open house at 4 Wood Street, Spitalfields, for all who loved the Lord Jesus in sincerity and could relish a glass of rich home brewed ale'.[2] And there was his grandfather's house, 9 Astley's Row, Islington, when Cannonbury, Holloway and all regions round about consisted of rich meadowland and Islington itself was regarded as a pleasant village. 'I well remember Cannonbury spring as I used to accompany old Betty every fine morning. Thence came all the water for the table use as the New River supply was not thought even in those unsanitary days, quite as pleasant or wholesome as fresh water from the spring'.[3]

His uncle Hale introduced him to friends with a wholesome haberdashery business – a Mr. and Mrs. Flower of 29 Friday Street, Cheapside, but he did not settle there, and, 'I decided for the trade of a bookseller. In my simple-hearted ignorance of the world I supposed that men who sold books would find time to read them; a notion in which, I need hardly say, the issue woefully disappointed my expectations'.[4] So a bookseller was found, one Samuel Burton of 156 Leadenhall Street, a man of decent reputation and member of the White's Row chapel congregation, 'but I found little there to make me love religion'.

He stayed with the bookseller for two years but then began to sound his father as to the possibility of following him in the ministry. His father responded, and suggested that he should seek entry to his own old college, Homerton, but David Everard Ford, unlike his father, did not succeed with the King's Head Society. A friend of his father's then suggested Wymondley College, effected the necessary introductions and got him accepted.

15. Wymondley College, near Hitchin.

David Everard Ford duly arrived at Wymondley College, near Hitchin in 1816 and his brother Joseph was to follow him, also having been unattracted by hard work in London. Though there is no mention of it, I think it can be taken for granted that financial help from the Everards was forthcoming because Dissenting pastors did not enjoy the affluence of many of the clergy of the Church of England, enabling them easily to educate their children.

In his autobiography, David Everard Ford gives a full account of Wymondley and the curious old characters who taught there. It was founded, like the Homerton Academy, in the mid-18th century to prepare Dissenters for their ministry and Dr. Dodderidge, whose life of Colonel Gardiner had so greatly affected him, was its first tutor. However, 'any young man of blameless reputation, who knew something of Virgil, Horace and the Greek Testament and thought he would like to be a minister' was admitted. As a consequence, some went on to the learned professions, some to the Established Church 'and not a few sank down to Unitarianism'. In other words, it was pleasantly liberal and that, combined with the fact that he had not been subjected to orthodox schooling, may have contributed to the lively, direct English which he wrote and a width of interests unusual in the restricted chapel world in which he lived and worked. He studied there from 1816 till 1821, when he was twenty-four.

One wonders whether Maynard, as a boy, ever had access to the autobiography of his great-grandfather and came across the passage which reads:

It was the year '16, when the new coinage was then of universal interest. During the long war which ended in the downfall of Napoleon the First, Britons were too busy with Iron and lead to think much about silver. The consequence was that the coinage had reached a stage of degradation all but incredible. Guineas had been sold out of the market and had disappeared. If my memory rightly serves, for those I had, I obtained from 24 to 26 shillings each.[5] Spanish dollars were allowed to pass as crowns and the name of shilling or six pence was given to any bit of silver beaten out or clipped into something like that shape and size. When, therefore, it became known that the old silver currency was to be stopped throughout all England in one day, great was the interest which was felt to see and obtain the image and superscription of his long forgotten Majesty, poor old George III, then insane and blind. Artillery wagons, well guarded had carried the treasure to every market town in the land and the day was appointed when the new coinage was to reach the eager grasp of the public.[6]

This was when he was at Wymondley. It was the practice to send students out preaching in village chapels. This was not as daunting to David Everard Ford as to some, as he had considerable practice in preaching in his father's chapel at Long Melford. His sermon register, which he had already started, shows that during vacations he preached widely in West Suffolk and North Hertfordshire. During term he was allocated to the hamlet of Wood End in the parish of Yardley, between Hitchin and Buntingford. He writes:

The reason for giving me this post was my great physical strength, an article which it required no small share. It was little short of nine miles from the college and a considerable portion lay over a road rugged at all seasons, but in the winter months almost impassable. It was a wild place inhabited by wilder people, a no-man's land where everyone might do as he liked without fear of the constable.

And in his notebook which he called 'The Case for Wood End', he writes: 'This spot was for many years totally neglected – the Sabbath was constantly profaned by the wickedness of every description and the poor villagers were sunk into the lowest degree of ignorance and vice'. There was a room in a private house which was used for services. It had been opened only a few years before his time, and on occasion the congregation was disorderly: 'Many people had scarcely ever entered a place of worship and knew not how to conduct themselves with common decorum'. On one occasion only one old woman was there. She told him the others had gone to watch a cricket match, so, with the pulpit bible under his arm, David Everard Ford went and stationed himself on the pitch. 'A stalwart fellow with a bat in hand eventually agreed with an oath, that if they must hear a sermon, they might as well hear it in the preaching room where they could at least sit down'. His power to put himself and his message over was such that he built up a congregation.

The increased number which attended, rendered their accommodation exceedingly uncomfortable. In addition a Sunday School of 60 children had recently been raised . . . so it is now proposed to erect a chapel capable of containing about 250 persons. A piece of freehold land had been purchased for £10 [£240] and the intended building will be erected in the very plainest style: it is hoped that the expense will not exceed £150 [£3,600].

This is in his notebook, which became his collecting book for the project, and there is a recommendation from the Rev. W. B. Collyer saying that David Everard Ford of 'outstanding zeal' was well-known to him and a list of 19 supporting local worthies from Bishop's Stortford, Buntingford, Ware, Walkern and Hitchin. There is the list of 265 contributors from whom he personally collected sums ranging from about five shillings to £1 and totalling £225 5s. 6d. (£5,400). He tells how he walked about five hundred miles collecting and, on one occasion, walked 30 miles for 15 shillings. He had no expenses and very often poorer people would offer him a meal or a bed in lieu of a subscription.

It was not always that I fared so well. On one occasion a most respectable gentleman took me for an imposter, said I was far too young to be the person I represented myself to be, that I had stolen my collecting book and was obtaining money under false pretences.

He even detained me for nearly two hours, locking me in his back parlour whilst he sent a messenger two or three miles to ascertain whether his suspicions were correct. On finding them unfounded he apologised and gave me half-a-crown.

Before he went down from Wymondley College in 1821, he was able to have the great satisfaction of preaching in the chapel whose building he had made possible, and which was fitted with an organ he had made with his own hands.

One of his last student preacher engagements was at Southwold in East Suffolk and also at Walberswick. He was at Southwold,

> when Queen Victoria, then an infant, lost within a few days her father, the Duke of Kent and her grandfather, George III. According to the custom of those times, I preached a funeral sermon for these royal personages – a foolish undertaking, perhaps, for a young man. But it excited great interest and gathered as large a congregation as could be crammed within those ancient walls. The throng was so great that fears were entertained as to the strength of the galleries. No harm ever came of the service. If any good, it never came to my ears.[7]

He was definitely looking for a pastorate and, on his usual Christmas visit to a London uncle and aunt, he heard that Lymington was in need of a pastor. He was told it was beautifully situated by the sea, but,

> 'The church there has a very bad name. They have been falling out for years and some people question whether they will ever agree. But if anybody can make them live in peace, I think you will. At any rate there can be no harm in paying them a visit for a Sabbath or two'.[8]

> I well remember my long journey, in those old days of coaching, when the rival *Times* and *Telegraph* used to placard Meets with monstrous handbills, headed 'Splendid Travelling from Southampton to Hyde Park Corner in eight hours, stoppages included'. On reaching Southampton I found I had yet 18 miles to go, by a pair-horse branch coach.

The bad name of the Lymington chapel was not undeserved and he was so poorly received that, after the first Sunday, he let it be known that he would leave at once. This effected an immediate change and more changes followed, so much so, that by 14 September 1821, he held a document calling him to his first pastorate. His ordination was fixed for October. His father came from Long Melford and his brother, Joseph, from Wymondley and it was done in style. The proceedings lasted for nearly five hours during which eight reverend gentlemen addressed 'an overflowing congregation whose attention was well maintained throughout'. There is no doubt that David Everard Ford was a good showman and, of course, the sermon, the lecture and the political speech satisfied the inborn appetite for the spoken word which is now satisfied by radio and television.

He got a local printer to produce a record of the occasion of which we have a copy. It comprises an order of service, an address by his classics tutor at Wymondley, amongst others, and his father's and his own address. They are all in exceedingly good clear English and the arrangement of their solid argument is excellent.

We have his account of the early days of his first pastorate:

> I began to realise the fact that I was indeed a pastor. My lot was by no means an easy one, and I have often wondered since how I managed to perform my duties. A young man, with no great stock beforehand, having to preach thrice on the Lord's Day and once a week-night, constantly to the same people, may expect to find he has enough to do. My old tutor used to say that to preach one new sermon a week required hard study; two, a decent measure of application; three, none at all. The good man was very fond of sweeping generalities.

> I was not long in learning that indiscriminate calling would never do. Yet, I knew not where to draw the line. I was anxious to give no offence to Jew or Gentile, or to the Church of God; but I soon found that a young minister may as easily have too many friends as too

few. The perils of my early pastorate were all the greater in consequence of my natural buoyancy of spirits. Temptations to levity, I could not resist, or at least, did not always resist. The young people of those days used to pay me the doubtful compliment of regarding me as the most entertaining minister they ever knew.

He added, 'Divine discipline cured me at last of my infirmity'. But when his wife later came upon that passage, she added: 'The cares of married life had most to do with it. My dislike to it, if I may say, had a considerable influence'.

He did not marry till he was 37 and those early years may have been the best of his life. He had comfortable lodgings where his landlady allowed him to play an organ and to keep a dog, Pompey. When Pompey was dying he was to write: 'The faithful companion of nearly 19 years of my life, now lies near his end. He is unable to eat but still knows his master's voice. May it be the same with me when my time comes'.

He was very active, politically, in the matter of the Reform Bill and, when it was passed, campaigned actively for the return of Lord Palmerston for South Hampshire and this Lord Palmerston never forgot. We have original letters of his to David Everard Ford and a copy of a long letter of March 1834 when David Everard Ford was pressing him on the subject of the registration of births and marriages of Nonconformists and Lord John Russell's Marriage Bill. Lord Palmerston believed 'that in the long run English politics will follow the conscience of Dissenters' and he came to regard David Everard Ford as an important representative of Nonconformist opinion.

It was in this period that he wrote hymns and hymn tunes. A book of his hymns, of which we have several copies, was related to the parables of Christ and was published in 1828 for a long list of subscribers (one of whom had the unsuitable address of Bagnio Court).

He also wrote a book on Psalmody with a view to improving public worship and a book on the *Elements of Music* which was to sell 10,000 copies. His book of hymn tunes, *Comprising One Hundred and Twenty-Eight Original Psalms and Hymn Tunes, Harmonized for Four Voices and Chorded for the Organ, Pianoforte, etc.*, is a remarkable work in which each is called after a place in which he preached. There is no date of publication and no specific reference to publication in his diary but it was most probably published in his Lymington days, that is, prior to 1843.

A friend, who is the organist at our village church, was kind enough to play some of the collection. They are what we would today call traditional hymn accompaniments embodying some very good tunes worthy of inclusion in any hymnbook. To these he added simple chants for singing. He was writing for the congregations he knew, mostly humble village folk in south-east England, not Wales.

His interest in music combined with his tendency to indulge in acts of showmanship led to an unfortunate incident. He had set an anthem to music to be sung in his chapel. In it occurred the words 'Hark the Trumpet'. He had, unknown to the congregation, placed the bugler of the Lymington Town Band just under the pulpit. When the words 'Hark the Trumpet' were sung, the concealed trumpeter blew a powerful blast which startled the elderly members of his congregation most horribly. It was left to the deacons to point out the unsuitability of such a thing, as he had not yet got a wife to do so, though he was soon to have one who most assuredly would.

David Everard's autobiography does not tell us why he visited Plymouth or of his courtship and marriage and the volume of his diary which might was destroyed. But we have letters which his wife kept and numbered and his sermon register shows that in December 1832 he preached on 12 occasions at Endless Street, Salisbury and that in May 1833 he preached 16 times at the New Tabernacle, Plymouth and thereabouts. The key letter is No. 4 of 14 June 1833 addressed to Miss Downe, 36 Tavistock Place, Plymouth.

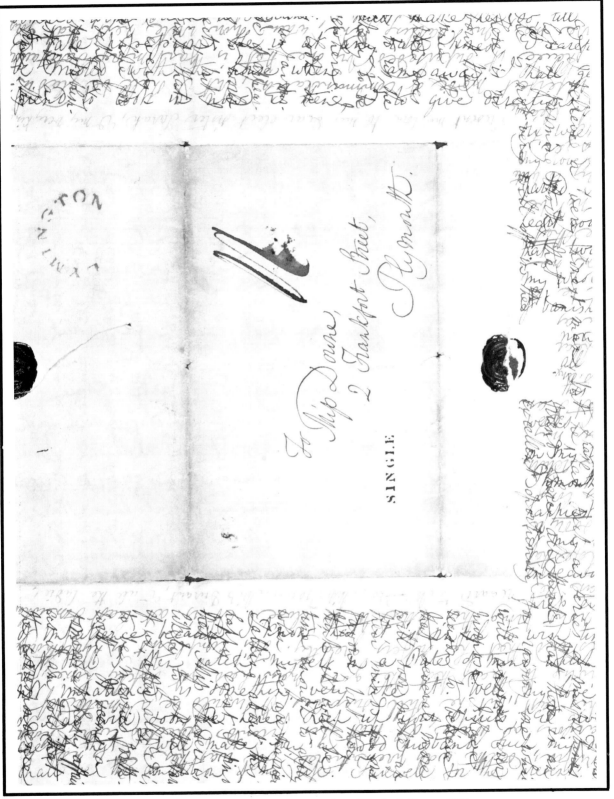

16. David Everard Ford's letter to Jane Elizabeth Down, 1834.

I thank you my dearest friend for keeping me no longer in suspense, but I want a word to express the satisfaction which I feel on reviewing the whole of your letter. I thank my God, whom I serve in the Gospel, that he directed my way to Plymouth and that he inclined you to accept my proposal. May we from this time forth, be helpers of each other's faith and joyfully walk together, blamelessly in all his commandments and ordinances. It was a trial of my faith and patience that I was treated so strangely at Salisbury but now I see the reason. Had I been invited thither, I certainly should not have visited the New Tabernacle (Plymouth) and in that case we had never met.

When at Salisbury he almost certainly met John Keynes, later the famous horticulturist and Mayor of Salisbury, grandfather of John Maynard Keynes. John Keynes, who was deeply interested in education, was at that time Superintendent of the Sunday School at the Baptist Brown Street Chapel and David Everard Ford's sermon register shows that he preached there on Wednesday, 9 February 1831 before preaching to the Congregationalists at their Endless Street Chapel on the succeeding occasions. There was much come and go between certain of the Dissenting bodies for David Everard Ford preached to Baptists no less than 52 times in his life and the Keyneses had been Congregationalists, and later became so again.

Returning to David Everard Ford's letters to Jane Down, there are some further passages of interest in letter No. 4 –

It seems unfortunate, if we may use so heathenish a word, that you should just now have taken a larger house, but the house *is* taken and must therefore be entered upon. Still I would have you go to no expense in the way of furniture, painting or repairs, beyond what may be absolutely required. For my own part, I care not who knows of our engagement. Why should I? But so far as you are concerned the case is different, for were it known that you are likely to leave Plymouth, it might injure your school during the remainder of your time there, as few parents would send their children with such an uncertainty before them. . . . I thank you for the readiness with which you have acceded to my proposal about a school. With regard to the prospects of success, I really think there is still an opening for a good ladies school at Lymington. Day pupils might not be as numerous as in such a populous place as Plymouth, but still we might reckon with tolerable certainty on some and I have little doubt that amongst my connexions we might find some boarders . . . If you could bring some of your young ladies with you, the circumstance would excite the public confidence and produce the conviction that a school in your hands is not a mere speculation, but one in which you have had considerable experience.

This letter is legible, but most of the 24 we have are hardly so. They are most extraordinary documents and I reproduce the face of one. When opened out, they measured 16 inches by 10 inches and the inside and back are completely covered with fine black writing one way and red the other. Even before the red faded, reading them must have been a laborious matter.

David Everard Ford and Jane Elizabeth Down were to be married in May 1834 but I think she must have had serious doubts. She was not the ordinary Protestant young woman for whom, in all the generations before our times, marriage was the only calling. At 25 she had built up her own business, a successful school, and was independent. David Everard Ford's extraordinary letters, his flamboyance, his readiness to tell her what to do about *her* school, must have made her uncertain and anxious. Evidence of this begins to appear in his letters. The fantastic criss-cross writing in red and black ink disappears and we get normal, easily readable letters. On 2 April, letter No. 28, he wrote:

Thank you for your kind and satisfactory letter. I said you wrote your last letter under a cloud which would soon pass away. *I am perfectly satisfied*: I see no reason for your disquietude. Some mischief-making body seems to have told your aunt some idle tales about me. Really I am quite unconscious of ever having borne *to any fellow creature* the intensity of affection which I cherish, my darling Jane, towards yourself.

She seems outwardly to have accepted this, but what that mischief-making body had said was tucked away at the back of her mind because to the entry in his diary about Salisbury which reads 'How nearly had that place been made the grave of my happiness', her annotaton of 1875 reads, 'he would not have met J.E.D. but would probably have had M.H.' Who was M.H. – one of the young people of Lymington who thought he was the most entertaining minister they ever knew?

The campaign of reassurance continued, on 7 April, letter No. 29: 'Cheer up my love and look on the bright side of your prospects, if you can find one', and on 21 April, letter No. 31, he had to write: 'Come my darling do brighten up. Remember that though you are going to leave your father's house, there is some prospect at least of your having an affectionate husband. Away then with your fears and misgivings'.

There is a normal letter, No. 32 about his travelling plans on 27 April and then a later, but obviously rather desperate undated letter, No. 33 in which he took the great risk of 'instructing' her.

All my arrangements, my dearest love, are complete, nor can I alter them without giving rise to all manner of unpleasant surmises. Prove your love to me, my beloved one, by making some extra exertion to be in readiness. If all be well, by the blessing of God, dearest one, I must *instruct* you this day week to fulfil the interesting and happy engagement under which you lie and for which I hope to have reason to bless God, now and in eternity.

He was a tall, well-built, vigorous man of 37 with brilliant brown eyes and a notable command of English and he clearly loved her dearly. She swallowed her doubts, and they were married on 7 May 1834.

They were married at St Andrew's Church, Plymouth and we have the certificate signed by John Hatchard, vicar. It was not till 1836 that Dissenters could be married in their own chapels, but, by means of a typical English fiction, 'occasional conformity' and typical English tolerance on the part of many clergy, they could be married in Church of England churches. It was a wise precaution because bastardy of children could otherwise be imputed and, indeed, this couple's son-in-law, the Rev. John Brown had to intervene in such a matter even a generation later.

As one reads on, in David Everard Ford's autobiography and diary, one wonders about their marriage. It is said that only three parties to a marriage – the man, the woman and the Almighty – perhaps only the Almighty – know its true content and that would seem to be so in the case of David Everard Ford and Jane Elizabeth Down. All his writings remain full of affection without a breath of criticism, but we know that he was highly eccentric, moody, an exhibitionist and that many people could not do with him. In her mutilation of his diary, her irritation is so intense that it burns brightly some forty years on. Was this the consequence of a conflict between two very remarkable personalities in the hard life they led? Did Jane come painfully to realise that her doubts during their engagement were well-founded and that she should not have married him?

Having destroyed the first volume of his diary, she wrote on the flyleaf of the second: 'Many pages are cut out either because they refer to *very many* who have fallen asleep or to matters strictly private'. On the next page she writes:

Sir A. Helps says: 'Now it would be hard for a man to live with another, who always criticised his actions, even if it were kindly and just criticism. It would be like living between the glasses of a microscope. But these self-elected judges, like their prototypes are very apt to have the persons they judge brought before them in the guise of culprits'.

But it is *her* continuous criticism of him which is the most striking feature of her annotations and not the text of his diary. She writes in continuation:

> The author of John Halifax says, 'I had a very useless, and sometimes harmful, and invariably foolish habit of a diary'. My husband's diary has been altogether a matter of surprise. He was always most kind and from his flattery in words and letters and from his thanksgivings and prayers, I thought he was almost unconscious of a fault in me. He wrote sometime after our marriage, 'I am perfectly satisfied that had He given me the licence and power of ranging through the universe to find a suitable companion, I could not have found another in all respects so calculated to make me blest'. It seems, however, he noted every fault, and often in a one-sided manner, but still nothing could exceed his affection for me.

17. The Red House, Lymington.

It is probable that her mutilation of his diaries may have concealed much from us for I cannot find, until the last volume of his diary, when old age was overtaking him, any trace of the criticism, direct or inferred, of which she writes. One does often notice in very capable driving personalities a morbid sensitiveness to criticism, the faintest breath of which, undetectable to others, puts them outside themselves, and I rather think this must have been her case.

Dr. John Brown said of her in his funeral oration of 1890: 'Of striking appearance, she had a singularly powerful intellect. With marvellous energy of character and resoluteness of will she filled her life-sphere with unwearied self-sacrifice. She seemed never to know what it was to think of herself. From everything like softness and self-sparing she had an almost unutterable shrinking'.

David Everard Ford wrote little in his autobiography about his early married life and the first entry in volume 2 of his diary is 12 July 1836, but we know from his father's letter of 23 September 1835 that they had their first child, Mary, and were thinking of moving to a bigger house and one which would accommodate his wife's school. The move was to be to the Red House, High Street, now the Lymington office of J. D. Wood, the auctioneers and estate agents. It was a courageous step for a young minister of an Independent chapel in a small town, with a wife and already one child, and it was not undertaken without much heart searching.

We have a letter of David Everard Ford's to his wife when he was away preaching in Devonport. It is dated 25 August 1835 and reads:

My own Sweet Darling,

If you knew how anxious we all are to hear your decision, I think you would at once relieve us from our suspense. Your father is always asking – 'Well, has Jane decided yet?' He wants me to write at once to Mr. Markew, but as I do nothing without my dearest love, that is out of the question. I certainly should feel mortified if the house should slip through our fingers, but I would rather run the hazard of losing it altogether than act without my darling, who is all the world to me.

Before he posted that letter he was able to add:

Wednesday, 26 August. – I thank you, my darling, for your letter which came to hand last night. I have been so anxious about the house. I cannot but wish you had been more decided, but as you have left it entirely to me, I must come to some conclusion. I will ask God to direct us and then I will go over to Torpoint and state the whole case to your father and mother, and then I will take that course which on the whole appears best. I confess that I feel *inclined* though not yet *resolved* to offer £60 [£2,100] a year. It, at present, seems to me to be our duty to take the house and trust to providence. We shall be much more likely to obtain pupils in a first rate house like that than in our present situation. If God should spare my darling's life and health I can see every reason to expect a prosperous school.

In that he was quite right. I think he knew that he married a most remarkable woman and he knew that she knew exactly how to run a school.

In less than a year, 26 July 1836, he was able to write in his diary: 'God has graciously disappointed my fears and realized my hopes concerning our school. We bid fair to attain the number which concluded last half year'.

Chapter Five

DAVID EVERARD FORD

Lymington 1836-1843

Churchwardens in every parish were entitled to levy a rate on the occupants of land in the parish for the maintenance of the church and churchyard. A Bill to abolish church rates, introduced by Melbourne and the Whigs, had been defeated by the Tories in 1834 and compulsory church rates were not abolished till Gladstone was in office in 1868. In David Everard Ford's Lymington days, therefore, Dissenters had to pay to maintain a church in which they could only be married by invoking a fiction, could not have the baptism of their children registered, and a churchyard in which they could not be buried unless they were ready to have the burial service of the Church of England read over the grave. On the defeat of Melbourne's Bill, David Everard Ford went into battle. We have no record of the first rounds as they were in the years of the destroyed diary, but we have a summons dated 12 September 1836 requiring him to appear before the magistrates on 14 September for non-payment of his church rate. In volume 2 of his diary he wrote: 'Tomorrow I am summoned before the magistrates on the church rate question. I wish they would commit me to prison,[1] but I suppose I shall only have a distraint put upon my goods. I hope to be able to keep my temper in subjection'. On 1 October, his dining room furniture having been seized, he records: 'A distress for church rates was levied on my goods. I have consequently published a manifesto which has given great offence'.

We have a copy of his manifesto. It took the form of a printed handbill addressed to the inhabitants of Lymington. It starts off aggressively by saying that if he had been ready to swallow his principles and accept the Prayer Book he might have occupied a very different station, but, 'I prefer Nonconformity in rags, to the old lady of the seven hills, with all her scarlet and her gold', irrelevant, since his dispute was with Canterbury and not Rome. He goes on, however, to accuse the Church of England of dangerous error and ministrations by unconverted men and of damning more souls than it saves. And so on through about 900 words of provocative theological argument. His final words made sure of the offence he intended to give: 'I have to ask my fellow townsmen, who are members of the Church of England, . . . that when next Lord's-day morning, they receive the communion, they would bear in mind, that the bread and wine with which they commemorate the death of Christ, were purchased for their use by the sale of my dining-table'.

On 13 October, he was able to write: 'My church rate affair has ended for the present, in the return of my tables, free of expense. They were purchased by some unknown friends and brought to my house at 10 last Saturday night. I have been vilely insulted by the pro-rate party but I have been enabled to take it joyfully'.

The next reference to the issue is on 30 May 1837, when he wrote: 'The ministerial church rate measure has been introduced by a majority of five !!!, a deep disgrace to a reformed House of Commons. Our relentless foes, the Tories would be very glad to burn us if they might. Ireland may yet be the saving of Dissenters, the Irish Catholics defending the English Nonconformists!!!'.

Three years later on 28 April 1840, he was again summoned to appear on 2 May and remarked: 'May God enable me to keep my temper and take joyfully the spoiling of my goods'. But having gone through the motions of enforcing the law, the authorities decided

Insert to be placed between Pages 36 and 37 of
DISSENTING FORBEARS

DAVID EVERARD FORD 1797-1875 Aged 46

It is possible to date this portrait (oil on canvas 29" x 25") from the book under the right hand in the picture. The book is D.E. Ford's *Damascus,* published in October 1842, after he had resigned his pastorate in Lymington, but before he left for Manchester in November 1843. The portrait was probably done by an itinerant painter at the instigation of some of his admirers.

<u>Provenance</u>: Old Town Meeting, St. Thomas's Street,
Lymington (now demolished).
United Reformed Church, High Street,
Lymington, 1847-1990.
Now in possession of the author.

not to gratify him with martyrdom, because against 20 May, we read: 'That annoyance never came. I have gone out and returned in safety. My dear mother accompanied me home by rail-road, which had opened the whole way on the Monday preceeding'.[2]

David Everard Ford was an author. His works were religious tracts, but when each appeared, he suffered all the anxieties with which many of his descendants will be familiar. His first work of importance was *Decapolis, or The Individual Obligation of Christians to Save Souls from Death*, and he wrote of it on 29 May 1840: 'I have today completed my final manuscript of *Decapolis*. It has been the subject of much prayer. 1 June: *Decapolis* has now gone to press. May God prosper it. 18 June: I have corrected and returned the first proof sheet of *Decapolis*. 11 July: *Decapolis* was published in London yesterday. Should it fall from the press still-born, it will be a great grief'.

Simpkin Marshall were his publishers and they got it out in six weeks having compositors who worked over 60 hours a week for 33 shillings (£46). By 3 September he was very depressed: 'After all *Decapolis* is a failure. I have disposed of nearly 900 copies but the publishers have sold only 115. It will never see a second edition', and on 10 September: 'The failure of *Decapolis* sank my spirits much'. But on 10 October:

> I bless God for a letter from my publishers this morning informing me that only 450 copies of *Decapolis* are on hand. The sale had been 1,500 copies in 14 weeks. As the supply in hand is only equal to one month's demand, I shall proceed at once to a second edition. 23 October: *Decapolis* is now re-printing. I have ventured an edition of 4,000 copies. Should it prove a failure my loss will be heavy. 24 October: Only 350 copies remain. God grant that while he is blessing my endeavour, my soul may prosper and be in health. The devil is very angry about my book and often comes at me in a great rage. Temptations of a very fearful character he is sometimes permitted to bring.

What the devil did when, by 1843, *Decapolis* had reached the 13,000th in a fourth edition and had been extensively pirated in America, we are not told. He certainly did not succeed in checking sales nor in stopping the flow of similar works. *Chorazin, or An Appeal to the Child of Many Prayers*, reached 8,000 by 1842; *Laodicea, or Religious Declension*, 4,000 by 1842; *Damascus, or Conversion in Relation to the Grace of God and the Agency of Man*, 5,000 by 1846 and *Alarm in Zion, or a Few Thoughts on the Present State of Religion*, 2,000 by 1848. Over the years, *Decapolis* was to yield him £174 19s. 5d. (£5,940).

One can hardly exaggerate what he owed to his wife. What an extraordinarily tough, courageous and gifted woman she must have been. In their years at Lymington, when she built up one of the best known girls' schools for Dissenters, she was either pregnant or recovering from childbirth most of the time. She bore a surviving child in each of the years 1835, 1836, 1837, 1839, 1841, 1842 and 1844. The entry in David Everard Ford's diary for 19 June 1839 reads: 'At 4.40 a.m. I had a third daughter born to me. My beloved held out till the last and packed all the boxes. This is the day of our breaking up, and all the ladies but one are gone. My dear wife's confinement seems to have been most opportune, as with God's blessing she will have the whole of the holidays for renewing her strength'.

She had much to contend with in the mercurial temperament of her husband. He wrote in his diary on 12 January 1839: 'I am lost in astonishment. The time was when nothing but ruin stared us in the face'. Her annotation reads: 'I know not when'. In the following August, he wrote: 'I have given the instructions for the purchase of £140 Consols [about £4,000]', and she added: 'This after all the complaints'.

She was obviously very touchy about her school. Almost any comment was taken amiss. In March, and again September 1837, pages are cut out of his diary with the note: 'School affairs cut: they ought all to be removed'.

He was allowed, however, to observe in August of that year: 'The arrival of cholera here would at once be our ruin as our school would be scattered in a day and we would not have enough in the world to keep ourselves for three months but for God's blessing on my darling's exertions'.

Apparently in October 1837 when she was expecting Ada Haydon, there was some commotion in the household. He wrote: 'I was dreadfully excited as to the effects on our unborn child. I fear already that the poor thing will have but one eye and in addition to this calamity, it should prove an idiot, we shall have a new triumph of faith and patience'.

In 1875 his wife wrote: 'My husband always anticipated trouble'. In addition to her annotation we find: 'She was not an idiot and had two eyes'. This addition is signed 'Ada'. Evidently the daughter shared the mother's irritation. She was, herself, a married woman with five children when the diaries came to light in 1875.

David Everard Ford transmitted his tendency to see things in over-dramatic terms to his great-grandson, Maynard Keynes. In Virginia Woolf's Diary (volume 4 1931-35) Friday, 3 June 1932, we read: 'I heard Maynard say to Mrs. Shaw, "Well, we're about as bad as we can be. Never been so bad. We may go over the edge – but as it has never been like this, nobody knows. One would say we must" – which was uttered in the low tone of a doctor saying a man was dying in the next room, but did not want to disturb the company'. Maynard provoked in her the same kind of reaction which inspired so many of the annotations of David Everard Ford's diary by his wife. Virginia Woolf continues, 'This referred to the state of Europe; well, we lunched – very well too'. My father also had a touch of the 'Ford Dramatic' but I am sure that neither David Everard Ford nor my father, nor Maynard, really believed their dramatic sallies nor intended them to be taken literally. It was merely their way of emphasising the point they were making. Maynard's great-grandfather would have approved when he wrote 'words should be a little wild, for they are the assaults of thought upon the unthinking'.[3]

By 1840, David Everard Ford was becoming unsettled in his pastorate at Lymington. We find on 12 October the entry: 'My brothers seem to think I ought not to continue here unless I undertake a roving commission for six months in each year'. In the midst of consideration of his problems, we get a shrewd appreciation of technical progress. He wrote: 'War with France appears inevitable. War now would be such as war has never been since the world began. The appliances of murder by means of steam would be so great as to render destruction sure on both sides'. Substitute another word for 'steam' and he is to the point, 150 years later. Then back to his own position: 'I feel that here my work is done. Nearly all who hear me are Christians and beyond the walls of the chapel I can make no impression'. Also, trade was falling off in Lymington and members of his congregation were leaving to find work elsewhere. Lymington had been a more important place than Southampton. It was a port of call for vessels plying between London and Plymouth and it was a port for France and the Isle of Wight. As, however, the size of vessels increased and steam packets appeared, Southampton grew and Lymington declined. On 29 December 1840 he wrote to Dr. Matheson to offer his services to the Home Missionary Society. He got no early reply and, in April 1841, was invited to visit Devonport. The best way was still by sea as the railway had not got beyond Exeter. 'My passage down was a season of great peril. It blew a hurricane, the vessel was leaky and we were nearly run down by an Indiaman. Mercifully, we reached Torbay. I landed at Brixham, walked to Totnes, and proceeded to Devonport by coach'.

It was not till November 1841 that his offer to become an itinerant preacher was accepted. 'It is a great satisfaction to find that everyone, even including my dear wife, thinks I am doing rightly'. The salary of £75 (£2,160) would do no more than keep himself. His travelling expenses would be paid and he could count on hospitality. He was to travel for the Society for six months in the year leaving the remainder at his own disposal and retaining his home at Lymington. But the maintenance of that home, the needs of his wife and growing children, would have to be found from the profits of her school.

He accepted on 30 December 1841. 'I preached my farewell sermon to an overflowing and deeply affected congregation. For my own part I was not as deeply affected as I could wish. The unkind few had weakened my affection for all and I feel that this is not as it ought to be'. All we know about the unkind few comes from a letter, in many ways malicious and inaccurate, but the essence of the matter may be in a sentence in it. A descendant of the King family, the Lymington printers, wrote: 'My father and Mr. Rutter were returning from chapel which they had both attended. Father expressed satisfaction with the sermon they had just heard. His companion briefly replied "All for effect". This was his opinion of the preacher he knew intimately'.

We can see from his sermon register the wanderings required of him by the Society. The railway network was in its infancy and most of his travelling would have been by coach and by gig. In 1842 he was drafted to Kent, Norfolk, Lincoln, Northumberland, Cumberland, Yorkshire, Staffordshire, Somerset and Devon. There is a very full account in his auto-biography. He was well-known by reason of *Decapolis* and his other books so drew good congregations but the ardours of the itinerant life must have been extreme and affected his spirits. The entries in his diary are full of gloom. '26 Sept. 1842. My heart sinks within me at the thought of leaving my dear wife to serve alone. She is longing to see me settled in a pastorate'. By March 1843: 'I resume my wanderings. Right glad I should be to find a pastorate where again I should have my family round me. I confess that I am almost in despair for hope deferred maketh the heart sick'. He suffered from serious depression in reviewing whether he had been right to resign from Lymington and wondering if he would ever again be permanently employed. His wife's annotation of June 1843 reads: 'My husband was more anxious for settlement than I'. He writes:

> My soul is sinking in deep waters. With six babes all in health and not a single unpaid bill which I cannot meet, I apprehended troubles which I may never see and distressing foreboding fill me with terror and despair. Moreover, my beautiful darling, the wife whom I love so tenderly reproaches me with want of decision which would throw us out of bread. She wishes to leave but whither should we go?

Her comment on this passage in his diary, reads: 'D.E.F. was in such wretched spirits. I had sometimes to sympathize, sometimes to urge to action, sometimes to blame'.

He did not foresee that some day his diary and his autobiography might be read side by side, for in the latter, which he hoped might be published, he puts a wholly different face on things, writing: 'Although at this time, I had begun to change my views as to the relative advantages of a roving commission and a settled ministry, I breathed not one word of dissatisfaction, nor did I feel it'.

He had to set out on his last tour in August 1843, and wrote: 'I leave today on the most hopeless journey I have ever undertaken. I am to go through Dorset and North Devon in harvest time when congregations on a week-night are impracticable. My heart dies within me on leaving home. My beautiful wife has long loved me so dearly and I cannot bear to leave her'. But it was this journey which led to a fateful opening. At Ilfracombe on 22 September 1843 he met a certain James Griffin of Manchester who wrote to recommend him to a 'newly gathered flock' in his town. On 3 October, a Mr. Bancroft of Manchester wrote inviting him to preach at Greengate Chapel there. He did so for four Sundays and was appointed pastor. We have the letter in which he was informed that he had been elected by secret ballot and that in the first year his salary of £200 (£6,900) and, thereafter, the whole of the pew rents 'so long as the church continues to worship in this place'. The letter, dated 26 October 1843 was signed by John Dracup, Chairman. Fortunately, he had some private monies inherited from his parents, for he could hardly have faced the cost of removal

Manchester, October 28. 1843.

My sweet little blackeyes,

I am much obliged to you,
for your letter. When I am so
many miles away from home,
I am very glad to hear from
my dear babes. You know what
a mile is, do you not? Well,
only think of poor papa, three
hundred miles away! This
distance would be very terrible,
if we only had coaches, as they
used to have, when papa was
a young man. They now have

what they call locomotive engines,
things which go by steam, &
which run a great deal faster
than a horse when it goes
full gallop. If you are a
good girl & learn your lessons,
I will promise to give you a
ride, some day, in one of these
wonderful carriages. You will
be surprised to see the road
on which they run. Sometimes
it goes over the chimney tops,
& sometimes under the cellars,
of the houses which it passes,

& a single train will take
scores, & even hundreds, of
people.

I have told you that I am
now about three hundred miles
off. This is saturday; but it
will be tuesday when you have
this letter. I hope then to be
in London, not quite one hundred miles away from home.
Tell dear mama I love her,
& ask her whether that is news.

Your affectionate father

Miss Ada Haydon Ford.

18.   David Everard Ford's letter to his daughter Ada, 1843.

from Lymington nor the maintenance of his large family on such terms. He accepted on 29 October.

He had travelled down to Manchester by the new railway which had only been opened in 1842. On 28 October 1843, he wrote a letter from Manchester to his six-year-old daughter, Ada, which began, 'My sweet little black-eyes' and went on to describe the most revolutionary invention of his age. His letter is reproduced as plate 18. He moved to Manchester in November. At the end of December his wife came to spend Christmas with him, returning to Lymington on 16 January. 'Her visit has been of much mercy and she *interested* the people'.

In February he got a pain in his side and an attack of 'Ford Dramatics'. 'Depression of spirit sadly unfits me for my work. Perhaps my course is almost run. This northern climate tears me to pieces and I begin to fear I shall never see my lovely family again'.

In March he wrote: 'Many will be my cares both as to our removal and its consequence', across which his wife wrote: 'They devolved on me alone: my beloved was in Manchester'. This is not strictly true. When she married in 1834, Mrs. Ford had brought her 13-year-old sister, Sarah, with her to Lymington. When they moved to Manchester, Sarah was 23 and must have been of considerable help in looking after her young nephews and nieces.

On 24 April 1844, we get the first criticism of his wife I have been able to find. He wrote: 'The sale of my furniture begins this morning. I feel anxious as to the result but my wife writes me such crazy letters that I fear she is going mad. One would think me the most desolate of our race'. This drew a stiff and well-deserved rejoinder, albeit over thirty years later:

> This page shows want of thought. My labours and anxieties were fearful at this time and my physical energies were impaired (she was pregnant with her seventh child). My husband's affection was intense but he did not estimate the troubles rightly. This diary shows that he was frequently cast down. He forgets all that I had to do. Here is no madness but great anxiety, great labour. I was left alone, to have a sale, to pack, to wind-up a large concern, with those young children.

We get the best account of her journey to Manchester with Sarah and six children of nine or under from an autobiographical note by her daughter, Ada, herself only seven at the time of the move. They went by coach to Southampton and then on to London by train, only to find that the bank notes of the Wilts & Dorset Bank[4] in which Mrs. Ford had her money for the journey were not legal tender in London, so they could not go to an hotel, much less travel to Manchester. Mrs. Ford landed the whole party on the doorstep at her sister, Mary Price, who had only been married for a year. The children had to sleep in one bed, three heads at the top and three at the bottom. Uncle Price changed the notes for them and they went on to Manchester the next morning.

Chapter Six

DAVID EVERARD FORD

Manchester 1843-1849

Manchester, Lancashire, is where industrial capitalism began. Such capitalism, and the techniques it developed, now cover much of the world and have yielded a standard of life beyond the dreams of visionaries. The process continues. Even in my time I can remember ragged children running about the streets of Manchester with no shoes and stockings and with feet covered with that black slime which the burning of raw coal in a humid atmosphere deposited on city pavements. Many of those ragged children are now driving their robot-assembled cars. In Stockport, one in 12 of the working population are university graduates.[1]

The population of Manchester in 1774 was 41,000 but in the census of 1841, when the Industrial Revolution had got into its stride, it had risen to 243,000.[2] The average weekly wage for cotton spinners and weavers was about 10 to 12 shillings (£14 to £17), a rate undreamed of by agricultural labourers who were sucked in, not only from rural England, Scotland and Wales, but also from Ireland and Europe. The *Manchester Guardian* of 25 October 1851 refers to 'enormous shoals of paupers from Ireland, that great Celtic incubus'. Other poor immigrants (and without English) were Jews, for England was a posting stage for persecuted Jews fleeing to America from Russia, Poland and Germany in the 1840s, as it was a century later, when Hitler was launching the most horrific persecution of all, intended to be terminal. In earlier times, when they were persecuted and intermittently massacred, they had no escape, but, in the 1840s, railways had made flight possible. Stettin was linked with Berlin and Hamburg by rail in 1844 and Lower Silesia in 1846. By 1844 there was a direct railway chain across northern England, Hull, Leeds, Manchester and Liverpool, where, in 1846, a steerage passage to New York cost £3 (£96). But many stayed in Manchester where their brethren already had a firm foothold.

Any immigrants, in addition to the domestic flood already submerging south Lancashire, accentuated the appalling conditions and life was turbulent and precarious. The Reformed Parliament and the first Factory Act of consequence were only 10 years old. The Prayer Book was still relevant when it said, 'From plague, pestilence and famine, good Lord deliver us'. As we shall see from David Everard Ford's diary, cholera was endemic and the potato famine about to occur.

Among his books there is a guide book to Manchester dated 1839,[3] which he presumably bought when he arrived. It is a surprising work rather smugly revealing a more organised community with a more highly developed civic consciousness than one would have expected. Manchester had clearly assembled more than cotton mills and railways and was, according to its lights, making efforts to deal with its problems. It had innumerable churches, chapels, 'benevolent, moral and religious societies', schools, libraries, town offices, law courts, and a Royal Infirmary, where the total number of patients rose from 1,662 in 1780 to 19,342 in 1838. But all this can only have touched the fringe.

David Everard Ford had got himself into a position when he, too, had to become an emigrant to the industrial north, the population and wealth of which were increasing by such leaps and bounds and new chapels were being built. At least he had not got to learn a new trade and, in spite of the loss of her school and the task of moving to the north of England with six young children, his wife recognised, perhaps more clearly than he, that they had no choice.

His appointment was to Greengate Chapel, Salford (geographically a part of Manchester), but it was the intention of the deacons, led by James Bancroft, to build elsewhere as soon as they had the opportunity: Richmond Chapel was to be the outcome.

It so happens that the Salford Local History Library at Peel Park, Salford, has a bound volume of papers No. 285/8121 which includes 'The Story of Richmond Chapel by the Rev. Bernard J. Snell, M.A., B.Sc.', who opens with the intriguing sentence, 'Though the story is not a very long one, its early development is known to very few persons'. Mr. Snell tells how at Chapel Street Independent Chapel, Salford, a splinter group developed and took over an old disused Unitarian Chapel in Dawson's Croft, Greengate:

> There were 97 seceding members of Chapel Street Church, who thus initiated the new Independent Church, from which Richmond sprang, and their new venture was cordially and formally recognised by the other Independent Churches of the neighbourhood at a meeting held on 25 May, 1843.

> The Rev. David Everard Ford of Lymington was invited to become the pastor of this little community in October 1943, and immediately on his entry upon the ministerial duties a scheme was drawn up for providing a more suitable structure. It was decided to secure a site in Broughton and by agreement with the agent of the landowner, Mr. John Clowes, a plot was chosen near Broughton Bridge (then a toll-bridge). But the proposal to erect a Nonconformist chapel in the select district of Broughton was scouted by the Church of England party as an outrage, and Mr. Clowes was entreated to withhold his sanction to the proposal to desecrate this Episcopalian preserve.

> . . . Being shut out from Broughton the Independents chose the most eligible site they could obtain in Salford, the garden of Mr. Thomas Agnew[4] called Richmond Hill, which was purchased in December 1844, on chief rent at the price of one shilling per year. The plans of Mr. Lowe were accepted. The foundation stone was laid in May 1845 by Mr. James Carlton, and the building was completed by Messrs. Southern in time for the opening services on 22 April 1846. . . . The building has lost its pristine beauty, but we are not surprised to read that it received high eulogium on its completion. The total expense was £5,136 [£181,300]; the final instalment was paid in June 1853, and the deeds were deposited in the muniment room of Lancashire College in November.

James Bancroft, no doubt, guided David Everard Ford to Villiers Terrace, opposite his own rather grand house and garden called 'Noah's Ark', on the other side of Great Clowes Street, Broughton. David Everard Ford was able to rent the right-hand house in Villiers Terrace. It had a good entrance and 10 rooms but the road was still unpaved and there was no gas. The rent was £42 (£1,465) a year which was appropriate. Until the Rent Restrictions Acts made it impossible, by drying up the supply, to rent houses, the guideline for middle-class families was a rent equal to about 10 per cent. of their income. Rates, if levied, were of no importance. On his income of about £400 a year (£13,900) they were able to rent this good house and keep a cook, a housemaid, a nurse and Mrs. Ford's sister, Sarah, as governess. This shows, I think, that the retail price index alone does not enable one truly to assess the standard of life in earlier times: so many other factors come in.

The best account of their arrival is to be found in their daughter, Ada's, biographical notes. She tells us how, when the young family first moved from Lymington, she, and her brother Everard:

> were received into the house of Mr. Ainsworth (one of the deacons) who had a silk mill and lived in Broughton Lane. I have a very vivid memory of what a delightful time we had there. Ours had been a strict nursery life with two nurses to keep us in order, at Mr. Ainsworth's, luxury and freedom were combined. Mrs. Ainsworth was a very kind mother and the servants were of the old-fashioned sort, very devoted to the family and most indulgent.

> Amongst the congregation there were an unusual number of well-to-do men. Some with large families and all very interested in the growth of the new place. To mention a few,

19. Ordnance Survey map of Manchester, 1850.

1. Villiers Terrace
2. Noah's Ark
3. Broughton Bridge
4. Richmond Hill
5. Greengate Chapel
6. Ducie Chapel (Park Chapel)

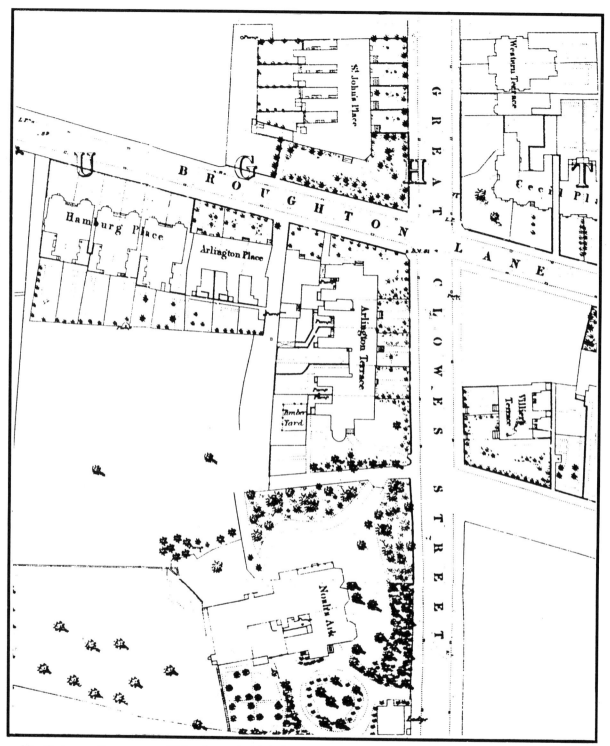

20. Ordnance Survey map of Manchester in 1850. David Everard Ford rented the right-hand house of Villiers Terrace from 1843 to 1860. Noah's Ark, on the left, was James Bancroft's house. All the old houses were demolished and replaced by back-to-back slums, a few of which were still standing in 1984, boarded-up and awaiting demolition. The area has again been developed, this time with small well-spaced houses and gardens.

Mr. Lowe, a leading man in Philips' Warehouse and a very generous personal friend, Alderman Bancroft, Vice-chairman of the London & North Western Railway Company, was a deacon and superintendent of the Sunday School. He was a workhouse boy and his first work outside was to help in digging the foundations of the gasworks. Having great force of character, he got promoted quickly and, when quite young, married a milliner, who supported the family, while he devoted himself to public works and rose quickly to a good financial position. When we came to Manchester he was living in a large house standing back in a garden nearly opposite to us. His wife was quite a lady, very charming and gave most delightful parties, especially dances at Xmas. Mr. Southern had a large business as builder and wood merchant. From a platform in his yard I witnessed several demonstrations. He had three sons and two daughters. Sam Southern was voluntary organist and his brother, William, was choir master. Miss Bancroft, who was married to William, the day of the Battle of Alma, and Miss Southern, afterwards Mrs. James Lee, were leading ladies in the choir. My father married Henry Lee to Miss Dracup and they lived on the opposite corner of Broughton Lane to where we were. He had begun life at Mr. Dracup's shop and then rose to partnership in Tootal, Broadhurst, Lee. His addresses were always on the subject of getting on in life. He seemed to think everyone could succeed, as he had, alone. Mr. Dracup was an older man who had a draper's shop in Chapel Street, with one son and two daughters. Mr. Crux, another deacon, had a fashionable shop in Deansgate and his wife gave some attention to the millinery part.

Some of these were already, or about to become, important Manchester families.

Philips' was one of the great wholesale warehouses of Manchester into which, through the good offices of Mr. Lowe, David Everard Ford was able to introduce his son, Everard. Rylands was another such warehouse and, when Mrs. Rylands established the world famous John Rylands Library in Manchester, she prescribed that Nonconformists should always be represented on the governing body. Hence, David Everard Ford's son, Gerard, and my father were, in succession, governors. S. & J. Watts was another of these great houses and we shall see that the James Watts of his day was a public figure. Before the development of Marks & Spencer and the big stores, the bulk of the clothing and household textiles passed from the mills to these great wholesale warehouses in Manchester, and thence on to the small private shops upon whom their travellers called assiduously, as we read in Arnold Bennett's *Old Wives Tales*. The Southerns referred to are now part of Magnet & Southerns, the nationally known timber importers and manufacturers of builders' joinery. Tootal, Broadhurst, Lee was one of the great firms of Manchester and we are still all familiar with Tootal handkerchiefs, shirts and other textiles.

In David Everard Ford's autobiography there was an interesting account of the problems which Dissenters, by their nature, had to face when they came to build a chapel. They had no diocesan architect to say what should or should not be done. Too many people wanted to have their say. The position of a window or pinnacle could cause serious disagreement in the Building Committee where the only qualification was a substantial contribution to the building fund. What dramas lie behind the facade of most Nonconformist chapels! Unlike the Church of England there was no hierarchy administering immense funds arising from pious benefactions of previous centuries and there was no court of appeal beyond the congregation of each chapel, dominated by its deacons. Those of Richmond Chapel, being chiefly men of business, kept their cards close to their chest, and even their pastor did not, at first, know the full extent of the liability involved in building. However, when the chapel was consecrated on 22 April 1846, David Everard Ford remarked, 'the cost had been kept secret by the deacons but the frightful secret could be concealed no longer – we owed £2,400' (£77,280). We know from Mr. Snell that the total cost was £5,136 (£181,280). Probably the deacons had paid half and left the congregation to pay off the balance over

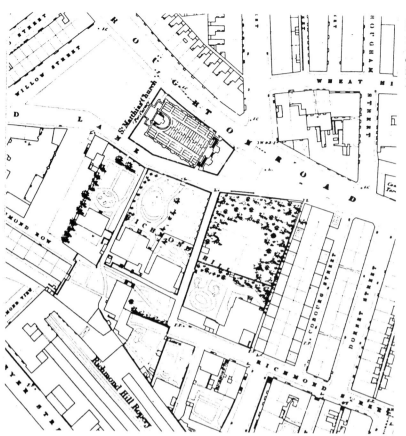

21. The Ordnance Survey map of Manchester in 1850 shows Richmond Hill as it was when the Greengate deacons acquired a site for their chapel in 1844. This site was on the Broughton Road face of the shrubbery.

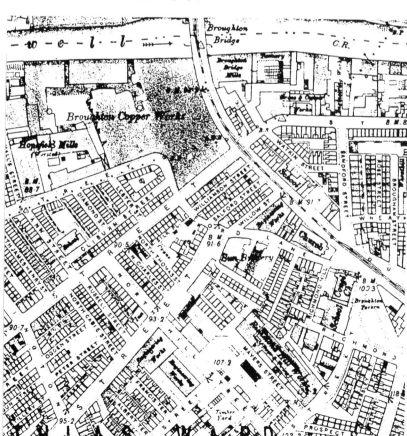

22. The Ordnance Survey map of Manchester in 1880 shows the chapel and the school (added after David Everard Ford's time). The back-to-back slum houses of the neighbourhood are evident. Today the whole of Richmond Hill is a pleasant public park, church, chapel and slums having gone.

the years. Most communal ventures are, in fact, largely financed by a few prosperous backers.

David Everard Ford was greatly impressed by the open-handedness of the Manchester people. The fact that the cotton industry was generating wealth enabled them to give effect to their generous inclinations.[5] For example, he records that Dr. Vaughan, the Principal of Lancashire Independent College (about which we shall hear more when we come to Dr. John Brown), preached the sermon at Greengate Chapel on the evening of 20 June 1844. The collection was £74 1s. 11½d., which he says 'was a very considerable sum when our present circumstances and prospects are taken into consideration'. It was, indeed, a very considerable

23.   Richmond Independent Chapel, Salford.

sum, today's equivalent being £2,582. What small chapel or church could today expect such a collection at evening service, albeit when a distinguished visitor is preaching?

A few months later he records another remarkable example of Manchester readiness to give, on 3 October, when he was called upon to second a motion of sympathy with Madagascar and Tahiti. He reports that the meeting: 'was disturbed by the sensualists miscalled socialists and with a Mrs. Martin at their head they succeeded in making a great uproar but the police officers soon put them to rout. Notwithstanding this scene of wickedness, we had a happy meeting. The chairman gave £1,000' (£35,000).

But there were other incidents in the spending of their new found wealth of which he did not wholly approve:

25 January 1845: Attended a grand dinner party. We had plenty of turbot, champaign [*sic*], claret and all delicacies in season and out but no family prayer. What would be thought of such a thing in the south? There were five present who 'lived by the altar'. What ought to be thought of it anywhere, but that Manchester Christians have very little religion and yet their munificence causes them to be spoken of throughout the world. On this occasion our host gave us £50 (£1,675).

All through the 1840s cholera was a continuing and terrible scourge. It had worried David Everard Ford in their years in Lymington, where any suggestion of its arrival would have emptied their school, and in Manchester he became dramatic. He was having trouble with his leg, and on 6 August 1846 wrote:

It may be that my leg will not much longer be wanted. Mortality is raging in Greenbank to a fearful extent, being 130% in advance of last year and three-fifths of the cases are connected with cholera – English cholera they say, but whatever may be its name, its characteristics are frightful. A man was seized with it yesterday at noon and at three he was a corpse. This was within a few doors of Richmond Chapel.

The agitation which led to the Repeal of the Corn Laws in 1846 stirred strong passions and the Manchester of Cobden and Bright was a focal point. Ada Ford writes in her autobiographical notes:

24.   Sarah Crellin (born Down), *c.*1847.

Aunt Sarah chose me as her favourite companion and I remember going with her to a meeting at Hanging Ditch to advocate the Repeal of the Corn Laws when I was eight-and-a-half. It was a wonder that one could object to such a beneficent Act but there was an organised plan to break up the meeting and men rushed in prepared to use force. Chairs were broken up and fought with and in the midst of the confusion women and children were pushed into a room and the door locked and, when safe, we were let out at the back of the building.

Aunt Sarah, herself, was only twenty-six. Evidently the whole family was interested in national affairs if she went to such a meeting taking her small companion.

Famine was also in prospect because on 18 August 1846 David Everard Ford wrote: 'The melancholy fact is becoming every day more apparent that the potato crop is an entire failure. Last year this visitation occasioned much distress, the present will probably prove a season of famine. Indeed, the plant appears to be dying out. What can be done to keep alive the teeming population of Ireland?: it seems impossible to say'. The following year was no better: '24 March 1847. Days are dark, very dark, and unless the potato should be restored there is no saying what the end will be. A loan of eight millions has been raised to keep Ireland from absolute starvation and this will not suffice till harvest'.

£8,000,000 would be £228,000,000 in 1986 and would be regarded as very substantial aid. Yet it is one of the main strands of Irish mythology, that even if the English were not actually responsible for the failure of the potato crop, they were unconcerned about the famine which inevitably followed.

On 7 May 1847, he was to write: 'Public distress is deepening fast. Many mills are already closed and many more will close this week. Provisions are still rising and trade is so bad that almost everybody is sinking capital. With all this the preparation of a new race-course is going forward as if the salvation of the world depended on its being finished by Whitsuntide'. Whitsuntide had, for centuries, been the Manchester 'Wakes' week. 'The commencement of our saturnalia. At Whitsuntide all Manchester goes mad. Who can wonder that harvests fail and that potatoes are blighted when men glory in their forgetfulness or contempt for all that is sacred'.

Like many others he was alarmed by the revolutionary violence on the Continent in 1848. This is referred to in his diary entry of 27 June: 'During the last few days, Paris has been the scene of awful carnage. Prague is now lying in ruins and probably Paris by this time in the same condition. Had the Chartists been able to prevail, London would have been as bad'. One would have thought that a Dissenting parson would have had some sympathy with the Chartists, all of whose six demands, with the exception of that for the annual re-election of Parliament, have since been granted. But it was the widespread revolutionary violence and the fact that the Irish, like the notorious Fergus O'Connor, M.P. for Nottingham and 'a redoubtable blackguard', joined in, which frightened the middle-classes. There were vicious riots in various parts of the country, and at Newport the Yeomanry had to be called out.

About France he was clear. He had written a month earlier: 'That wretched country, France, is again in a state of combustion. Yesterday was expected to be a bloody day in Paris. Blessed be God for the Straits of Dover'. One wonders what his reaction would have been if he had lived into the next century and read André Maurois's remark: 'When I consider that the English were nurtured on the Old Testament, I thank God for the Channel'.

On 26 July of that year we find: 'I have this day agreed to purchase for £400 [£13,120] my brother's share of our freehold in Kingsland Road (this must have been Everard property inherited from their mother) and if, as is very probable, I should fall in the next bout of cholera, it is a happy thought that neither widow nor my babes will have to ask shelter in the workhouse'. His wife was not going to let him get away, even posthumously, with this touch of 'Ford Dramatics', for she wrote firmly across the page: 'There was never, thank God, much fear of this'.

His eccentricity was becoming a little more evident, for on 4 August he tells us: 'I have today sent copies of my *Alarm in Zion* to Lord Brougham, Miss Burdett-Coutts, His Grace, the Archbishop of Canterbury'. A few days later, the Duke of Wellington and Prince Albert were similarly favoured.

On 20 March 1849 we get the first indication of the troubles ahead. The entry reads: 'A testing question will now arise whether Chapel Street and Richmond can both prosper. Or perhaps, the question may take the more trying form of whether I am the man to build the walls of Zion. My wife, who generally looks on the bright side of things, alarmed me not a little by diverse hints of the probability of my removal'.

In 1849 there was a visit of the Congregational Board of Education and David Everard Ford was appointed to their Manchester Committee. His comments are interesting:

> We shall do nothing. We cannot compete with the Government Schools because we cannot offer similar emoluments as a reward for their diligence. But even the Government Schools are not half full: the supply is everywhere greater than the demand. It is my firm persuasion that the entire question is very much misunderstood on all hands. Something beyond education is necessary, even to render educational advantages a blessing.

Had he perceived that the standard of life for the working classes was so low that the small income children could bring in when employed, could not be sacrificed, or was he pursuing some religious contention? It was not till 1880 that school attendance was made compulsory.

On 6 September 1849, he records:

> The cholera grows worse and worse. In the midst of life we are in death (and he then could not resist adding), the most incontrovertible proposition in that contradictory volume the Prayer Book. It now stretches over a large proportion of our island and few places are exempt, and from day-to-day the numbers assume a more appalling character. Bath is invaded by the destroyer and at Ramsgate my brother tells me the grave-digger can hardly work fast enough.

The endemic wave which the country was suffering ran from 1840 till 1849 and reappeared in 1882. It is now known that its bacillus is both air- and water-borne. The death rate was from 40 to 60 per cent. of those infected. There is a report to the General Board of Health on the Sanitary Conditions in Broughton in 1850 in which the Government Inspector wrote on page 12:

> Many of the large houses have covered cess-pools beneath them or upon the premises, into which the refuse from the water-closets and sinks is turned and there are many privies,

with open cess-pools behind and beneath them, where the refuse, such as ashes and leaves of vegetables is thrown, and the accumulation is allowed to go on for months together. The danger to health, and the nuisance arising from these privy cess-pool-middens, is very great. The present water supply is principally obtained from the local pumps and wells which are generally sunk on the premises.

David Everard Ford's diaries constantly refer to illnesses in his family which were obviously caused by such conditions. For example, Ada was supposed to have had a mild attack of cholera, and, having suffered no deaths of infants in Lymington, they lost Gerald in 1848 and Geraldine in 1852 in infancy in Broughton.

The same Inspector who wrote the report of 1850 also pointed out the danger of lead poisoning through drinking rain water collected in lead cisterns and, indeed, we find in David Everard Ford's diary an account of the death of the Richmond Chapel Treasurer, Mr. Ainsworth (who owned a silk mill and had entertained the Ford children immediately on their arrival from Lymington). On 20 January 1852, David Everard Ford wrote: 'The new surgeon testifies that they have all been poisoned in consequence of drinking rain water. Three died in three weeks with precisely the same symptoms'.

In spite of cholera things were going well with his own pastoral duties in 1849. 'Romanism is more potent for ill, because more consistent in its errors than Anglicanism can ever be. My work is to seek the prosperity of that section of the church where providence has placed me. The demolition of the citadels of Satan I must leave to younger men than I, capable of braving the terrors of death in the breech. Garrison duty is enough for me'. And he was apparently doing his 'garrison duty' very well. One of his anxieties had been that the new chapel at Richmond Hill might not permanently hold those who had seceded from the Chapel Street chapel. On Christmas Day 1849 he was able to write: 'It is well to bear in remembrance disappointed fears. I was sadly afraid that the attractiveness of old bricks and mortar would draw away our resources to the quarters from whence they came. Not so it proved, Chapel Street has prospered. So have we'. And that day he received the largest sum for a quarter's salary that he had ever had – £64 (£2,233). 'Many devout servants of Christ would think it a special mercy to receive such a sum for a whole year's labour. My salary for the closing year has been £282 12s. 0d. [£9,862]. Still, if I had no private resources, I could not live upon my income'.

Chapter Seven

DAVID EVERARD FORD

Success 1850-1857

With the passing of the 'Hungry Forties', the Chartists, and revolutionary violence in continental Europe, the benefits of the industrial revolution were becoming increasingly felt. The railway network was nearing completion though that amazing work had been the cause of great upheaval. For example, David Everard Ford wrote, 'It is reported that the Eastern Counties Railway will shortly grab our property in New Sun Street'. This was for the building of Liverpool Street Station and was John Everard's property which came to him through his mother. Railway Companies, operating under their Act of Parliament, rarely paid what the owners of property thought a fair price. One has heard the same complaint in our times, when land is acquired for a motorway.

When David Everard Ford was appointed the pastor of Richmond Hill chapel he was to have the proceeds of the seat rentals. His income was, therefore, directly connected with the size of his congregation and, at the end of 1851, he laid out a schedule showing what it amounted to during the preceding six years.

Year	£	*1986 Equivalent* £
1846	148	4,765
1847	234	6,692
1848	229	7,512
1849	239	8,341
1850	242	9,026
1851	258	9,958

If a pastor was popular with his congregation there were also not inconsiderable presents. At the Christmas of 1851 he was able to write of the gifts from his people, 'In addition to two geese, three turkeys and four hares, providence has sent my wife a shawl and me £5' (£192), and at the Christmas of 1852, we read, 'My soul praise the Lord. Mrs. Carlton sent yesterday a beautiful silk dress for my wife and my wife is now herself again'. But, he was more fortunate than many of his brethren because he had Everard monies. Thus, on 6 January 1851, he calculated his total income as follows:

	£	s.	d.
Digitalial	289	11	11
Patrimonial	82	4	4
Literary	14	7	3
Specialities	13	2	0
	£399	15	6

(1986 – £15,430)

'Digitalial' is a word of his own invention, though it sounds as if it belonged to our computer age. I think he meant monies which had to do with digits, with numbers – the numbers of people paying pew rents.

Competition between chapels was very fierce and certain of them employed door-to-door canvassers which David Everard Ford scorned. There was also touting because we read on

2 August 1852, 'One gentleman intimated a wish to settle with us but probably the other people will get him. They keep a sharp look-out and we cannot compete with them, and if it is necessary to use such means as they employ', I cannot'.

I have not given extracts of David Everard Ford's religious writings and we have no text of any of his sermons. In his diary he lapses, on occasion, into what might have been a passage in a sermon. There is an example of this on 18 November 1852, when he was writing about the funeral of the Duke of Wellington:

> The bones of the illustrious Duke are now on their pathway to grace. If the weather is in London as in Manchester, his obsequies will be the death of thousands.
>
> Mortals burying their dead! Each attending that funeral will soon want a grave!
>
> A more glorious spectacle awaits the faithful, from which no barriers or policemen can keep them away.
>
> Angels and the spirits of just men made perfect, welcome an illustrious saint to everlasting habitations; in solemn march proceeding. Not to the cold dark grave, which even in the crypt of St Paul's is a melancholy place, but to the right-hand of the glorious Redeemer. 'Well done! good and faithful servant!' The very deep gives back the sound, in mighty echos. A throng (compared with which the dense masses which watched our warrior to the grave were only a mere handful) responds in the thundering of angelic harmony 'Well Done'.

This was a soliloquy. He was evoking fantasies for his own pleasure, writing in his diary, and not his autobiography, which he thought might be published. And he goes on to put the old Duke in his place and to give himself and his calling a round of applause.

> 'Amidst such grandeur, earth and its little heroes are not forgotten and they that turn many to Righteousness shine as the stars for ever and ever!'

As I have said, this was a soliloquy and not a sermon. But how easily could it have become part of a sermon or funeral oration delivered to a rapt congregation with dramatic pause and gesture. There is no doubt that this is what his sermons were like, delivered with all the devices of, alas – that den of infamy – the theatre.

With these gifts went, in the case of David Everard Ford, a large measure of eccentricity and peculiar tricks. One of these was the addressing of letters in a manner which required co-operation from the Post Office. I have 16 examples and there are probably more amongst other family papers. Of course, in Manchester he was a well-known personality and possibly there were post office sorters who were members of his congregation at Richmond Chapel.

Much was going on in the Manchester of the 1850s. It was the time of the great agitation in favour of the Free Trade following the triumph of the Repeal of the Corn Laws. David Everard Ford wrote, on 2 March 1852: 'The Leaguers today subscribed £27,000 [over a million pounds] to protect free trade. When will our wealthy Christians be equally in earnest for the faith?' And there were lectures at the Free Library for which there was a great rush to get tickets. 'The most notorious [sic] authors of the day – Dickens, Thackeray, Sir Bulwer Lytton, Moncton Milnes, the Cambridge Professor of History, Lord Shaftesbury and others. Most of the speakers were very poor. A village missionary would usually command more eloquence. These men of mighty pen make a poor show when called to speak. Thackeray fairly stuck and sat down'.

Working through his diary for the year 1852, we find on 17 November, a record of another contact with a Keynes ancestor. David Everard Ford wrote: 'I have this day had the pleasure to forward to the Rev. Richard Keynes of Blandford a cheque for £22 5s. 0d. [£860] on behalf of Mrs. Palmer, whose husband resided in Herts., and whom I knew in connection with Wood End. Left with an income of £5 [£190] per annum to support herself and six children she had powerful claims on the churches'. Evidently, the Rev. Richard Keynes had circulated a general appeal for the widow of a Congregational pastor. He was the

25. Two examples of letters sent by David Everard Ford: a challenge for the Post Office.

Keynes referred to by Geoffrey Keynes in his *The Gates of Memory*, who became a Congregational minister at Blandford. He was the uncle of John Keynes, before whom David Everard Ford probably preached at the Salisbury Brown Street Chapel in 1831.

Things had been going so well with Richmond Chapel that they were able to pay off the balance of their debt. 'Dr. Harris declines to preach the funeral sermon for our debt apprehending that it would not be long before someone will have to render him that service'.

Not only was the congregation supporting the chapel generously, there were also marks of appreciation for their pastor's wife. These, in particular, came from Frederick V. Lowe. As will be seen, Lowe was David Everard Ford's staunchest supporter in the troubles which led to his resignation. I do not think that he, himself, attracted the loyalty Lowe was to show, but rather that Lowe was much attracted by Mrs. Ford.

David Everard Ford notes in his diary on 7 October 1853:

> At the close of the meeting, Mr. Lowe presented my dear wife with a purse of 60 sovereigns [£2,200] expressive of admiration of her *pastoral qualifications*. On my return home a watch arrived from Mr. Dracup which had been his son's, Robert, who died whilst a student at Exeter College. I had long desired that very thing and had designed its purchase. This morning my dear wife has been into town with me to procure a gold Albert chain that I might realise the *first fruits of her toils*. Altogether, it was a blessed commencement of the decade of my Manchester pastorate.

David Everard Ford suffered severely from attacks of gout. He also had serious trouble with the knee which had been dislocated. At times, in his late 50s, he could not walk without crutches and doubted whether he could continue his pastoral duties. There were frequent references to members of the congregation and others transporting him in their carriage. On one occasion, the descendant of Black Ben, 'Sir Elkanah Armitage, brought me homeward åin his carriage'.

26. The Rev. David Everard Ford: an engraving reproduced in the *Evangelical Magazine*, 1854.

There were in the Manchester cotton trade two great families by the name of Armitage. One of these families was descended from a certain Black Ben and the other from a certain Red Ben, both of whom figured large in Manchester folklore. A descendant of Black Ben, 'Sir Elkanah Armitage gave us a great spread yesterday of diverse meats and drinks to follow-up the dinner at the Royal Hotel given by Mr. James Watt'. Mr. James Watt was a member of S. & J. Watt's, another great wholesale house, comparable with Philips's. In my days in Manchester in the 1920s and '30s there were still descendants of these families, together with those of Red Ben, of which the firm Armitage & Rigby was best known – and very gifted they still were. From the days of David Everard Ford there was still a century to run before the final eclipse of the cotton trade and Manchester leadership.

Until 1914 Manchester had enjoyed a pre-eminence amongst provincial cities to which there is no parallel today. This was based, not solely on wealth, but also on its Liberal and entrepreneurial outlook. Its contact with other civilisations, by reason of its worldwide export trade, produced a culture wholly different from that of Birmingham. Its Scottish, German and Jewish merchants read *The Manchester Guardian* and supported the Hallé concerts, whilst all its

27. (*right*) The Rev. John Brown, the young minister at Park Chapel.

28. (*below left*) Ada Haydon Ford, from a daguerreotype.

29. (*below right*) The young Mrs. John Brown.

citizens would unite in a venture as remarkable as the Manchester Ship Canal. There was some element of truth in the cliché 'What Manchester thinks today, London thinks tomorrow'.

David Everard Ford's children were beginning to grow up. Mary was 19 and about to go teaching, Everard was 18 and at Philips's and Ada, only 17, was already teaching far from home. Laura, Emiline, Palmer and Clara were still in the schoolroom whilst Gerard, at five, was happy being spoilt (they had lost Gerald and Geraldine). That the three eldest should be gainfully employed was good, but the resulting independence led to the usual worries, for, on 17 January 1856, we read:

> Dancing is the very pest of this neighbourhood. Mary, Laura and Everard were at Mrs. Lees' party till three this morning and they were amongst the first to leave. Ada, poor child, would have gone with all her heart, if she could only have been carried thither. (She had had a fall). It is astonishing to me how our children acquired the love of such a folly as we never allowed them to see a dance or to learn. I suppose that, like depravity in general, it is indigenous.

There had already been anxieties, for on 6 December 1850, he had written: 'This is my Mary's hour of peril. She is now in London, without friend or guide, going from Euston Square to the Great Western terminus. God grant she may reach Taunton safely'.[1] He need not have worried: she grew up to be as formidable as her mother and there is no doubt that, at the age of 16, she knew how to button-up her face and also had the gift of the dismissive crack. When my father was a small boy, he was reading whilst his mother and Aunt Mary were gossiping. Aunt Mary said, 'I hear that Harold is doing very well'. When my father looked up, hopefully, she said, 'No, not you young man'.

Ada was 20 when she got engaged, and we have two versions of her engagement: there is that of her daughter, Florence Keynes (born Brown) and that of her father.

Florence writes:

> John Brown, who was considered a specially promising theological student, was released shortly before the termination of his college course in order to save the situation. He came full of enthusiasm and quickly gathered about him a body of devoted adherents to form the nucleus of a church. This young man was naturally introduced to the family of David Everard Ford, one of the senior ministers of the denomination locally. It was also quite natural that he should fall in love with one of the reverend gentleman's charming daughters. His choice fell upon the second – Ada – a young girl who had the courage to be one of the first to break away from the confines of the Victorian poke bonnet and to shade her fine dark eyes under a wide leghorn hat trimmed with black velvet ribbons and a pink rose, to the scandal of all right-minded females. Ada, on her part, was not unwilling to throw in her lot with that of the brilliant young minister who was ever trying to subdue, as unsuited to his chosen profession, his dramatic instinct and his wit which had been the joy of his fellow students.[2]

Then we have David Everard Ford's account:

> Ada this afternoon received an offer from Mr. Brown of Park Chapel. She hesitates and asks my advice. I have told her to follow the example of Hezekiah, in relation to a letter of different purport. Lay it before the Lord. Like many foolish girls she had often said that she would never marry a minister. And, if she would only wait a little, it was likely that an opportunity of better settlement as to this life, would be submitted to her discretion: but I will not be the father to oppose the marriage of a child to one who saves souls.

He gave it only second place in his entry for 26 February 1857. Perhaps, he and his wife had been hoping she would marry into one of the prosperous Manchester families who were members of his congregation,[3] and he must also have had some natural antipathy to a promising young man who had just taken over a competing chapel. It is doubtful, however, if he foresaw the disaster to his own personal position which was to flow from Ada's engagement.

Chapter Eight

DAVID EVERARD FORD

Pastoral Bereavement 1858

During 1857 trouble was brewing at Richmond Chapel. It was very natural and very probable that, where a pastor was as idiosyncratic and flamboyant as David Everard Ford, a congregation would, after 14 years, want a change. Irritation with his style and mannerisms must have been building up, but as usual in such situations, it is some particular matter or incident which lights the fuse. I think it was lit by the appearance of my grandfather, John Brown, at the neighbouring Park Chapel and the fact that this personable young minister was carried off by one of David Everard Ford's pretty daughters, Ada.

Mr. Dracup was the chairman of the deacons at Richmond Chapel and certain of his unmarried women-folk also had their eyes on the young Rev. John Brown. We read in David Everard Ford's diary for 10 November 1857:

> I thought myself to be the happy pastor of a united and affectionate flock, but I find myself mistaken. Mr. Dracup told me, last night, that there is a strong feeling against my ministry, especially among the young people. Mrs. Tom Dracup leaves us for Mr. Muncaster's, in consequence of Ada's engagement to Mr. Brown. This I have long expected, but she is trying to injure me by alleging as the reason, the importunities of her young people, who she says, find my sermons too elaborate for their comprehension. If so, she must sadly have neglected their education.

It was not only the Dracups who were sore, for: 'Emily Askew hates me because she failed to enamour Mr. Brown'.

On 11 November there was a very clear indication that the underlying situation was serious. His generous and steadfast friend, Mr. Lowe, asked him if a salary of £700 (£20,000) would tempt him to leave. He reports that he said 'no', but he did not apparently grasp the significance. This was a clear hint by a loyal friend that he should, perhaps, look elsewhere. He did, however, become exceedingly worried, and wrote: 'My nights are very gloomy, but my *beloved wife greatly cheers me now*. I need to be comforted'.

On 22 December he wrote: 'Yesterday was a dark one. My poor darling wife was sadly upset by a visit from Mrs. William Dracup, who returned her borrowed cushions to the door. That poor spiteful woman will do me all the injury she can, but no devil can go beyond the length of his chain'. His wife made a pertinent note: 'Coming events cast their shadow before. The result proved I was right'.

The year 1858 opened badly. 'During the morning I had a lecture from Mr. Dracup, as the note of preparation for a fatal fray, about his foolish and spiteful daughter-in-law'. Mrs. Ford noted, 'My husband was now very excitable and not without reason'. And he wrote, 'At the house of Mr. Lowe, his compassion for my wrongs produced a champagne supper'. Mr. Lowe was, no doubt, gratified by the animation which the champagne and sympathy produced in Mrs. Ford.

There had been changes amongst the deacons and five new men came in. He continued to be exceedingly worried and his wife wrote:

> Everything annoyed him. The trouble in the church was decidedly approaching though he wished not to believe it and, in addition, he was sickening for smallpox. To attempt to console or stimulate a decision was equally in vain and taken badly, and no wonder I can

now thank God for the Richmond affair, which then nearly cost me my life and reason, as it prolonged the life of my husband several years and increased its usefulness.

This is a most interesting comment. Apparently his wife had come to the conclusion that he was not ideal as a pastor of a chapel in charge of a congregation, though he had great powers as a preacher, and it was in the succeeding years that he continued to preach as a 'supply' preacher all over Lancashire and Cheshire, which she regarded as increasing his usefulness. A 'supply' preacher is a substitute and it was the custom for the cost of engaging a 'supply' pastor, when the resident pastor was away preaching elsewhere, to be borne by the resident.

On 21 January the symptoms of smallpox appeared and the deacons ordered David Everard Ford at least five weeks' holiday, adding that they would not charge him for supplies – meaning that they would pay the cost of his substitutes. His good friend, Mr. Lowe, sent him a dozen bottles of port and a pheasant. A week later he was much better in spirit, and he reported, 'The goblins are gone', and on 3 February he went to Blackpool and, later, on 6 March, to Torpoint.

His diary during the painful early months of 1858 is not very explicit and is, naturally, full of extreme expressions of indignation and distress. It is to his autobiography that one must turn for a coherent account of events, though that account may have been written up to 10 years later and there are occasions when it is difficult to reconcile the two.

It was when he was on the last week of his holiday staying with his wife's parents at Torpoint that he received a letter signed by the 10 deacons of Richmond Chapel, which eventually led to his resignation. We have the original: it is a lengthy document which, much abridged, reads:

Richmond Chapel Vestry
24 February 1858.

Dear Sir,

During your recent indisposition the affairs of the church rendered it necessary for us to meet and confer together.

One of those meetings disclosed the existence of a feeling of dissatisfaction among the members of the church and congregation.

A place of worship so commodious ought to be well filled and to this extent at least there are all the indications of prosperity, but little increase has taken place and, in fact, we are on the wane. Some families long connected with the place are dissatisfied, and it is feared are on the point of removal.

The reasons assigned for this state of things are – that your ministry does not interest, or command the respect and affection of the young – and that it is not understood by, or adapted to interest and attract, the labouring classes.

We assure you that nothing but a sense of duty forced us to make this communication following so soon your serious illness, and need hardly say that we shall be glad to meet you for a mutual explanation should you desire it.

Commending you to the divine guidance.

We are Dear Sir,
Yours Faithfully,

John Dracup
James Bancroft
S. A. Dewhurst
Henry Lee
Josh. B. Lever
Geo. Crux
Robt. K. Lee
Isaac Bryant
Rober Acheson
John A. Moss

He reproduced this letter in his autobiography and wrote:

I was astonished, bewildered, overwhelmed. At first I doubted the sanity of the writers and then my own, it seemed like a hideous vision rather than reality. No, I would not, I could not, believe it. But believe it I must, for these were their signatures. The document was no forgery. One name, however, was not there and that missing name was one distinguished for gentlemanly honour and Christian liberality. If that signature had stood here, I should now have said in my haste, 'all men are liars'.

The missing name was Lowe, his faithful supporter.

As soon as I had sufficiently recovered from my surprise, I managed to write the following brief letter. Its tone was certainly far milder than subsequent events would have justified, having always acted on the principle – never to give offence if I could help and never to take offence under any circumstances whatever – I determined to use only words of kindness and here they are.

His first rough draft is reproduced as plate 30.

He returned to Manchester on Friday, 5 March, having told no one but his wife, preached as usual on the Sunday and arranged to meet the deacons on Tuesday, 16 March. The meeting was unsatisfactory because they would make no specific charges but only a statement of general dissatisfaction, 'But, as Mrs. Ford had, during my absence, called on 52 families or individual seat-holders, and all of them expressed themselves as earnestly looking forward to my return. . . .' Considering the firm character of the lady, this was not surprising, but as the deacons would give no names, he was nonplussed. 'They intimated that they would treat me generously and that no decision on my part was expected for some time to come'.

His diary during March is filled with accounts of sleepless nights and doubts as to how he should proceed. He had reassurance from friends and supporters and it looked as if the matter would blow over. But his daughter, Ada, nearly had hysterics because he looked so ill during a service and her fiancé, 'Mr. Brown, is profoundly astonished and says that every minister in Manchester will shake in his own shoes as to his own position'.

On 31 March, John Dracup died. He was the chairman of the deacons and one of the chief malcontents. 'His death will tend to set matters in a new light, but whether that light will be permanent, I cannot see'. But on 1 April he had to record: 'Miss Dracup flew at me last evening like a lady bulldog – her father lying dead the while! I went to comfort her mother in her affliction and she began to abuse me about Mrs. Williams and Mr. Brown'. The critical part of his diary, between 4-11 April has been cut out. It is to his autobiography that we must turn for the continuation of the story:

I had even begun to entertain the question, how far it would be compatible with my character, as a Christian minister, to allow matters to resume their usual course, without a more definite understanding as to the limits of pastoral endurance and diaconal interference. This was precisely the position of affairs when, on Saturday night, I received a letter of resignation from the deacons.

Some of his friends thought that this was a good thing, but he did not know what the deacons were doing, or what he should do. At a church meeting at which eight of the nine recalcitrant deacons were on his left, and the only one who supported him, on his right, 'One could not but be forcibly reminded of the unequal array of the Syrians and the Children of Israel'. The leader of the malcontents who had succeeded Mr. Dracup was absent, but his second-in-command was abusive to David Everard Ford's supporters, though courteous to him. The deacons claimed that they did not wish to divide the church on the question of their pastor's retirement and their resignation as deacons was accepted. He gave them credit for sincerity so far as the disclaimer went and almost began to fancy their difficulties were past.

30. David Everard Ford's draft letter to the deacons of Richmond Chapel, February 1858.

Soon I was undeceived. The following Sunday week was the church anniversary and was the occasion of the grand collection of the year. As the church had been run by, and as the monies had been spent by, the men who had only just resigned, it was assumed that they would contribute their fair proportion. Not they indeed! So, when the collectors carried round the boxes, these men, with all their families and dependants, buttoned-up their pockets and shook their heads, while some of them had the cruelty to laugh outright! So well had they perfected their plans that the entire collection realised less than £40 [£1,276] (instead of the £140 [£4,466] requested and expected). I then understood their tactics: they intended to starve me out by creating a deficit on the incidentals and charging it on the pew rents, and they made no secret of the matter.

Since he derived his income from the pew rents, they were, as he said, in a position to starve him out.

At the request of the sole office-bearer, he called another church meeting for 6 May, to elect deacons. The same nine recalcitrant deacons were re-elected.

It afterwards transpired that there had been canvassers, intimidation and all the worst features of a parliamentary election. When the meeting was over, I retired to the vestry. The daily companion of my sorrows, my noble-minded wife, followed me and said, 'Your course is now quite clear. You must resign'. Before I had time to reply, our generous friend entered the vestry [this was Mr. Lowe]. 'What think you of affairs now?', he said. I knew what the question meant and, as he had previously advised me by no means to retire, and had informed me as to his readiness to sustain both the pastor and the place, if needs be, to an extent beyond any parallel in Manchester. 'As dark as they can be', was my reply. 'Never mind, cheer up. In that pulpit or out of it you shall have £100 [£3,200] a year from me for four years to come'. God only knows how welcome or how timely was that assurance. It saved me from despair.

Expecting my mind to be greatly disturbed, although not anticipating all that I was called to endure, I had previously arranged with a friend to exchange pulpits on the following Lord's day. The exchange was made and I left, in the hands of my substitute the following letter, which he publicly read, both morning and evening:

TO THE
CHURCH AND CONGREGATION
ASSEMBLING AT
RICHMOND CHAPEL
MANCHESTER
———

FRIENDS AND BRETHREN

Recent events have prepared you for the announcement, that my ministry among you, belongs only to the memories of the past.

For fourteen years, I pursued the even tenor of my way and thought no pastorate happier, or securer, than mine. With fond and affectionate zeal, I laboured for your welfare, wept with you in your sorrows, and rejoiced in your prosperity as if it had been my own.

As to my life and ministry – before my gracious Master I have much to confess, and much to deplore. But, before man, justice is all I ask. To Him, I have no apology to offer. Instant in season and out-of-season, with an amount of pastoral labour which left me little time for other occupations, it has been my study to adorn the gospel and to make full proof of my ministry.

And now, brethren, I know that ye all, among whom, I have gone preaching the kingdom of God, will hear my voice no more.

Among you, there are some whose generous kindness I shall never cease to remember. The Lord reward them abundantly, both now and in His heavenly kingdom!

If any have occasioned me pain, I condemn them not. No hard words have yet escaped my lips; and it is not likely that they ever will.

Although I am leaving you, I doubt not that I shall find some sphere of usefulness, where I may turn to good account the pastoral and ministerial experience of former years. The time – the place – I leave in the hands of Him who walks amidst the golden candlesticks. I have loved His service from the age of 14; and He will not forsake me now.

As for any formal leave-taking, my heart is too full to allow it. The hour of separation is over. The bitterness of death is past.

Farewell, brethren, sisters, friends! – my last farewell! We shall soon meet again. The Lord grant that we may find mercy of the Lord in that day!

Allow me to subscribe myself, with such sorrow of the heart as no one, never placed in my circumstance, can possibly comprehend.

Your once faithful and affectionate

Friend and Pastor

Villiers Terrace, Broughton
DAVID EVERARD FORD
Saturday evening, 8 May 1858.

Chapter Nine

DAVID EVERARD FORD

Supply Preacher 1859-1875

His letter of resignation was not only read, but also printed. As we have seen from his Lymington days, he was a great believer in the printed broadsheet. In his autobiography he writes:

> The impression produced by the public reading of this letter was such, that the authors of the mischief were alarmed as to probable consequences. Already, several of the members and seat-holders had taken away as many of their books as they could conveniently carry – and told the apparitor when they would send for the remainder – and, had left the chapel, declaring that they would never enter it again. That such proceedings should go no further, it was thought advisable to take immediate steps. Accordingly, on the evening of the next day, my friend called to tell me that the late deacons, then deacons-elect, had deputed one of their number, to wait on him, to inquire whether I would be willing to accept a testimonial of £500 [£16,000], as they did not wish for us to part on bad terms; and as they thought it only right to mention such a sum as would render it unnecessary for me to take the first pulpit that might offer.

He regarded this offer with grave suspicion and wrote, *timeo Danaos et dona ferentes*. He proved right, because in the event, after rather sordid negotiations which occupy the remaining half-dozen pages of his autobiography he, in fact, only received £150 (£4,785), which he contemptuously describes as 'six shillings in the pound'. It was, indeed, only a little over six months' pew rents.

He did not carry his autobiography beyond his 'Pastoral Bereavement' chapter and for the next 14 years we have only his diary and sermon register. In his diary, as we might expect, there are many despairing entries, such as: '16 May. A silent Sabbath in possession but not in enjoyment of perfect health and strength. God grant that I may not have many such. My poor darling is sadly distracted. She will have it that I have ruined myself by my patient submission'. Then, her characteristic annotation, 'Rather too gloomy a picture'. But, of course, she wrote that 20 years later with the benefit of hindsight. 'No light yet breaks. Surely, it never will and yet I ought not to give up all for lost. I fear that my mind will give way, if not my bodily health. It is, indeed, a wonderful thing that I have been sustained as I have been, but some times I get near the gates of death. My poor darling chides me with being "cast down"; my wonder is that I am not destroyed'. And again, her annotation, 'She did not chide, but she wished to rouse her beloved to face the evil. She wished to act rather than to mourn'.

On the same day he remarked, 'It is no small mercy that I get some supplying to do'. Then we get, on the day after, 'No deliverance appears: but my dear wife withdraws her determination not to open a school in Manchester' because, she wrote, 'I preferred one elsewhere (but) two desirable openings presented themselves'.

Here we have in two short entries the pattern of the balance of their lives. He, at 61, was to turn to supply preaching and she, at 49, to her original skill in running schools.

At the end of the year he worked out what his income had been. It was rather higher than usual by reason of the once-and-for-all payment arising from his resignation from Richmond Chapel. As usual he describes each item by some odd word, such as, 'Patrimonial', 'Digitalial', 'Filial' and so on. Then there is a new item described as 'Thimble-rig' – £150.

Treasurer's Pew Rent Account to March 25th 1859.

Dr.   Cr.

	£	s.	D.		£	s.	D.
To Pew Rents	241	17	8	By Cash to Rev. D. E. Ford, balance of Salary	40	0	0
„ Contributions from the Deacons for special vote of the } Church	118	2	0	„ do. do. special vote of the Church......	150	0	0
„ Balance due	18	19	10	„ Cash to Supplies	188	19	6
	£378	19	6		£378	19	6

Treasurer's Incidental Cash Account to March 25th 1859.

	£	s.	D.		£	s.	D.
To Collections last Anniversary............	37	12	10	By Balance last Anniversary..................	72	15	11
„ Contributions for Tea Service............	9	19	3	„ Chief Rent................................	56	0	0
„ Rent from Sunday School	20	0	0	„ Printing, Advertising, &c	16	7	9
„ Balance due	156	15	4	„ Attendance, Cleaning, Lighting and Insuring Chapel	51	0	3
				„ Sundry Incidental Expences including new Tea Service..	28	3	6
	£224	7	5		£224	7	5

Audited and found correct,

HENRY LEE,
WM. KAYE.

AMOUNT REQUIRED THIS ANNIVERSARY.

Balance due to Treasurer	156	0	0
Current Expences, including £56 for Chief Rent, say	124	0	0
	£280	0	0

31. Richmond Chapel Accounts for 1858/9. (Multiply by 30 to get 1986 equivalent.)

This was the settlement Richmond Chapel had made with him and his description is a reference to the swindle operated at fairgrounds with a pea and a thimble, rather like the 'three card trick'.

The Local History Library at Salford has, as I have mentioned, a bound collection of Richmond Chapel papers, amongst which is their accounts for the year 1859, which I reproduce as plate 31. It will be seen that, in fact, the deacons had no surplus on which they could draw after allowing for supply preachers and, indeed, had to put their hand in their pocket to the amount of £118 2s. 0d. (£3,658) to meet, what he called, their 'thimble-rig' settlement with him.

Things really took a turn for the better on 8 March 1859, when a certain Mr. Barfoot, who had been one of his congregation at Richmond Chapel, died and left him £3,000 (£94,000). This relieved his financial worries and his self-respect was restored by his success as a supply preacher. In the first four months after leaving Richmond Chapel he preached 26 times and had gone as far afield as Croydon, Poplar and Billericay in Essex. From September onwards, a local Presbyterian church employed him for spells of 23, 9, 11 and 13 services and he doubled their congregation. His fees for this first year of supply preaching amounted to £87 (£2,723). By 1860 he was much in demand all over the north of England. He preached 88 times and this pattern was to continue for another 14 years, but it did not yield an income on which they could live.

The school project of his wife's was slower in starting. They must have been discussing it because she complains that she could not get him to make up his mind and on 17 February 1860, when he was having an attack of his glooms, we read: 'And lower still I am getting, even to the border of despair. And my poor wife is at me continuously about opening a school. I sometimes feel my reason will give way. Yet surely the wonder which God has wrought for me ought to fill my soul with praise'. One could say that the wonder was his wife, whose annotation about the school project read, 'A wise and necessary step which my dearly loved husband long opposed'. Then we get a surprising annotation. She actually wrote, 'I am sorry I took the leaves out. They contained the discussion about removing and opening a school . . . necessary if he did not get a pastorate'. A biographer can only wish that she had realised earlier that some of her mutilations might be a mistake. Pages between 25 April and 28 July 1860 have all been cut out: it must have been during that period that she got her way, because he then wrote, 'How our house will ever be ready for use, I am at a loss to think'. To which she added, 'He was so morbidly fearful of non-success. Timidity as to every step characterised him'. By 8 September they were in the new house, for he wrote, 'The first sentence in my new abode. As to the school, about which I was so anxious, it was a *glorious* success, providing us, not only with the means of subsistence, but enabling us to make good provision for the time to come. It went on until the death of my landlord occasioned a notice to quit our residence at Merryfield House'.

By April they had six boarders and eight day scholars and David Everard Ford was getting plenty of supply work, but they were worried about the consequences of the American Civil War for Lancashire. The supply of raw cotton was drying up and though, at first, he records that the better employers kept their people on short time, they could not do so indefinitely. A relief fund of over one million pounds (30 million pounds) was raised. As more and more mills shut down, depression spread through Lancashire and Manchester, its merchant capital. David Everard Ford reported that he had to compete with 18 other 'job-preachers' in the Manchester area and wrote that he and his wife were 'likely to lose one-third of our school by the pressure of the time'. He even managed to dent his wife's buoyancy, for she wrote, 'When my precious one saw nothing but ruin all around, could I fail to be depressed?' She knew that she was facing, not one of his moods, but an economic disaster with widespread consequences. By August he was writing: 'Trade is getting worse and worse and there seems to be no hope of improvement until we can become independent of American slavery. That sin belongs no less to the North than to the South and to pretend that Northerners are fighting to put it down is sheer humbug. It seems, however, that they are determined to fight till the country is ruined'.

In 1865 the great excitement was the addition of another house, Glen Villa, to give extra accommodation for the school which now had 30 pupils.

I reproduce the prospectus adding the approximate 1986 equivalent for the fees charged. Merryfield House was in Smedley Road off Queen's Road, Cheetham, and Glen Villa was in Church Lane, Harpurhey, overlooking Moston brook. Queen's Road was at the top of Cheetham Hill and as early as 1830 it had been forecast that 'Cheetham Hill would become a favourite area for gentlemens' residences. It has always been the most healthy of all the environs of Manchester'.[1] Mrs. Ford had good business sense, for Queen's Road was less than half-a-mile from an area to which the most successful immigrant Jewish families were soon to move in considerable numbers. They would be anxious that their daughters should have genteel English education and there was much in the character of Mrs. Ford which would commend itself to them. Mrs. Ford must have had great confidence in her eldest daughter, Mary, who was responsible for Glen Villa, which was some distance from Merryfield.

The happiest account of Merryfield and Glen Villa is to be found in Florence Keynes's

GLEN VILLA,

MOSTON;

AND

MERRYFIELD HOUSE,

CHEETHAM;

MANCHESTER.

Mrs. and the Misses FORD, assisted by competent Governesses and Professors, receive a limited number of YOUNG LADIES.

TERMS :

For a Comprehensive English Education, with the use of Library, Globes, &c.; Two Guineas and a Half, per Term of Ten Weeks.   Pupils, under Ten Years of Age; Two Guineas.

Inclusive of Board, with Home Comforts; Thirty-five Guineas, per Annum.

Pupils, under Ten Years of Age, or Weekly Boarders; Thirty Guineas, per Annum.

Laundress; Three Guineas, per Annum.

French, Music, Drawing, and Dancing; each One Guinea, per Term.

Latin, German, and Italian; each One Guinea and a Half, per Term.

Singing; Half a Guinea, per Term.

GLEN VILLA, and MERRYFIELD HOUSE, are both pleasantly situated within their own Grounds.

Accounts settled Quarterly.   A Quarter's Notice, previous to the Removal of a Pupil.

---

32. Prospectus for Glen Villa and Merryfield. The fees quoted would now be:

	£
Two Guineas-and-a-Half	79
Two Guineas	63
Thirty-five Guineas	1,100
Thirty Guineas	942
Three Guineas	94
One Guinea	31
One-and-a-Half Guineas	47
Half-a-Guinea	15

Gathering up the Threads, and I cannot do better than quote from it at length. Florence was of an age to remember David Everard Ford who died in 1875, when Florence was 14, whereas my father was an infant, so we are indebted to her for a contemporary account of Merryfield, rather than the legendary stories which I heard from him. She wrote:

When the boys and girls were becoming young men and women, their father gave up his pastoral work and the time had come for the wife's gift for teaching to contribute an important share of the family income. She returned to her earlier interest with zest. Again, a large house was obtained, standing in a shady garden, called Merryfield, not altogether an appropriate name for such a strictly disciplined educational establishment. The unmarried daughters were brought up to help in the teaching and, again a successful boarding-school was built up. When the number of pupils outgrew the accommodation at Merryfield, a second school, Glen Villa, was opened in Harpurhey, another suburb of Manchester, and two of the daughters – the eldest and the youngest – were established there. This house was the background to the picture of my aunts as I remember them when I was a child.

The eldest, Mary, handsomest of the bunch, a wilful girl, had always been idolised and indulged by her father.

She had many admirers and many flirtations – not a conventional school-mistress, but her girls adored her, and she certainly taught them manners. The bulk of the more serious teaching was done by her valued assistant and friend, Miss Sophia Caldecott, sister of the artist who devised the most fascinating illustrations to nursery rhymes that ever beguiled youthful fancy. Aunt Mary, in addition to teaching her girls how to behave like ladies, must have inspired them with a love of what we should now call Nature Study, for she was an ardent student of botany and a most successful gardener. Aunt Mary was, in fact, very clever; she could do anything well in which she was interested[2] [including acquiring husbands; N.B. Parentheses are mine.]

I like to remember my aunts as they were when I used to pay my long visits to Glen Villa, sometimes for three months at a time. They formed a charming group when sitting on the lawn, their beauty set off in the fashion of the day by sheer muslin coatees with coloured ribbon run through the hem, their hair arranged in huge chignons, from which hung a long curl over one shoulder. When they went out into the road, their coiffure was crowned by a minute bonnet, flat as a pancake, covered with tiny flowers, rosebuds and forget-me-nots, and tied with velvet ribbons under the chin.

My visits to my grandparents at Merryfield were something of an ordeal for a shy little maid, for my grandmother was very much the critical school-mistress. My grandfather, often immoveable in his study from gout, sat by the fire, smoking a long church-warden clay pipe, the whole room and the forbidding-looking books round the walls being saturated with the fumes of tobacco. He was a strikingly handsome man built on a massive scale, with fine features, brilliant dark eyes and a mass of white hair. When free from his ailments and able to walk, he was an imposing figure as he strode down the broad flagged hall at Merryfield House, clad in a long frock-coat, a tall silk hat, in his hand a stout malacca cane with a silver top inherited from his grandfather, John Everard.

When my sixth birthday [1867] came round, I was sent upstairs alone to pay my respects to my grandfather. As I timidly opened the door of his study, I could barely discern through the clouds of tobacco smoke the form of my grandfather, with his gouty leg stretched out, in a remote corner of the large room I had to cross, while from behind the church-warden came a stentorian voice: 'Do you love Jesus?' At this point my memory fails me, but there was nothing in my grandfather's appearance to mitigate this unusual form of address, and I am quite sure that I should have been thankful to sink through the floor.

Among the terrors of childhood, of which I was the victim, two were especially connected with my visits to Manchester. I had heard of 'Fenians', a name almost forgotten now, but then applied to a 'Brotherhood' formed first among the Irish in America in 1864 for overthrowing English rule in Ireland. Later, there were Fenian riots among the Irish, if not in Manchester, no further away than Liverpool, and the name itself was enough to

33. David Everard Ford.

34. Jane Elizabeth Ford (born Down).

frighten a child. But still worse were the tales of 'garrotters', who sprang upon solitary
foot passengers from behind and throttled them in order to rob. I dreaded the lonely road
outside the rather gloomy Merryfield garden, where garrotters might be prowling and was
happy when, duty done, I went back to the cheerful atmosphere of Glen Villa.

One can well imagine that Glen Villa in charge of the flirtatious and gifted Aunt Mary
had a wholly different atmosphere from Merryfield where David Everard Ford must have
generated gloom. For example, on 26 September 1865, he was writing: 'My precious wife
has of late been unusually calm; but she finds the crushing course of our two establishments
almost too much for her. Her anxiety for riches is to me distressing, but how much worse
must it be as to her own soul! Food and raiment are the assigned boundaries of Christian
contentment and when we go beyond them we leave our fatherland for a foreign and
dangerous soil'. Her comment was remarkably restrained because she put a small cross
against the reference to her desire for riches as distressing and merely noted, 'I never knew

this fault'. He seemed oblivious to the fact that he owed his comfortable standard of living and security to her enterprise and hard work.

He preached his last sermon on 27 June 1875, but had been feeling this time, genuinely, and not merely to be dramatic, that his end was near, for we have the entry in his diary on 2 February 1875: 'To that pass I have already come: my work is done. Am I going home?' And on 27 February: 'My sight is now failing so fast that I shall not be able to see much longer to read or write. God grant that my latest breath may be to testify His praise'.

They had decided to move to Bedford as most of their children were now there. They arrived in July 1875, but David Everard Ford died in October, aged seventy-eight.

In Jane Elizabeth Ford's last annotations, which must have been written shortly after her husband's death, she wrote:

> I believe he loved me always fondly but he has been at some pains, in this diary, to show up my faults. I believe few loved as we did and now I am desolate. He has already said he loved me more than life, that he was a perfect 'maniac' in his love for me, etc., etc. Undoubtedly my fault was constitutional excitability, he never names another. This he knew before our marriage. My sanguine impulsiveness was the character just suited to counteract his morbid despondency. By bringing us together the wisdom of Providence was seen.

Though she mutilated his diary freely, she filled three-quarters of the last volume with copies of letters he had written to her from their marriage in 1834 till his death in 1875. They number hundreds. I confess I have read only a few: they are love letters, and though they might fill gaps in the story, they are of a quality which makes one feel that one is prying into things which should remain private between the two.

Chapter Ten

JOHN BROWN
(1830-1922)

Manchester 1855-1864

John Brown introduced into our heredity strains which had been lacking, tolerance and homely north country common sense. Unlike the Downs, he was never censorious, unlike the Fords, he was always on a level keel.

Like David Everard Ford, he left us an autobiography. It was written between 1910-14, when he was over 80, and he called it, 'Life Recollections'. His outlook was much wider and, though a devout believer, he was not confined within narrow evangelical limits as were the two Fords. His approach was that of a humanist, of a scholar. Like the others, he left a sermon register which is lodged with the County Records Office at Bedford.

His father was the second son of Alexander Brown of Stewarton, Ayrshire, who was born in 1764. Robert Burns was a fellow citizen and the poet spent much of his time there. His mother was Agnes Brown and though Browns are thick on the ground in parts of Ayrshire, kinship between Alexander and Agnes Brown is not impossible.

> O wad some Power the giftie gie us
> To see oursels as ithers see us!

was alike the philosophy of Robert Burns and John Brown.

John Brown writes, 'My grandfather (Alexander) like so many other Scotchmen before and since, as soon as he attained to manhood, wandered southward', to Bolton-le-Moors. Bolton was so strongly Puritan that it became known as the Geneva of Lancashire. In the Civil Wars, after driving back the Royalist armies in 1643, it was besieged by 8,000 men under Prince Rupert who, when he captured the town, put the inhabitants to the sword in continental fashion. Even the Royalists themselves were later to admit that this was beyond any atrocity previously committed by Englishmen upon an English city.

In that town, he wrote, 'Alexander Brown met with my grandmother, Sarah Wyld, then a vivacious young person of some 18 summers and they were married in the parish church above the river in 1789. The wife he chose was a person of considerable energy, of character and strong and marked individuality. I remember her well, for she lived to be 81 and I was 22 when she died'.

They had 10 children. John the eldest was active in town affairs and on incorporation of the borough in 1838, was elected on the Town Council and for many years took a prominent part in all municipal affairs as an Alderman.

David Everard Ford's diary records the horror of endemic cholera – a dirt disease – and the flood of refugees and others which was pouring into Lancashire. Bolton had no public bath house, so Alderman John Brown set up a private company to build and maintain one, and we have a fine silver salver dated 1854 which was presented to him in recognition of this work.

Our John Brown was the son of William Brown, that is of Alderman John Brown's younger brother. William Brown married a Hodgkinson of an old Preston family. Her father organised hand-loom weavers to take advantage of the great quantities of cheap cotton yarn produced by Arkwright's invention of power spinning. Tens of thousands of workers all over Lancashire were drawn into this largely domestic industry only to be left without work when Cartwright developed power weaving to be carried on in factories. The old hand-loom weavers could not learn to work power looms, though their children could. Unemployment caused by technical progress is not a new problem.

William Brown, like his elder brother, John, was very public-spirited, but a more retiring character. He was a deacon of his chapel for 50 years and the Sunday School superintendent, but he could not afford protracted education for his children. His son, John, therefore, started as an office boy in a solicitor's office, where he was was so under-employed that he had ample time to read *The Edinburgh* and *The Quarterly Review* and also *Blackwoods* and *Fraser's Magazine*, to which his employer subscribed. He wrote: 'These were at my service and introduced me pleasantly to new and varied fields of literature greatly to my advantage and, perhaps, I learned more than if I had remained longer at school'.

He was then apprenticed to a bookseller:

> In a small way he was a publisher as well as a printer. Here again, I was in congenial surroundings for the constantly arriving parcels of books and periodicals were, to me, a personal source of interest and the brisk talk of travellers who came for orders from the great London Publishing House, seemed to me like the opening of a new world. Though I afterwards turned to another walk of life, yet the practical knowledge I thus gained, both of men and business, has since often proved of service to me.

> Looking back over bygone years I have ever counted it a happy circumstance for me that my father's relations with both church and school brought to our home fireside godly men and women who were his colleagues in Christian circles and whose talk was, quite naturally, about the things of a better life. In my opinion no one can be truly said to know the real inwardness of the Nonconformist churches of England and the work for God they are doing, who has not come into close continued and personal contact with the quiet, worthy, godly people of whom they are mainly composed. I feel sure I am the better for knowing these people and hearing their talk, even though it was often beyond me.

It was natural for him to take a class at the Sunday School of which his father was a superintendent and then to give short addresses at functions connected with the school. Little by little he began to think of the Christian ministry as his vocation. He mentioned this to his minister, who, without either encouraging or discouraging him, arranged to give him lessons in Latin.

It so happened that at the time he was released from his apprenticeship, the Lancashire Independent College in Manchester arranged for a course of study preparatory to entering the college. This preparatory course was carried on in Lancaster. The Lancashire Independent College was a 19th-century version of Homerton: it had been opened in 1843 as the continuation under enlarged conditions of the Blackburn Academy established in 1818 for the training of students for the Congregational ministry.

He applied for this course and, after being carefully interviewed by the college committee in Manchester, was accepted on probation and told to proceed to Lancaster.

In the same way that David Everard Ford, when at Wymondley, had been sent out as a student to preach in village chapels, so John Brown was sent out to Galgate, a village on the old Preston to Lancaster road. He writes:

> My congregation consisted of some 50 or 60 persons including the schoolmaster of the neighbouring parish of Ellel and his wife, the manager of the neighbouring mill and his family, a tall, white-haired old man who was a gamekeeper and a number of village folk of the north Lancashire type. I was not altogether without fear as to my being able to fill up the regulation time, for I remembered that my sermon was short and the rest of the service far from elaborate. Chants, much less anthems, had not as yet appeared upon the horizon of Congregational worship, save here and there in some progressive city church. Still, I do not remember that any of my congregation reproached me afterwards for letting them out too soon. In the afternoon I took heart and grace from the fact that I had not

foundered in the morning and I preached with some of that glow of feeling which I have experienced many times since. At the close of the service some of the people spoke kindly to me, and the burden of the day being lifted, I turned homeward with a lighter heart than that with which I had set out in the morning.

He was fortunate: the shrewd and kindly people of north Lancashire were infinitely to be preferred to those in the 'bad' villages of Hertfordshire, whom David Everard Ford had to face a generation earlier.

He found that he could keep up with such training and with the work of his classes and have time to spare, so resolved to enter in the Matriculation Examination of London University. The subjects were Virgil's *Georgics*, Xenophon's *Anabasis*, the First Book of Euclid, some Algebra, Natural Philosophy, English and History. This must have been a formidable undertaking for one with his sketchy educational background, when already engaged on a theological course. The examinations were then held in Somerset House, London. Whilst waiting for the results, he visited the Great Exhibition of 1851.

'When the list came out my name was there: so with a light heart I made my way back to Lancashire again'. He tells the story modestly, but it was a notable achievement, indicating great resolution and a good brain.

One is impressed by the greater educational opportunities open to John Brown in 1850, as compared with those open to David Ford in 1787, or David Everard Ford in 1816. The standard of life of 1850, after another 50 years of the industrial revolution, was obviously higher than that of 1800 and all that went with that rise, such as improved, though still limited, educational facilities, was becoming evident.

At the end of that summer he received a letter from Dr. Vaughan, the president of the Lancashire Independent College asking him to appear before a committee as a candidate for admission. Having passed his Matriculation Examination, he was exempted from the ordinary entrance examination and was accepted and went into residence at once. Fortunately for him, arrangements had been made that very year for junior students to receive their classical training at the newly opened Owen's College in the house, once occupied by Richard Cobden, in Quay Street in the centre of Manchester. John Brown records that it was to become Victoria College, but writing in 1910 he did not know that it was later to become the University of Manchester and that he was, therefore, one of the first students in what was to become the first and, perhaps, the most notable of our 'red brick' universities.

> There was this advantage also of our going to Owen's College, that in the classes there we were brought into more and more varied competition with other minds than we should have been if we had been restricted to our own college, which, I cannot but think, resulted in a broader and more healthy spirit of emulation. Most of the men we met there had greater advantages than we had, by being trained in the public grammar schools of the time, there was thus much more incentive to work and when, at the end of the first year's course, I succeeded in carrying off the Second Classical prize, I was prouder of that achievement than I have been of some things since which were, perhaps, greater.

Apparently Lancashire Independent College relied for its examinations and degrees upon London University, for he tells us:

> During my first and second years in college I was mainly occupied in reading for the B.A. Degree of London University which I took in October 1853. The Classical subjects in that year were, in Latin – The Odes, Epistles and the Ars Poetica of Horace; and in Greek – The Great Oration of Demosthenes on the Crown. The examiner, in Greek and in Greek and Roman History, on that occasion was Dr. William Smith, the great Master of Classical Dictionaries and Editor of the *Quarterly Review*.
>
> After graduating I entered upon my theological course at Lancashire but still kept up some connection with Owen's, on my own account, joining a Master Class under Professor

35.   Richard Cobden's house in Quay Street, Manchester.

Greenwood for reading the Ethics of Aristotle and also a Political Economy Course under Professor Copley Christie, afterwards, Chancellor of the Diocese of Manchester.

One gets the impression that the lead the Dissenting academies had established over Oxford and Cambridge lasted well into the second half of the 19th century and that many Nonconformist pastors, with the thorough and varied education which John Brown obtained, were far ahead of the average Church of England clergy. They also had the spur of ambition lacking in young men who went to an Oxford or Cambridge college and who could look forward to a living in the gift of their college or family.

Whilst still a student, he was invited, in March 1855, to become the pastor at Oak Street Chapel, Accrington, but had to decline as he had another year to remain at college. Meanwhile, certain events were taking place in Manchester which were, in fact, to hasten his departure from college.

Just beyond Victoria Station, Manchester, a road takes off to the higher ground to the north-east. It was originally known as York Street, but the name was later changed to Cheetham Hill. Immediately on the left is a very fine classical building in Portland stone. It is now listed as of architectural interest and is much esteemed by its present occupiers, Laidlaw Thompson Ltd., door furniture wholesalers. It was built in 1840 as Ducie Chapel and was a part of the Church Extension movement in the suburbs of Manchester. When it was built it was feared that it would be too far out in the country to be successful. Green fields stretched away behind it as far as Stangeways Hall, the seat of the Earl of Ducie, and now the site of Strangeways Prison. Manchester was expanding so rapidly, however, that these fears were groundless and a large congregation gathered together, of which a certain Alderman Burd was the leading spirit. He died in 1848, and there is an entry in David Everard Ford's diary of 19 August of that year: 'Alderman Burd died yesterday. This removal is an awful calamity to Ducie Chapel. Should it teach Little Nolan to lay aside his buffoonery, it may be overruled for good'. 'Little Nolan' was a certain Rev. Dr. Nolan, the pastor at Ducie Chapel, and David Everard Ford had made up his mind about him. We have the following succession of entries in his diary:

> 2 March 1849. At present the tide of immigrants flow towards Chapel Street. Nolan has lost several families who go there. Things at Ducie Chapel are in a very unsound state. I should not be surprised, any day, to hear that the place is all in ruins.
> 27 August. Confusion worse confounded is now the order of things at Ducie Chapel. What injury is done to our churches when the working of their discipline falls into bad hands!
> 30 August. Nolan's re-election was carried, *vi et armis*, on Monday night. He stood at the door, backed by the police, daring the objecting members to force their way into the meeting and threatening to fight every 'blackguard' among them. The row outside lasted an hour-and-a-half, and, when it was over, the 'church' (Acts XIX 41) unanimously re-elected their pastor.
> 27 October. Nolan's trial before a select committee of bishops and deacons commenced last night.

I do not understand the reference to bishops as there are none in Nonconformist sects. Perhaps he means respected elders.

> 7 November. Nolan was expelled from our ministerial circle on Monday morning. He appears to have indulged in low language and indelicate hints, with various females, where he could take such liberties. His defence is that the whole is a conspiracy to ruin him, but *that* he has failed to show.
> 30 May 1850. Nolan's trials have ended in his utter disgrace and ruin. His fall is not half so strange as the concealment of his sin.
> 25 November 1852. Nolan is in gaol. It would have been better for his reputation had he always been.

No congregation could survive such a pastor. 'Little Nolan' was presumably Irish, or of Irish descent, and would have relished and prolonged the fight with all the rhetoric at his command. Meanwhile, the congregation scattered and the chapel was closed down by the trustees who had a debt of £600 (£22,000) to shoulder.

The Congregationalists of Manchester rallied round and it was reopened and renamed Park Chapel and services were continued by various Manchester ministers, including Dr. Vaughan, the head of Lancashire Independent College.

It seems probable that Dr. Vaughan had been asked by the trustees if he had a qualified student who could pull Park Chapel together and that he had nominated John Brown, because the College Committee took the view that, since the honour of Congregationalism in the city was at stake, they should consent to John Brown leaving the college a year before the usual time. This he did and preached his first sermon at Park Chapel on Sunday, 27 May 1855.

There was a later public meeting presided over by Sir James Watt, a leading merchant in the city, and attended by many ministers and friends from other congregations to express interest and good wishes. At that time the average congregation was 120, but a month later it was 160 and by December, one hundred and eighty.

The Rev. John Brown does not tell us how he met Ada Haydon Ford, but as her father, the Rev. David Everard Ford, was pastor of Richmond Chapel on the same side of Manchester, their meeting was to be expected. We know nothing of his courtship, but his letter of proposal, undated, was received on 27 February 1857.

36. Park Chapel, formerly Ducie Chapel.

76 Elizabeth St.
Thursday morning.

My dear Miss Ada,
  I hope you will be none the less favourably disposed to this communication of mine because I am determined to be brief and to the point.
  Of late I have been growing sensible that my feeling towards you has been something far deeper than mere friendship. To be plain and direct, I love you dearly and I feel that if I am to have any peace of mind I must tell you so. *May I venture to hope that my love will be reciprocated?*
  I have not determined upon this declaration without serious thought, and, may I add also, much fervent prayer for guidance – in such matters above all others we need our Father's wisdom to direct and His blessing to attend us. These I have desired and sought for, and if I have understood the indications of Providence aright, they have led me to you – most truly I do desire that events may prove that I am right.
  I do not wish to hurry your reply in a matter of such grave importance, but suspense in such matters is proverbially hard to bear and I am sure that in your kindness you will not forget this. Waiting your reply.

I remain, my dearest
Most affectionately Yours,
John Brown

Miss Ada Ford

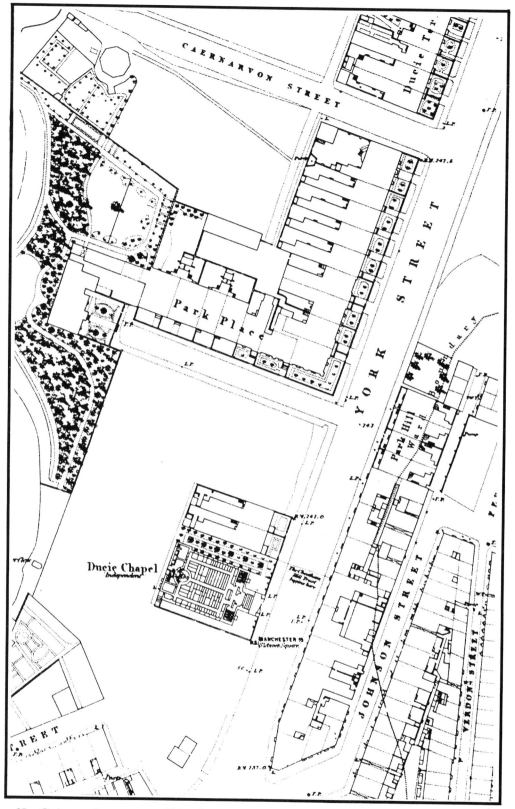

37. Ordnance Survey map of Manchester, 1850. Ducie Chapel was renamed Park Chapel in 1854 and was a synagogue from 1890 to 1928. York Street was later renamed Cheetham Hill.

The underlying tone of his letter is somewhat authoritarian, more so than most of David Everard Ford's a generation earlier and perhaps reflects the further development of Victorian attitudes. Miss Ada was told that the Almighty had been consulted and approved of his suit. The implication was that if she refused him she would be going against the Will of God. But she did not, and since we have the letter, it was treasured.

John Brown found, as did so many others, that the intellectual climate in Manchester was stimulating, but in 1864 we find he heads a page, 'The Hebrew Multiply in the Land', and writes:

> With so many kind friends around me I was naturally unwilling to entertain thoughts of leaving this my first ministerial charge. Yet, as time went on, circumstances arose from outside which almost forced this question. In these seven or eight years Manchester business made great strides towards the suburbs altering the character of the neighbourhood where we were. But another fact, more important still, issued considerable social change. The City Corporation ran a new street from Market Street to Cheetham across the site on which had hitherto stood the Jewish Synagogue, the result being the erection of a new Synagogue quite near to Park Chapel and the migration to the neighbourhood of an increasing number of Jews, and a second Synagogue was necessitated and built. At the head of this migrated colony was the Rabbi, Dr. Schiller Szinessy,[1] with whom I had frequent walks and talks, and whom I came to know again as Keeper of Oriental MSS in the University Library at Cambridge. The coming of the Hebrews grew to become a real invasion. When a Gentile vacates a house, it was usually a Jew who became the next tenant. As in Egypt of old, 'The Children of Israel increased abundantly and multiplied, and waxed exceeding mighty and the land was filled with them'.[2]

Manchester would not have attained its remarkable position had it not been for its immigrants and of these the Jews were a notable element. I am much indebted to Bill Williams whose book, *The Making of Manchester Jewry*, is the leading work. He told me that a small community fleeing from pogroms in Western Russia set up a place of worship, the Chevra Walkawischk, in a house in Fernie Street, Red Bank (an area now demolished) immediately opposite Park Chapel, and that Michael Marks the founder of Marks & Spencer Ltd. opened his first shop just opposite Park Chapel.

Bill Williams also gives in his Appendix B a good estimate of the Jewish population in different areas of Manchester. Whereas in the Red Bank area there were only 21 Jewish families in 1851, by 1861 there were 149 and by 1871, two hundred and thirty six. These were poor immigrants who continued to flow out of Eastern Europe. Their onward passage to America was checked by the American Civil War which broke out in 1861.

Red Bank had once been a middle-class residential area, and it was to serve the inhabitants of that area that Park Chapel had been built. John Brown's fears as to the future of the district were justified and it is interesting to note that Park Chapel, itself, became a Synagogue in 1890 and remained so until 1928.

Chapter Eleven

JOHN BROWN
(1830-1922)

Bedford Pastorate 1864-1903

The Rev. J. Jukes had been the pastor of the Congregational Chapel in Bedford for nearly 25 years. It was known amongst Independent chapels as Bunyan Meeting because it originated in a barn in Mill Lane where John Bunyan preached (when he was not in gaol for so doing). It had been rebuilt in 1850 which had been the cause of some dissension and strain for Mr. Jukes, who did not enjoy good health and had long been seeking, what in the Church of England is called a curate, to assist him. A Mr. Kent of the British and Foreign Bible Society thought he knew the right man, a young Mr. Brown whom he knew to be fearful for the future of his congregation by reason of the Jewish influx in north Manchester.

John Brown, himself, was writing:

> Taking all things into account and forecasting the prospects of the future I began now to think that to make a change might be the path of wisdom. Still I had many searchings of heart at the thought of separation from a people with whom I had lived and worked happily for eight years of my life. Moreover, it was my first pastorate and every minister knows what that means. I, therefore, shrank with almost superstitious dread from taking steps myself which might issue in a removal.

When, however, he received an invitation to preach at Bunyan Meeting, he accepted. 'Thus, it came about that on Saturday evening, 20 February 1864, I found myself with misgiving heart in a town I had never seen before and where I did not personally know a single human being, but in which, as God so willed, the main part of my life-work was to be done'.

He preached on the Sunday and again on the following Thursday. The impression on both sides was favourable and an agreement reached, so that we read:

> 'With my Manchester people it was sore parting when parting-time came. A Farewell Tea-Meeting was held on the 7 June when they presented me with an illuminated Address[1] in a Morocco case and a cheque for £100 [£3,000], expression of their affectionate regard. I went away with my heart torn and bleeding, taking my wife and two young children, one of them a babe scarce two months old'. [These were Florence and Alice.]

Of his reception in Bedford, the *Bedfordshire Times* of 20 June 1864 wrote:

> A most interesting event took place on Monday afternoon in connection with Bunyan Meeting, Bedford, it being no less than the public recognition of the Rev. John Brown, B.A., late of Park Chapel, Manchester, as co-worker with the Rev. J. Jukes, the venerable pastor of this old Meeting. Mr. Brown cannot but be gratified with the hearty reception of Monday afternoon. By his general manner, gentlemanly bearing, and Christian deportment, he has won for himself in a short time the good wishes of the people among whom he is called to minister. At five o'clock no less than 450 persons sat down and partook of an excellent tea. Mr. Town, confectioner, of the High Street, was the purveyor, and the manner in which he discharged his duty gave the utmost satisfaction.

Not only Mr. Brown, but also Mr. Town must have been gratified.

He was 34 when he moved to Bedford and his still youthful erudition, combined with a width of outlook, soon became recognised.

38. Bunyan Meeting, Bedford.

39. A view from the gallery in Bunyan Meeting.

On the approach of winter I started a series of Sunday Evening Lectures on Life and Worship in the Early Christian Church as seen in the history of certain prominent church leaders. . . . These lectures excited a good deal of interest and brought crowded congregations the evenings they were delivered, and being printed *in extenso* in the *Bedfordshire Mercury* as they appeared, they were also widely read outside my own congregation, and, indeed, may be said to have given me a wider introduction to the town and country.

I had been at work about a year when the people began to give me gentle hints that they were looking to me to lead them in the much needed enterprise of erecting school buildings. The old three-gabled Meeting House erected in 1707 had been taken down in 1849 and the present chapel erected on the site in 1850. It was decided also that the proposed enlargement scheme should include the erection of an organ in the chapel and the installation of hot water heating apparatus. The entire cost ultimately came to £3,436 [£102,700].

The school hall they erected is a remarkably fine and lofty building and was requisitioned by the BBC as their principal studio, together with the Corn Exchange, when the BBC was evacuated from London during the 1939-45 War and must have been the scene of many historic broadcasts. The architect was John Lilley Anthony, who was to marry Mrs. Brown's sister, Emeline.

Unlike David Everard Ford, John Brown never mentions his stipend but the minute book and accounts of Bunyan Meeting are carefully preserved at the Bedford County Hall. He started with a stipend of £100 a year plus £235 from the pew rents (Mr. Jukes received £200), that is a total of £335 (£10,000). A statement put before the Finance Committee, which is reproduced as plate 40, shows the potential and actual income from pew rents.

He wrote of his duties:

It was a pastorate of many activities, for besides the work incidental to the town congregation, we had six village chapels worked from this as the centre, namely, Elstow, Kempston, Oakley, Goldington, Stagsdon and Fenlake. Lay preachers carried on the Sunday services and teachers went out from Bedford to work in the Sunday Schools in four out of these six villages. On week evenings I went out to hold services in these places in succession, so that normally the work was considerable and this having been increased by the extra demands necessitated by our building schemes, by the beginning of 1868 the strain began to tell on me.

Impaired in strength and suffering from a relaxed throat as I was at the time, my people with that kindness which they have always shown me, made arrangements for my taking a six weeks' rest with a tour on the continent.

This kind congregation must also have provided people upon whom they could rely to look after his three infant daughters. Their tour was extensive – Brussels, Cologne, up the Rhine, Baden-Baden, Munich and over the Brenner Pass to Italy. The railway had only been opened the previous year and at Brenner Station the rustics came out with wonder to gaze at the train. 'There is a delight about one's *first* entrance into Italy, which, perhaps, cannot be quite repeated'. They went to Verona where they found, from the hotel register, that John Bright had stayed there just before them. The Roman Amphitheatre had the same effect on them as on many of us – visions of horrors. No doubt they visualised Christians being thrown to the lions. But John Brown being a scholar was precise. 'It was erected about A.D. 290 under the Emperor Diocletian, the last great persecutor of the Christians'.

They went on to Venice, of which he wrote with charm and discernment, and then back via Milan and Como. At Bellagio they found a small group made up of an Irish judge, the Dean of Ardagh, an American officer and their ladies, and an old school friend of his wife's.

Our way home across the Alps was by the great Splügen Pass, the diligences making the journey by night. We, who had travelled from Milan together, were all eight of us grouped as one party and described in the way-bill as 'The Brown famille'. In the grey of

Bunyan Meeting.
Sittings in the Chapel.

Assessed Sittings in the Body of the chapel	406
Sittings free " "	30
Assessed Sittings in the Gallery --------	192
Sittings free " "	94
Total	722

Income

Floor.	52 Side pews at £3.	£	156 — " — "
	33 Middle pews at £4.		132 — " — "
Gallery.	60 front seats at 8/-		24 — " — "
	64 Middle do 5/-		16 — " — "
	68 Back do 4/-	£341-12-	13 —/2 — "
From the Trustees of the estates			100 — " — "
Weekly offerings			83 - 8 — "
			525 - " - "

Disbursements

To Rev. John Jukes	£	200 — " — "
Rev. John Brown		235 — " — "
Incidental expenses		90 — " — "
Total	£	525 — " — "

40. Bunyan Meeting financial statement. (Multiply by 28 to get 1986 equivalent.)

the early morning as we slowly travelled up the mountainside, and as the rich notes of the Italian church bells sounded across the valleys calling the people to prayer, the Dean and I left the diligence and went on foot for some miles together.

While we went on and talked, on and on came the slow procession of diligences and travellers till we all reached the snow-line on the Alps. Then came the exciting change from diligence to sleigh drive across the snow. At one sharp turn of the road my wife and I were both thrown out of the sleigh on to the snow, but as the snow was softer than the mountain road would have been, we were, fortunately, none the worse for it.

He had already made his mark in Bedford. Sir William Harpur, an Elizabethan merchant, had established an Educational Foundation in his native town and John Brown was elected to serve on the Harpur Trust in 1869. Bedford School was the first of the Educational

Foundations having over £10,000 (£300,000) a year to come under the Endowed Schools' Act of 1869. The Mayor, the Members of Parliament and representatives of the Harpur Trust, of whom John Brown was one, formed a Vigilance Committee to ward-off damaging outside interference under the Act.

In 1869, he and his wife went on another continental holiday, spent mostly in Switzerland, returning through Germany.

The next summer, that of 1870, his wife was expecting their fourth child, so John Brown set off on his own for a short run up the Rhine as far as Heidelberg visiting Bonn on the way and falling-in with various celebrated German professors and remarked on the great deference shown to distinguished chemists and physicists. He then came down the Rhine visiting Rotterdam, The Hague, Leyden and Amsterdam, but was anxious about the Franco-Prussian War obviously about to break out.

The expected child was Walter Langdon Brown, their first son, and as soon as he was well launched in the world they were off again on another continental holiday. This time, in 1871, visiting Oberammergau and the Passion Play, by way of Würzburg and Nürnberg. They were in Munich for the celebrations of a victorious German army, but had also remarked from the train in which they travelled that at station after station: 'Young men enfeebled in body and shattered in limb were returning to their Bavarian village homes. It was a saddening sight all day long and recalled the saying of Wellington "that there is nothing so terrible in war as a victory, except a defeat"'. By ancient tradition this country was anti-French so it was not surprising that nothing was said by John Brown about the vindictive peace the new German Empire had imposed on France. It was their grandson, Maynard Keynes, who was to witness, with such deep revulsion, the inevitable French revenge in the Treaty of Versailles.

One can well understand the attraction which the infinite variety and beauty of Europe and its people held for him. In his time the motor car, universal steel or concrete construction and the package tour had not reduced Europe to overcrowded uniformity. Though much of interest is embedded in his accounts of their foreign travel, their recital becomes somewhat tedious so I shall now only note them (other than those in North America).[2]

One finds it very difficult to understand how on an income of only about £10,000 in 1986 values, he was able, with a wife and four young children, to indulge in foreign travel on the scale on which he did. He does, on occasion, mention help from kind friends and I think that, as in the case of David Everard Ford, whom we know had substantial presents from members of his congregation, John Brown also was helped in the matter of holidays and travel. There were many prominent and prosperous citizens amongst his congregation. There was Barnard, the banker, Rose, the leading draper, Carruthers, a wholesale merchant, Hobson, a timber merchant and Anthony the architect. These were men born in Bedfordshire, attached to the town and inspired with a high sense of civic duty, very different from the transient managers of the big banks and multiple stores who have, in our days, replaced them everywhere. The loss to the communal life of small towns is great.

Bunyan Meeting, Bedford had a very unusual advantage for a Nonconformist chapel – the patronage of a great nobleman. The ninth Duke of Bedford had told John Brown that the first book his mother had given him was *Pilgrim's Progress* which moved him, on his accession to the title, to erect a public statue in Bedford to John Bunyan. This was unveiled in 1874. It was followed by a further gift in 1876 to the Bunyan Meeting of bronze doors in the manner of the Ghiberti doors in Florence. With his oratory and historical feeling, the Rev. John Brown must have played his part in all these celebrations with distinction.

In politics he was a valued and effective supporter of the Duke, who, until he inherited the title, had been Hastings Russell, the Liberal Member of Parliament for Bedfordshire from 1847 till 1872. The *Bedford Bee* which was the local *Private Eye* did not regard the Rev.

John Brown nor his congregation as sufficiently radical, for in their cartoon, it will be seen that the pews are Marked 'Reserved and Cushioned' and inscribed '£ s. d.', and that play is made of the ducal coronet with J.B. apparently shown as a wolf in pastor's clothing, mounted upon it. My father told me that in one campaign, when his father was electioneering in support of Hastings Russell, he worked in tandem with William Howard Russell, who had made a name for himself as war correspondent for *The Times* in the Crimean War. It was the task of these two, one after the other, to keep meetings going until the candidate arrived, which they did by, amongst other things, telling funny stories. One evening when my grandfather was following Russell round a number of village halls, he found his stories were greeted with groans and boos. The next evening he happened to be going round first and, guessing what had happened on the previous night, told all Russell's stories.

John Brown much enjoyed his mid-week visits to the six village chapels connected with the Bunyan Meeting.

41. The Rev. John Brown in *Bedford Bee*, 8 October 1879.

> It is indeed a pleasure to preach the Gospel to the poor. The simplicity and reality of the piety of the peasantry who made up these villages' audiences, has often humbled me while it has gladdened me. I feel that they were taught of the Spirit and their religion was all in all to them amid the struggles and hardships of their life. God sometimes reveals to such as these what he often hides from the wise and prudent.

In his relations with the Established Church, the Rev. John Brown compares favourably with the Rev. David Everard Ford, in that it was possible for him to have friends as well as opponents amongst the clergy, particularly in the villages where his work might have been resented. There was a vicar of the village of Stagsdon, the Hon. and Rev. Alan Broderick, who always insisted on his taking supper with him at his vicarage after having preached in the village chapel.

There were other less happy relationships, notably, in 1872, when the Rev. John Brown was told that the Rev. H. Hocken, the curate of Bedford's parish church, St Paul's, had said from his pulpit that those who had been married in Nonconformist chapels were living in sin. This caused great distress to many of his people and, failing to get satisfaction, John Brown sent the correspondence to the press. Column after column of the old *Bedfordshire Times* almost glow today with the heat of the battle which followed. Here are a few extracts:

THE TEACHING AT ST PAUL'S CHURCH

Sir, – I shall feel obliged if you will allow me through your columns, to lay before my fellow townsmen, the following correspondence which has recently passed between the Rev. H. Hocken, the curate of St Paul's and myself.

'Bunyan Meeting, 29 April 1872.

Sir, – Towards the close of last year I heard a report that you had said in the pulpit of St Paul's Church that "all married persons not married according to the rites of the Church of England are living in a state of adultery". I was willing to believe that your words had been misunderstood, but having met with the report again lately, I should be glad if you would favour me with a denial or an affirmation of its truth.

I remain, yours truly,

JOHN BROWN

To the Rev. H. Hocken.'

I received the following reply:

'Sir, – Your letter, which I received this morning has caused me much surprise.

I am at a loss to conceive in what capacity you put the question to me. The question itself also is a strange one. For you must be aware that I cannot be answerable for any outside interpretation put upon my teaching, or for the shape in which other persons choose to present it. Whatever opinion may be held on the point on which I was speaking by persons outside the Church, I have very little fear of being misunderstood by church people referring to the blessing which the Church pronounces on the married state. It was as a minister of the Church that I was speaking on the occasion you allude to; and for the gist of my teaching at the time I can only refer you to the Prayer Book. In teaching, it seems to me, that one positive is worth a hundred negatives.

Believe me, yours faithfully,

HARRY HOCKEN

Bedford, 30 April 1872.'

John Brown's broadside which followed was prolonged and devastating and I quote only a few rounds:

You seem surprised at my thus desiring to know directly from yourself whether the offensive remark imputed to you was really uttered by you or not. . . . You have felt it right in the exercise of your calling as a minister of the Church to affirm publicly that honourable men and chaste and virtuous women, to the extent of half the nation, are living in deadly sin, and the only explanation you have to give of this monstrous assertion is that you 'have very little fear of being misunderstood by church people'. In other words you think they will agree with you when you say the most contemptuous thing that can be said of their friends and neighbours. Pardon me if I suggest that you are a little too sanguine. If I am not misinformed, some indignant churchmen walked out of the church when the assertion in question was made.

For the gist of your teaching on the occasion you alluded to, you refer me to the Prayer Book. I am, perhaps, not profoundly versed in that manual, but I have yet to learn that even the Prayer Book repudiates the marriage laws of England.

Nonconformists regarded the Prayer Book merely as the manual of the Established Church: their faith was founded on the Bible to which many of them attributed divine inspiration. In their dedication of the Authorised Version of the Bible to James I, the translators stressed the value of a 'more exact translation of the Holy Scriptures into the *English* tongue and had great hopes that the Church of *England* should reap good fruit thereby'. In fact, it was the Puritans and their heirs, the Nonconformists, who seized upon it. This comes out clearly in John Brown's battle with the Bedford curate when he wrote:

I want you, on one of the gravest questions affecting social life, to refer me to God's Book and you refer me to man's. This is after the manner of your kind; priests, both Anglican and Roman, have always been rather shy of the Bible and always exalt the protean abstraction which they call 'the Church' and its corrupt traditions. They seem to feel instinctively that God's word creates an atmosphere in which priestcraft cannot live.

He ended in fine form:

I have simply to add that I shall feel it my duty to inform the Bishop of the Diocese of the manner in which the priestlings of the Church venture to insult Englishmen, Englishwomen, and their children in the sacred name of religion.

I am, Sir, yours truly
JOHN BROWN

To the Rev. H. Hocken.

And, in fact, he did put the whole matter before the Bishop of Ely and in his *Recollections* writes: 'He wrote me a courteous letter in which – bishop-like – he tried to agree with both of us, saying that the curate in question "could not mean that the marriages of the heathen are valid". This, of course, was not saying much, but I suspect that he gave the offending curate a severe wigging behind the door, for he remained quiet ever after'.

In 1881, after 17 years of work and achievement in Bedford, he felt he would be justified in taking three months off to visit the United States, of which I treat in a later chapter. His congregation thought so too and gave him a hero's welcome on his return.

We now come to the undertaking which was to secure John Brown a place amongst literary historians of note. *John Bunyan – His Life, Times and Work*, published in 1885, is still, a century later, the standard work on Bunyan. It had involved much research and the use of sources not tapped by previous biographers. His daughter, Florence tells us, 'When the material had been collected, he escaped for weeks at a time, except for Sunday work, to a cottage near Woburn Sands, where he could do his writing undisturbed'.[3]

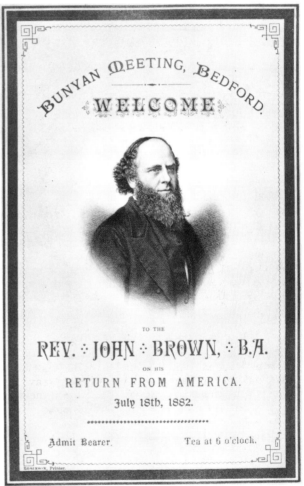

42. Ticket of admission to the celebration of John Brown's return from America, 1882.

The book was dedicated to the Duke of Bedford and published at one guinea (£40) by Isbisters, who took great pains in its production and secured the services of Edward

Whymper, of Matterhorn fame, to illustrate it. When it appeared in November 1885 it had a reception far beyond its author's expectations, both here and in the United States. The first edition appeared in November, but it had to be reprinted in the following May and then, two years later, a second cheaper edition was issued at 7s. 6d. (£13.90) and this was reprinted in 1888 and 1890.

When passing through Milan during the Italian holiday of 1889 John Brown happened to see in their hotel a copy of the *Christian World* and in it the fact that his name had been put forward as Chairman of the Congregational Union for 1890. 'I trembled at the thought of such a possibility, but as I read on, found that on the second ballot . . .' he had not been elected, but he was the year after.

He explains that:

> Congregationalism, being a simple democratic system of Church Government, devoid of hierarchical pretensions has no great prizes of distinction to offer to ecclesiastical ambition. The chairmanship of the Union is the highest honour our churches have to offer to any who take place among them. Its value, therefore, consists in the fact that it is freely conferred by brethren to some brother among them as their recognition of service rendered to the Great Cause they have at heart together.

Though he justly denies hierarchic pretension, the position, albeit tenable only for a year, did carry with it, in the Nonconformist world, the prestige and standing of the Archbishop of Canterbury in the Church of England. There were also, of course, the other Nonconformist churches such as the Wesleyan, the Baptist and others. Together, they represented a body of opinion no government could ignore and the economic success, which their individual members so often attained, tended to give them power out of all proportion to their numbers. To be the elected spokesman of one of their principal churches was, therefore, a position of national importance.

We get an indication of the prosperity and vigour the Nonconformists attained towards the end of the century from the following:

> My first duty on returning to Bedford [in 1891] was to take part in the holding of a bazaar to meet the cost of building new classrooms and a church parlour to meet additional needs in the working of our Schools. This bazaar was held in the New Corn Exchange which was transformed so as to give a representation of Ancient Bedford and picturesque Elstow; and was formally opened by the Countess of Aberdeen who was accompanied by Lord Aberdeen, by Mr. Whitbread and Lady Isabella Whitbread, and the Mayor and Mayoress of Bedford. Our people took up the matter with great spirit so that about £900 [£34,000] was realized towards the amount of £1,500 [£59,000] required for the proposed buildings.

The population of Bedford was only twenty-eight thousand. Where in England today could a single group in a small county town raise £34,000 at one event?

In 1893 there were Tercentenary Celebrations of the Elizabethan Congregational Martyrs of 1593 who were hung at Tyburn for spreading their faith and the Rev. John Brown lectured on the subject in many parts of the country. He also preached in the Channel Islands for the London Missionary Society. At St John's in Jersey he remarked that a collection from a congregation of 50 yielded five £5 notes (£200), which was remarkable coming from a farming community whose land, he was told, was only worth £5 per vergee.[4] The Congregational Church in St John was then French speaking and had connections with the French Église Réformé but was obviously responsive to the Chairman of the Congregational Union preaching for a good cause, even if he did so in English.

His year ended with a luncheon with the great William Ewart Gladstone at Hawarden on the occasion of the presentation of a memorial which he, himself, had drawn up. This prompted him to dwell on his recollection of a debate in the House of Commons which he happened to attend that year:

. . . when there was keen conflict between Mr. Gladstone and Mr. Chamberlain. With that bitterness of personal attack of which the latter was a perfect master, he assailed Mr. Gladstone, and which was enough to raise a storm of passion in return. The only reply he received was that soft answer which is said to turn away wrath. Instead of dealing with the personal matters at issue, Mr. Gladstone proceeded to congratulate his opponent on an admirable speech which his son, Austen, had recently made in the House, a speech, he said, it must have been very gratifying to a father's heart to listen to, as showing a son to be so full of promise.

43. John Brown (*centre*) at a Sunday School tea party.

The age of Mrs. Thatcher and Mr. Kinnock is less polished: neither would be capable of using such an elegant device.

Most of the material we have about John Brown relates to his public and literary work, his foreign travels and the position he made for himself in New England. We have to look elsewhere to learn why he was so greatly loved and respected by the people of Bedford as a whole.

In the files of the *Bedfordshire Times* there is a letter dated 23 May 1872 from a parishioner of St Paul's, Bedford; that is the church at which the Rev. Henry Hocken, with whom John Brown did battle, was the curate. A passage reads:

Well, I am not much acquainted with Mr. Brown, but I am with the poor and needy of Bedford, for I have not only lived amongst them all my days, but have for many years been in the habit of visiting them. I am, therefore, in a position to say that I believe they have not many kinder hearted friends in the town than Mr. Brown and 'some of the ladies of his congregation'. And as to those afflicted with smallpox, why it is well-known – that Mr. Brown did not shrink from visiting the dying under the most appalling circumstances.

And I have found amongst his papers two illuminating letters. The first is dated 19 May 1880 and reads (mistakes included):

19 May '80

Bedford

Revd. Sir

    At a meeting of the late employees of the Victoria Iron Works mill St It was proposed and carried unanimously that we attempt to settle the Dispute existing between us and our employers by arbitration and that you Sir be respectfully solicited to accept the post of such Arbitration. a deputation has been appointed to wait on you we are Sir Yours

Respectfully
the late employes of firm
Joseph Appleby
William Sherman

He appears to have been unsuccessful but not to have lost the confidence of the men, for in a second letter we read that they were unable to raise a deputation to see their employers, 'Not liking the idea of humiliating themselves before them'. Would the Rev. John Brown say for them that they were willing to offer concessions? They would accept a $12\frac{1}{2}$ per cent. reduction to work 54 or 56 hours a week, or even the old hours of 59, including Saturday afternoons, in order that the old hands might be taken back and that there might be an end to the prolonged dispute. 'Trust you may be successful for the unhappy men and families'.

    We do not know the outcome but they were clearly sure of the kindly understanding and persuasive powers of a man they chose to make their surrender and seek clemency.

Chapter Twelve

ADA HAYDON BROWN (born Ford)
(1837-1929)

Mary and Ada Ford, born in 1835 and 1837 respectively, were remarkable girls. As Ada's daughter, Florence Keynes has told us, her Aunt Mary was exceedingly clever and could do anything in which she was interested, and their Aunt Sarah Down saw, when Ada was still a child, that she had not only acute intelligence, but also strength of character.

Ada was quick to realise the strain under which her mother laboured with seven children and a limited income, and in her own autobiographical note, wrote:

Looking back I cannot imagine how she accomplished so much. Everard was sent to Silcoates as a boarder, and Palmer went to Mrs. Lamb's Preparatory School, but all the others were taught at home. Then we only had two servants, and all the washing was done without extra help. The needlework alone was more than enough for one woman. In those days there were no sewing machines or ready-made under-clothes. Even gent's shirts and collars were homemade. It was the fashion for shirt fronts to have numerous narrow tucks. My part used to be to draw threads in the linen

44. Ada Haydon Brown (born Ford), c.1860.

and run the tucks, also to back-stitch collar and cuffs. While sewing at a great speed mother used to hear our lessons. We spent a great deal of time in committing things to memory, and that we could do while mother was directing the servants' work and giving orders. We were educated largely by reading aloud – history books of England, France, Spain and Germany – poetry, *Young's Night Thoughts – Paradise Lost* and *Paradise Regained –* Pope's translation, *The Iliad.* Conversational books, one teaching astronomy and another physical geography – selections of poetry – History of the Reformation. We used, after the custom of that time, to learn geography on a terrestrial globe and astronomy on a celestial

91

one. After Aunt (Sarah) left we had a master for music and I went to Mrs. William Dracup's school for drawing. I so desired to have thorough school life, that I am afraid I did not appreciate enough my mother's really valuable instruction.

From 8 a.m. till 10 p.m. she never gave herself a moment's rest.

She does not say that she, herself, was pressing in seeking to help, but we can be sure that she was.

When I was a little over 16 a great change came in my life. Through an advert it was arranged I should go as governess-pupil to Mrs. Hailey, Dean Cottage, Hanwell.

The journey was no easy matter. At that time the Railway Companies were compelled [by Act of Parliament] to have one train a day at 1d. a mile called the Parliamentary Train. What would third class passengers say now to the accommodation provided? Carriages open all through. No windows, only shutters, no cushions, no heating. Trains left Bank Top, Manchester at 8 a.m. and arrived in London 6 p.m. At Blisworth, near Bletchley, trains were shunted for the express to pass. There was often a long waiting time, and passengers got out and climbed up the banks; and women from houses near-by brought out cups of tea or coffee and buns.

The luggage was put on the top of the carriages if going through to London at the charge of 1d. a lb., if at an intermediate station in the one luggage van 1½d. per lb. I left the train

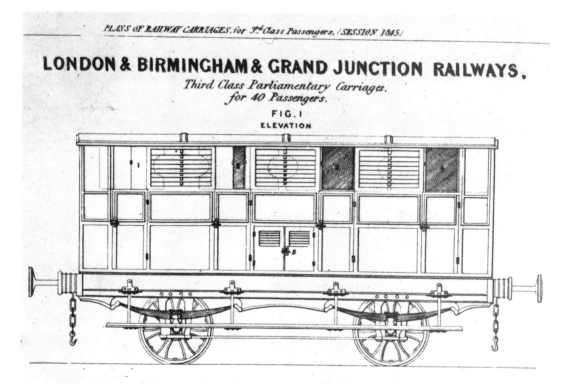

45. In 1851 Ada Haydon Brown travelled from Manchester to Harrow on a London & North Western Railway Company train. This design of a third class railway carriage, one of those submitted by various companies for parliamentary approval in 1845, shows the type of carriage she describes. It may, nevertheless, have been regarded as more comfortable than the top of a coach.

at Harrow to prevent going through London and there a fly would meet me and a drive of seven miles landed me at Hanwell. At that time Hanwell was quite a country place, few houses and only four shops.

I was much astonished to find what was required of me. Some of the pupils were my age and more, and Mrs. H. told me I must not let my age be known. The beginning of life there was no easy task – I heard the girls say as they looked at their new teacher, 'She is a young one, we will tease her', and so they did. Sometimes I went to Mrs. H. in tears, though the girls never saw me give in, and say I could not go on. She always expressed surprise and told me I was doing wonderfully, and thus kept my courage up.

Mr. H. usually conducted family prayer in the morning, Mrs. H. in the evening. One day when she was confined to her room I asked her what was to be done. She looked astonished at the question and said, 'of course, you will take it'. I asked for a prayer book but there was none and I remember to this day how I felt when there was gathered to listen to me more than 20 girls and four servants.

In time I had devoted friends. I was never allowed to make my own bed – indeed, there was often a quarrel as to whom should have that honour. And so it was as to who was to be my companion in walks. Lately I have come across loving letters from old girls, very gushing.

The holidays gave me great pleasure. We only had two terms, but a week's holiday mid-term, and on those occasions I went either to Aunt Mary's (Mrs. Price), or Aunt Sarah (Mrs. Crellin) at Clapham or Hackney. Uncle Langdon, a medical student, lived with his sister, Sarah, and was most kind in taking me to see the sights of London. [Uncle Langdon was, as Dr. John Langdon Down, later to become famous for his identification of 'Down's Syndrome' in infants (see Chapter Three)].

When she came home after an uninterrupted spell of two years, the young Rev. John Brown, who was in the sights of numerous young ladies in several congregations, steered past them all and proposed to Ada. She accepted him and they were married in 1859. When they moved to Bedford in 1864, she had already borne two of her six children.

Mark Rutherford was a novelist of great repute in Congregational circles. His real name was Hale White and his ancestors were connected with William Hale, our John Everard's partner. One of his best known works was entitled, *Revolution in Tanner's Lane*. Tanner's Lane was Bunyan Meeting. In the final pages it is recounted how a new young pastor was appointed who had a very gifted wife, possessing a knowledge of foreign languages. That was Mrs. John Brown; it was not surprising that, when she set about educating her three daughters, she was pressed to start a school.

The Cambridge Higher Local Examinations were being organised in the 1870s and she worked closely with the Syndicate, and her daughter, Florence, was one of the first candidates. From her knowledge of her

46. Ada Haydon Brown (born Ford), *c.* 1887.

mother's schools, Merryfield and Glen Villa, Mrs. Brown knew exactly how to reassure parents and control her staff to the benefit of her pupils. Eventually, a school of some size

47. The garden at The Manse, Bedford.

48. Ada Haydon Brown, aged 87, in Bowdon in 1924 with her great-grandchildren, Polly, Janet, Maurice and David Hill.

grew up, a new wing being added to the Manse to house it, and foreign resident governesses and outside masters brought in.

John Brown's attitude towards his wife's school was very different from the constant fussing in which David Everard Ford had indulged in a similar situation. He wrote: 'It meant a strenuous life for her, but it was work of a congenial sort; and she valued it most of all for the influence it gave her in the formation of character of those under her care. Many and many a time have they spoken with gratitude of what they owe to her, and this is her most valued reward'.

Her school, like her mother's, was profitable. Both added greatly to the potential of their husbands, their dignified retirement and the advancement of their children. I once asked my father why his mother's school was so profitable. He replied, 'She fed them on sausage rolls with a lot of roll and very little sausage'. The high thinking was clearly combined with plain living. Florence, in *Gathering up the Threads*, remembers the Manse chiefly for its large, very cold rooms.

She also wrote that love of education, rather than financial gain, had been her mother's incentive in running her school. I am sure this was so, but as her family increased and her husband's income did not (except through his literary earnings) her determination to have the means to set her children up well in the world must have been at work.

She was, of course, exceedingly active in chapel matters and in affairs in Bedford. As we have seen in the last chapter, there were public references to 'the extreme kindness of ladies of his congregation'. These would have been under the leadership of Mrs. John Brown.

There are still Harpur Trust Almshouses for old women in Dame Alice Street, opposite where the Manse once stood. John Brown was on the committee of the Harpur Trust and I remember my father telling me that his mother was particularly interested in the welfare of the inmates.

She was setting up a tradition by which her daughter, Florence, was to become the Mayor of Cambridge and her grand-daughter, Margaret Hill, was to devote many years, as a councillor of the Borough of Hornsey, to its housing problems, and to the founding of the Hill Homes for old people.

Women of great character, no less than men, perhaps more often, tend to overpower those around them. My father used to say that he recognised early the forceful character of his mother and welcomed the suggestion that he should join his uncles Palmer and Gerard Ford in Manchester, for he feared that he would otherwise be dominated by her. That he may have been right is substantiated by the rather unhappy lives of Alice and Kenneth, who never married. Indeed, it was felt that Alice and her mother almost conspired to keep Kenneth at home. Mrs. Brown did not entertain for her children and Walter had already married unsuitably.

We have seen the interaction of those two decided characters, Jane Elizabeth and David Everard Ford, in the writings they left. We have nothing about the relationship of John and Ada Brown and can only judge from the impression made on their family. My father told me of his father's great skill in joinery – and there was a magnificent book case in Hampstead to show it, of his love of sea voyages, of his standing in Bedford, and of his literary work. He told how his father bought some shares in the Hudson's Bay Company without consulting his wife, how they fell in price, and how he never heard the last of it.

Not only my father, but other members of the family give the impression that the Rev. Dr. John Brown was merely a retiring scholar: but that is not what the record shows. This impression may have been the consequence of an attitude adopted in the interests of domestic harmony, but it is also the kind of legend which springs up in matriarchal families such as ours.

My grandmother was endlessly kind to those in trouble and was always giving generously to pastors in distress, missionary societies and the like. When she died in 1929 she left about ten thousand pounds (£200,000) to everyone's amazement. One can only suppose that she had cherished the profits of her school and that Dr. John Brown's books went on selling. Nonconformists were both prosperous and literate, and he had tapped the American market with his books on Bunyan and the Pilgrim Fathers.

Chapter Thirteen

JOHN BROWN
(1830-1922)

The American Connection 1881-1905

John Brown does not tell us in so many words why, in 1881, he decided to visit the United States. America was not yet recognised as the Athens of the world where 'all spent their time in nothing else but to tell or to hear some new thing'[1] and to which a visit was a part of every intelligent man's or woman's education. The attraction for him was more specific: it had to do with his religious beliefs and his historical interests.

This comes out very clearly in his *Pilgrim Fathers of New England*, published in 1895, with many subsequent editions. He wrote (I have abridged):

> The modern movement of government by the people began not, as is sometimes supposed, with the 18th. century, but with the 16th, and was religious in its origin.
>
> On the Continent, democracy, as springing out of the Reformation, was arrested by the power of the princes, and delayed for centuries; in England also it came into conflict with the aristocratic forces, and was defeated for a time; but carried across the Atlantic by the Pilgrim Fathers, it found a virgin soil in which it spread its roots freely, and grew vigorously. American self-government was not the sudden birth of the Declaration of Independence. It really sprang from the organisation which the Pilgrim Fathers gave to the first colony.
>
> The hundred exiles, who in simple heroic fashion crossed the Atlantic in the *Mayflower*, their little barque of 180 tons, while merely aiming at freedom of worship for themselves and their children, were really bringing the fruits of a long and resolute struggle of centuries. We can see now that they were almost unconsciously pointing the way to a broader, freer life for the English-speaking people on both sides of the sea.

Twilight did not fall for American Puritanism during his lifetime. Though from the 1880s till 1914, immigrants poured in by hundreds of thousands from Germany, Southern Italy, the Balkans, the Ukraine and Poland – largely Catholic and many Jewish – they were, like the Catholic-Irish, to build railroads and stoke blast furnaces. It was not until the second and third generation that their descendants were to have any impact on American culture. In John Brown's day New England was still the country of Nathaniel Hawthorne, Harriet Beecher Stowe and Louisa M. Alcott. Freud and Jung were only hatching their revolution in far away Vienna. Norman Mailer, Saul Bellow *et al.* and, what Malcolm Muggeridge described as the scented smog of sex from California to Stockholm, was still two generations away. One can speculate on the future of the American mix, but I should doubt if the view John Brown expressed in 1895 has been wholly invalidated by subsequent immigration. In his *Pilgrim Fathers of New England*, he wrote:

> With the advent of power of the Long Parliament in 1640, and the consequent downfall of Archbishop Laud, the reason for the Puritan exodus ceased, and the exodus itself came to an end. Since the arrival of the *Mayflower* in 1620, the population had grown to 26,000 souls, and after 1640 for more than a century there was no considerable migration to this part of North America. These 20 years and these 26,000 people constitute the formative period and the determining element of New England and American life. Those who believe in a philosophy of history[2] and seek to trace it in the course of events cannot fail to see the special significance of the time. The Dutch had already erected Fort Amsterdam on the island at the mouth of the Hudson, which was afterwards to bear the great commercial

city of New York. The French had settled at Port Royal, in Nova Scotia, and had established a trading-post with the Indians at Quebec. If, therefore, the power of England and the English spirit of freedom were to become dominant on the great continent of America, the beginnings must be made during the years with which we have been dealing. Not less significant were the men than the time. Those who came over were almost without exception deeply religious men. It has been truly said that it was religious enthusiasm that secured the preponderance of the continent for men of the English race. Had the emigration not started when it did, the solid and godly element there is in American life would not have been what it is.

49. S.S. *Gallia*.

This is the greatest historical 'if' I have ever heard formulated. If the inhabitants of the United States did not speak English and had not been imbued with the democratic ideas which they embodied in their Constitution, might the world not have had another South America?

His *Pilgrim Fathers* appeared in 1895, after another visit to New England, but it was in 1882 that he paid his first visit lasting three months. He had just preached in Oxford with such success that he was invited to the pastorate there, and he then sailed from Liverpool.

On Saturday, 22 April I set sail for America in the Cunard Steamer the *Gallia* and greatly enjoyed this my first Atlantic voyage. There were interesting people on board and as a ship at sea is a sort of floating republic intercourse is usually free and informal. One of my fellow-passengers was Mr. McCarthy, formerly one of the Masters in the Bedford Grammar School. He and two ladies, one of them Principal of the Birmingham High School were going on commission from Birmingham to study the school system of America.

I made the acquaintance also of Miss Motley, the daughter of the author of *The Rise of the Dutch Republic*, and sister of the wife of Sir W. Vernon Harcourt, who told me much that interested me about her father whose works I had read with much pleasure – There were aristocratic people also on board – the Duke of Manchester and his son, Lord Mandeville, Lord & Lady Randolph Churchill and Lord Elphinstone. Lord Randolph was far from well at that time and for some days did not leave his cabin, but I had a long talk with him once as we sat on deck when he gave somewhat freely of his opinion about Mr. Gladstone whom he regarded as 'worn out', an opinion which proved somewhat previous in the light of after events.

On Sunday evenings he held services for the steerage passengers.

At Yale, John Brown made what was to prove one of the friendships of his life with Professor Fisher, the Dean of the Theological Faculty, and then set out on his travels. Rather like a Benedictine in medieval Europe, an English Nonconformist pastor could travel New England and be welcomed in house after house. He covered the usual triangle – New York, Chicago, except that he also sailed 500 miles down the Ohio River and visited St Louis, then Montreal and Quebec, rather than Washington, D.C. He was persuaded by Dr. Fisher to return to Yale for their Commencement Day, where he made a speech which the New York press said was 'enthusiastically received'.

The succeeding years had seen his name become known all over the literary and Nonconformist world by reason of his *Life of John Bunyan*, but it was not till June 1887 that he received a cable from Dr. Fisher of Yale, to say that the university had conferred on him the honorary degree of Doctor of Divinity.

My modesty shrank from the idea of my being placed among the learned Doctors of the Christian Church and my first impulse was to decline the honour. The only thing that deterred me from doing so was that it would seem an ungrateful return for their great kindness. Yale was the University founded next after Harvard, its date being 1701, and the degree conferred upon me had only been granted to a few on this side.

The Constitution of the University provided that 10 members of the Corporation should always be Congregational ministers belonging to the State of Connecticut. In 1887 there were 1,100 undergraduates. There are now about 5,000, but including post-graduate, there are over 10,000 students.

His year of office as Chairman of the Congregational Union in 1891 was marked by an International Congregational Council held in London. There were 100 representatives from the United States, 100 from England and 100 from the rest of the world. They came down to Bedford by special train, duly worshipped at the shrines of John Bunyan at Elstow and Bedford, listened to addresses, were given luncheon by 'my people' – all with such efficiency that the special train left Bedford on time to visit Scrooby, from whence the Pilgrim Fathers originated.

Scrooby is a village about a mile-and-a-half south of Bawtry on the Great North Road. It was the birthplace, in 1566, of one, William Brewster, a leader of the Pilgrim Fathers. The Puritans were so savagely persecuted by the Established Church that in 1607 a number of them escaped to the Low Countries where about one hundred were allowed to settle in Leyden. There, their preacher, John Robinson, acquired a house and a Puritan community collected. Life in Leyden was hard and they felt themselves to be aliens in the midst of a strange, if tolerant, community and could not regard their situation as permanent, yet it was not till 1620 that they were able, after much negotiation, to organise the sailing of the *Mayflower* and the *Speedwell* from Plymouth.

Some of the party visiting Bedford in 1891, after their visit to Scrooby, went on to Leyden and John Brown went with them. As a keen student of Puritan history he was deeply interested and he happily extended his American connection.

In 1892 he was requested by the Congregational Union to represent them at the Triennial Council of the American Congregationalists. In August, therefore, he was again at Liverpool boarding the White Star liner, *Teutonic* for New York. As usual he made acquaintances on the voyage, so made a round of visits and preached for his hosts at Auburndale and Dorchester, near Boston. He stayed with Miles Standish at Higham, Duxbury and went on to Plymouth, Massachusetts, upon whose Rock the Pilgrim Fathers had landed from the *Mayflower* in 1620. Coupled with his existing interest, it was this visit which inspired him to write *The Pilgrim Fathers of New England and their Successors* in 1895.

He was invited by Professor Fairbanks, formerly of Dartmouth College, to stay with him at St Johnsbury, Vermont, where there was a Garden City with workmen's dwellings. Mrs. Fairbanks and another lady were going to a Missionary Committee Meeting 500 miles away and invited him to join them. On their way to Minneapolis he passed through Chicago and preached at the church of his host there. *The Chicago Tribune* reported him as the lineal descendant of John Bunyan and he was once billed at a Brooklyn chapel as having written *Pilgrim's Progress*. One should not be too hard on transatlantic reporting because the Browns did rather tend to talk of Bunyan as if he were a family property. Indeed, my brother-in-law, Wilfrid Dimsdale, used to say that I was the only member of the family who did not believe that John Brown was the author of *Pilgrim's Progress*.

50. Congregationalists from New Hampshire, Rhode Island, Massachusetts and Connecticut – Elstow 1896. (The Rev. Dr. John Brown is in the front seated row and his wife, with the black bonnet, is seated at his feet.)

We are apt to think that speedy travel only appeared with the aeroplane but immediately after delivering his lecture, John Brown boarded the State Express Night Service to New York, the liner *Majestic* at 3 o'clock the following day, reaching Liverpool a few days later at 6 p.m. and Bedford at midnight. But in those days time was not wasted with customs, immigration and terrorist controls.

In June 1896 there was one of the many visitations of Americans to Bedford and he and his wife had to prepare to receive representative Congregationalists from each of the four States of New Hampshire, Rhode Island, Massachusetts, and Connecticut. They visited Bunyan's birth place at Elstow and were photographed before the Moot House. It was all a great success.

One of the visitors was to write, 'Somehow while there and looking upon the village green, or listening to the words of Dr. Brown, or going into the quaint little cottage . . . I was lifted into a kind of ecstasy. I saw John Bunyan as I had never seen him before, and felt the strange spell of enchantment which will, I trust, abide until the day of death'. This confirms what we must already know – that John Brown had the power to evoke visions and to transmit the things of the spirit.

Two years later, in 1898, he was invited to fill the Lyman Beecher Lectureship at Yale. He suggested that the usual eight lectures which comprised the course should be on 'Puritan Preaching in England'. In 1899 the Second International Council of Congregationalists was to be held in Boston, so there were two good reasons for his visit in the autumn of 1899.

He and his wife duly sailed from Liverpool on 5 September in the *Oceanic* of 15,000 tons and reached New York on the thirteenth. They then approached Boston, not along the coast by rail, but by steamer up the Hudson to Albany and then across to Boston by night train. By now he was well-known in Puritan circles all over New England and wherever he went he was asked to speak. He met Sankey of Moody & Sankey, the authors of famous 'pop' evangelical hymns, and was interested to learn that Sankey was a fellow Boltonian. They visited friends in Philadelphia and Washington and were then at Yale for the installation of a new President. In view of his lectureship, he found he was accorded full academic rank, and took part in a number of interesting ceremonies, and ended by preaching the University sermon on 15 and 22 October.

As I have said, the culture of the eastern seaboard of America was, at the end of the 19th century, still predominantly Puritan and the Rev. Dr. John Brown, D.D.(Yale), a respected figure in the circles in which he moved. He lived to see the first but not the second of the two terrible wars in which the United States was to save us. He must have felt that he played a not unworthy role in fostering memories of the Pilgrim Fathers, whose beliefs were, in the final analysis, responsible for that American intervention.

Chapter Fourteen

JOHN BROWN
(1830-1922)

Active Retirement

The Manse in Dame Alice Street had been the residence of the minister of Bunyan Meeting since 1830. Dame Alice Street is one of Bedford's main thoroughfares and in 1897 the site of the Manse, with its large garden and rear access, was needed for a new general post office. Recently, this in its turn was pulled down to make room for shops. Mrs. Brown's school had been sold some years earlier so they moved to De Parry's Avenue, wide and pleasantly bordered with trees and also in the centre of the town. The new Manse was number 46, a large, ugly, double-fronted house now broken up into flats.

In 1903, at the age of 73, the Rev. Dr. John Brown felt the time had come to retire. In his long letter of resignation he was able to say:

> No one has ever interfered with my freedom as a 'Teacher of God's Truth'. I have never been under any temptation to keep back any part of the Counsel of God which might be revealed to me and I have proved by my own experience that in a Congregational church the outspoken utterance of an honest conviction is the surest passport to the people's goodwill. I am grateful to God for the brotherly unity and peace which have so long prevailed among us.

I am sure that he did not realise that he was, in fact, writing a 'character' for himself. My father told me that John Brown had found himself unable to accept certain evangelical doctrines such as the verbal inspiration of the Scriptures, that is, that every word was dictated by the Deity. In his early days such an admission might have ended his career, but he was so unaggressive about his personal views and so unwilling to quarrel that he was, as his letter of resignation shows, always able to say what he believed without attracting persecution. That he never had dissension in his pastorate was not only due to his distinction, but to the fact that he had the gift, which he passed on notably to Florence, Harold and Kenneth, of being able to stop people quarrelling.

I was too young ever to have heard him preach, but my cousin Geoffrey Keynes did and wrote: 'I can still see my grandfather in his pulpit, high above the congregation, with his white pointed beard, healthy pink face and piercing blue eyes, preaching in his silvery voice to a rapt audience'.

His resignation came as a shock to his congregation and, at first, they tried to persuade him to stay with an active young assistant. We have a moving account of his last sermon and much of the text and an account of the speeches, testimonials and presentations from many leading figures, not least, from local Anglican clergy, the vicars of Stagsdon and Goldington.

His *Life Recollections* are not like those of David Everard Ford, loaded with references to 'My Dear Wife', but in the Bedford farewells the part she had played in the life of the town, as well as in her husband's pastorate, was fully recognised. When John Brown resigned from Bunyan Meeting he thought it proper to leave Bedford, where he and his wife would overshadow any successors. Like many people contemplating retirement, they wanted to be nearer to their children and, in their case, near a Congregational community of some standing. They, therefore, bought the balance of the lease of 10 Upper Park Road,

51.   The Browns, *c.*1902. Standing (*left to right*): Florence (41), Walter (32), Harold (29). Seated (*left to right*): Jessie (36), Rev. Dr. John Brown (72), Mrs. Brown (65), Alice (38). Front: Kenneth (23).

Hampstead, near Lyndhurst Road Church and Upper Park Road became the focal point of the family, to be followed, in the next generation, by Harvey Road, Cambridge.

Of course, retirement from executive responsibility at the age of 73 did not mean retirement in the accepted sense and John Brown writes, 'For the 10 years after leaving Bedford I had but few vacant Sundays when I was not preaching in various parts of the country – east, west, north and south'. His services were sought by many committees of which he tended to become chairman and his old pattern of transatlantic commissions continued.

Some of his American friends were shocked to find that there was no memorial to John Bunyan in Westminster Abbey and, when they got home, wrote to the Dean. The Dean, Dr. Clifford, came to Dr. John Brown to draw up an appeal: this he did and the appeal was signed by:

The Duke of Bedford; Lord Tennyson; Lord Roseberry; Lord Morley; Augustine Birrell; Prof. Butcher; Holman Hunt; Sir Oliver Lodge; George Meredith; A. C. Benson; Henry James; Andrew Lang; Frederick Harrison; W. Hale White; Prof. Dowden; Stopford Brooke;

52. Ada Haydon Brown, *c.*1900.

53. The Rev. Dr. John Brown, D.D. (Yale).

J. M. Barrie; A. T. Quiller Couch; H. G. Wells; Thomas Hardy; Watts Dunton and Mrs. Thackeray Ritchie.

There were also bishops and deans of the Anglican Church – The Bishops of Hereford, Truro, Durham and Ripon; Deans Weldon, Wace, Barker and Archdeacon Sinclair.

But there was scarcely an inch of space left on the walls. It was, therefore, agreed that there should be a stained glass window, showing scenes from the *Pilgrim's Progress* story, in one of the windows on the west aisle of the north transept. At the meeting in the Jerusalem Chamber of the Abbey to further the scheme, the Archbishop of Canterbury stated: 'What modern Christendom owes to Bunyan it is hardly possible to estimate'. John Brown could not resist writing in his *Life Recollections*:

So spake the Archbishop of Canterbury of John Bunyan in 1908, and the coming centuries will perhaps ask why a predecessor of his, Archbishop Sheldon, urged with such bitter determination those Conventicle Acts of 1664 and 1670 that kept that same John Bunyan for 12 long dreary years in Bedford Gaol. That day there was a discreet silence observed in the Jerusalem Chamber on this mysterious point.

Dr. John Brown and his wife lived to see and enjoy the successes of their children and grandchildren. He was 89 and his wife 82 in 1919, but they grasped the importance of Maynard's *Economic Consequences of the Peace*. Mrs. Brown had been bitterly opposed to the Boer War and realised that in condemning the Versailles Peace Treaty, which was to brew another war, her grandson had written a book, a fruit of their tradition, that was to influence world opinion.

That John Brown remained alert and active in old age is clearly shown by the text we have, in his own firm hand, of a paper he gave to a Hampstead Book Society in March 1914, when he was eighty-four. Though it is entitled *Brief Reminiscences*, it must have taken about an hour-and-a-half to deliver. His opening paragraph sets the theme:

I came into the world in 1830, just one week before George IV went out of it, so my life, running through the reigns of William IV, Queen Victoria and Edward VII, connects the time of George IV with that of George V. Going back to the start one may see that during the 15 years between the Battle of Waterloo and the death of George IV, England was slowly recovering from the devastating experiences of the Napoleonic Wars. The year 1830 was the time of a new departure, a dividing line between an old world and a new. During the next 10 years there were to be great changes. New modes of travel would bring a new civilization: an industrial revolution would change the face of England, and the Reform Bill of 1832 would bring in a new era of Parliamentary Government.

And so it continues, full of interesting detail and a fine example of his breadth of vision and sense of historical perspective. It ends with the kind of story he loved telling:

When Thackeray went to Oxford to deliver his lectures upon the Four Georges he called upon some of the heads of colleges. Among others, he waited upon Dr. Plumptre, the Master of University College. This gentleman said, 'But sir, what have you done?' To which Thackeray quietly replied that he was the author of *Vanity Fair*. 'Sir', said Plumptre, 'Isn't there some mistake, didn't John Bunyan write *Vanity Fair*?' The story got about, and, of course, people were laughing, when one morning Professor Thorold Rogers met Dr. Plumptre and asked him how he came to make this mistake? 'Well, you see', he said, 'I had not read the *Pilgrim's Progress*: in fact, I never do read novels'.

———

I did not see very much of my grandfather because he was in London and I was in Manchester, but I do remember, in my early teens, an overpowering Sunday afternoon at his house in Hampstead, when he, my great-uncle, Gerard Ford, and my father stayed on in the dining-room telling stories. Those of the two ex-chairmen of the Congregational Union were pastoral: those of my father's, Jewish, collected from his Manchester Jewish acquaintances. It was rather as if the Archbishops of Canterbury and York and the Chief Rabbi were passing the time capping each other's stories. Cockney wit seeks astringently to show up the folly of some third party, but their stories were Lancashire in flavour, kindly, inviting us to laugh at ourselves as much as others. I only remember one, told, I think, by my grandfather: 'A minister had just received an invitation to take up a better pastorate, when a neighbour happened to call. The door was opened by his small daughter. The visitor asked, "Are your mummy and daddy in?" The child hesitated and then replied, "Well, daddy is in his study praying for guidance: mummy is upstairs packing!" '

It was Jane Elizabeth who said to David Everard Ford after a church meeting at Richmond Chapel, 'Your course is now quite clear. You must resign', and perhaps it was her daughter, Ada Haydon, who told John Brown that he must look beyond Park Chapel, Manchester.

Chapter Fifteen

FLORENCE ADA KEYNES (born Brown)
(1861-1958)

Florence Ada Brown was born at 76 Elizabeth Street, Cheetham, Manchester in 1861, but was taken to Bedford in 1864, when her father, the Rev. John Brown, was appointed to Bunyan Meeting.

Her very capable mother ran a school at the Manse, where the excellent teaching, combined with her own natural abilities, secured for her, when she was only 16, an Exhibition to Newnham Hall, as Newnham College, Cambridge was then called. When she went up in 1878, it had only been open for three years and there were 30 students. She wrote in *Gathering up the Threads*:

> It is difficult to make young women of the present day who have the satisfaction of complete membership of the university, realise the thrill it gave to their grandmothers to be allowed to come humbly to Cambridge for teaching on university lines, and the intense gratitude they felt towards those who had fought the battle for them. Some of them were women who had been waiting with impatience for an opportunity which had been denied them in earlier days, others were young and unsophisticated but just as eager for the new experience. This combination added to the interest of the community.

I used to imagine that my uncle and aunt had met when he was supervising her studies, albeit in the presence of a chaperone, as was then required, but this was not so. A certain William Bond was a large Congregationalist grocer known to both John Brown and John Keynes. He was a public figure and his son, Henry Bond, who became Master of Trinity Hall, had been at school with Neville Keynes. It was at his hospitable house that Neville and Florence met. They married in 1882. Thirty-four years later (29 October 1916), their son, Maynard, was to write to his mother saying that he had met Constance Garnett: 'She told me that she last saw father when he was about my age. He had very blue eyes and was always smiling. You were "serene". When you became engaged, people said that it was a great waste for two to marry who both had such perfectly good tempers, "when they might have made two homes happy"'.

The Cambridge world into which the young Mr. and Mrs. Neville Keynes entered was not easy. Six Harvey Road was built for them in 1882 and only 11 years had elapsed since Parliament had had to pass a Bill to require Oxford and Cambridge colleges to drop exclusion by religious test of Nonconformists and others from college fellowships. But the Church of England still had a firm grip on the colleges, and rank, and the shibboleths of the landed gentry still dominated university society. Florence, herself, paints a picture in her *By-Ways of Cambridge History*:[1]

> Social life still had much of the formality typical of Victorian days, especially emphasized perhaps in university circles where order of precedence was a ruling feature. Before the influx of new life in 1882,[2] few had been admitted into the inner circle beyond Heads of Houses and Professors with their ladies. The young brides were, however, received hospitably and formal dinner parties were graced by them one at a time in turn, sometimes to their embarrassment. Etiquette demanded that the bride should appear in her bridal gown and be taken in to dinner by the host. For this occasion only, she was the leading lady; she had to be on the alert to catch the hostess's eye when the suitable moment came for the ladies to withdraw, and hers it was to rise and precede the train of stately dowagers into the withdrawing-room.

54. 'Going in to Dinner' – Gwen Raverat.

When it became her duty to return this hospitality, it was a real puzzle not only to provide the seven or eight courses of the dinner but also to arrange the guests at table in proper order. The husband usually had to solve the problem by explaining exactly how the expected guests would walk in an official procession.

If the husband made a mistake his colleagues would forgive him, but their wives would not.

Gwen Raverat, a daughter of Sir George Darwin, and sister of Margaret, who married Geoffrey Keynes, gives an enchanting picture of the Cambridge of the 1880s in her well-known *Period Piece*.[3] But her mother was American and she, herself, a rebel. Florence was not; her background and education at the Manse had equipped her for the notable work she was to do, but had not prepared her for the social ritual she had now to face. She had to feel her way: she and her husband were Nonconformists – chapel – and, though he had

£1,000 (£34,000) a year which helped, it came from trade.

It is possible that Florence may have shared the family characteristic of a certain lack of confidence till later in life – my father certainly complained of it, saying it had been one of his greatest handicaps. None of them had brassy self-assurance: its absence was part of their charm. In any case she was probably shy, facing a new and difficult world, but being game, as well as very intelligent, she did not withdraw but built up a manner with which to face the world. In later years, with the assurance of great achievements, she was wholly natural and the same with everyone.

I remember when I was staying at Harvey Road in 1922, she came in from a meeting. As always, she was kind and welcoming, but her manner was that in which she had chaired her meeting. On the table was a pile of press cuttings about Maynard which an agency had sent her and which she pasted into albums. She went over to the table and started fingering these and talking about Maynard. I was only 18, but the way the manner dissolved and the intensely warm, loving woman shone out, is still vivid before me.

Geoffrey Keynes contributed an essay on his brother, Maynard, to his son, Milo's delightful collection.[4] In it there are passages which tell us much of the family life Florence and Neville built up.

My father took his bride to live in a newly-built semi-detached house on the outskirts of the town. At the end of Harvey Road to the east was Fenner's cricket ground. Not far away to the south were open fields where our butcher, Mr. Bulman, grazed his cattle. The house and small garden were without charm or character, but the place suited our unexacting standards, and my mother died there 76 years later at the age of ninety-six. Our home was unmistakably and inevitably 'victorian' in character. The walls of the rather dark dining-room were clad in deep blue and crimson Morris paper of such quality that it never needed renewal during our tenancy. The furnishings were undistinguished, but comfortable, some having stood in my father's rooms in Pembroke. The pictures were conventional specimens of period taste, the most vividly remembered being a large reproduction of Raphael's 'Virgin and Child', such as might have been in 100 other homes of the same class. . . . Our parents, as I now look back on them, had a lovable aura of perfect integrity and goodness without stuffiness or pomposity; they were affectionate without sentimentality, and were careful not to interfere with the personalities of their children, while always fostering any worthwhile interests as soon as they discerned them. . . . It may seem odd, but I do not recall any family squabbling. Maynard's supremacy was accepted and there was no ground for quarrels to disturb our happiness, a reflection, perhaps, of the perfect harmony between our parents; a tribute, too, to our mother who directed all our lives with loving tact and understanding.

This understanding was lifelong. When Maynard was distraught beyond measure by what was being done at Versailles in 1919 in the drafting of the Peace Treaty, his letters to his mother were more than those of an affectionate son: nor were they the letters which might have been written by a man to his wife seeking solace. They were letters written to an equal who could grasp, as he did, the probable evil consequences of what was being done, and who could share his distress.

Such understanding of her children has been the admirable sum of many women's lives. In 1895, however, when the children were 12, 10 and eight respectively, Florence became the honorary secretary of the Cambridge Branch of the Charity Organisation Society (now the Central Aid Society), which aided the poor and needy of the town. To engage in such work flowed from the beliefs of the Manse and the view held strongly by Nonconformists that it was a duty to do what one could to alleviate misery. But, further, Florence had married into those circles in which the late-Victorian liberal intellectuals were laying the foundations of much of the social fabric we know.

The fathers of Professor Henry Fawcett and Dr. Neville Keynes were old Salisbury friends. It had been in the Fawcett's drawing-room, in 1869, that Dr. Henry Sidgwick had, in the presence

55. Florence Keynes on an early visit to her inlaws in Salisbury.

of John Stuart Mill, propounded his plan to persuade the Cambridge Higher Local Examination Board to allow girls who were over 18 to sit for their examinations. It was also the year in which John Stuart Mill's book, *The Subjection of Women*, appeared.[5]

It was to become evident that if the candidates for the Higher Local Examination were to do reasonably well, they would need to attend lectures, but it was unthinkable that girls of 18 from all over the country should, in the 1870s, have to seek lodgings in the town.

56. Miss Clough and Florence Brown, 1880.

57. Dr. John Neville Keynes, 1905.

Therefore, Henry Sidgwick organised the setting-up of Newnham Hall in 1876 and nominated Miss Jemima Clough as the first Principal.

Sidgwick, consequently, was a pioneer in Florence's eyes before she married and became a close friend of the family, often dining and golfing with them. Neville Keynes noted in his diary on 26 April 1900, a few months before Sidgwick's death: 'Maynard played golf with Sidgwick at Royston. He enjoyed Sidgwick's talk as much as his golf'. Sidgwick was one of the great figures of his time, and Maynard, a youth of seventeen.

Florence was, thus, at the heart of the thinking about the equality of the sexes which flowed from John Stuart Mill, through Henry Sidgwick, and which was to liberate Englishwomen from semi-medieval subjection and to enable them to play their proper part in the next century.

After a number of years as chairman of the Cambridge Branch of the Charity Organisation Society, Florence saw that there were areas, traditionally reserved for men, which were more suitable for women and, in 1907, stood for the Cambridge Board of Guardians. Her appeal reads today as a lucid statement of the obvious, but, 80 years ago, it was bold. It was, in fact, in the great tradition of reforming Englishwomen from Florence Nightingale onwards.

58. Florence Ada Keynes' appeal to the Cambridge electors.

CAMBRIDGE BOARD OF GUARDIANS ELECTION
1907.

TO THE ELECTORS

OF

New Town Ward.

6, HARVEY ROAD,
5th March, 1907.

LADIES AND GENTLEMEN,

I beg to offer myself as a Candidate for election to the Board of Guardians as one of the representatives of New Town Ward.

Some portion of the work of Poor Law Guardians is clearly more suitable for women than for men, and I hope to receive the votes of all who think that the presence of women on the Board of Guardians is desirable.

If you do me the honour to elect me as one of your representatives, I shall endeavour to pay special attention to the needs of the women and children in receipt of relief, and to the aged and sick in the Infirmary.

I am,

Ladies and Gentlemen,

Your obedient servant,

FLORENCE ADA KEYNES.

59. Florence Ada Keynes, 1905.

She was elected the first woman Guardian but began to find she needed the powers of a town councillor to get things done. This, however, was impossible because only householders could become town councillors and that, in practice, excluded married women. She, therefore, set to work to lobby M.P.s: she finally succeeded, and the law was changed in 1914 when Asquith was Prime Minister and Sir Samuel Hoare was at the Home Office. Maynard was a friend of the Asquiths and one is tempted to think that, having taken care to lose to Margot at bridge, he might have mentioned the barrier to women which his mother was seeking to lower. But the dates are some months out, so the reform was principally a triumph of Florence's skill and persistence.

After the war she became, in 1920, the first woman Justice of the Peace in Cambridgeshire and an Alderman and the Mayor of the Borough of Cambridge in 1932-3, mayoral office, till then, being held by very few women, indeed, in the whole country.[6]

Her work for the Cambridge Charity Organisation Society led her to found the Cambridge Juvenile Employment Organisation, the first in the country, anticipating by many years what became recognised as an essential part of the national framework. She was to become Chairman of Visitors at the huge Fulbourn Asylum, placed well outside Cambridge. Whether the work she undertook was depressing did not weigh with her, if it needed doing, or she would not have become a Poor Law Guardian.

Papworth now connotes heart surgery, but the origin of the hospital goes back to 1917, when a small group, of which Florence Keynes was a founder-member, honorary secretary and chairman of the House Committee, established the Papworth Village Colony for those suffering from tuberculosis. Dr. Varrier Jones and Sir Sims Woodhead were leading figures, and Geoffrey was its surgeon, and there was world recognition of its pioneer work.

Having served on the Committee of the National Council of Women for many years, she became its President, and, hence, the President of the National Council of Women of Great Britain, when the International Council of Women met in Vienna in 1930. In 1951, the National Council celebrated her 90th birthday with a luncheon in her honour. In the middle of her excellent speech, she had to apologise, pause, and search for her glasses to decipher a passage in her notes she could not read.

I never saw Florence in action outside the family circle, but I think I know the way she worked, because I saw the same qualities in my father. They were much the nicest of the Browns. Like the others, they grasped the essential point in a flash, but were never aggressive. They were rather thinking of the feelings of whoever they were dealing with. Florence had had a better education than my father, lived in a more stimulating atmosphere and achieved much more, but their approach, and the respect and devotion they inspired, was the same.

It was Florence who persuaded the Cambridge Council, in 1932, to approve the present Guildhall. The demolition of the old and inadequate building and its replacement by a costly new structure, at a time of deep depression, was thought by many to be improvident, if not folly. The belief that those were just the times in which such schemes should be carried through, was cardinal to Maynard's economic doctrine, and he supported his mother with much ammunition. They were a formidable combination, and the whole complex was completed in 1939, just in time to be of most important service during the 1939-45 War.

Another achievement, this time of national importance, was the introduction of women police. Maud Darwin, an American, whom Sir George had married, had come back from a visit, just before the 1914-18 War, greatly impressed with the work women police were doing in America and she made speeches and wrote articles on the subject. Her daughter, Margaret, was to marry Florence's son, Geoffrey, in 1917, so Florence, no doubt, became informed at first-hand and she knew, from her many years as a magistrate, how real was the need in this country. She, therefore, set to work: it took years of patient and persistent lobbying of Members of Parliament and others. When she judged the ground well-prepared, she arranged for a deputation from the National Council of Women to wait on the Home Secretary and the Secretary of State for Scotland on 2 December 1929, asking that the Police Acts should be extended to include women police, and also that a woman should be appointed to serve on the Police Council. Thus it was that, in February 1930, a Miss Peto was appointed as an Adviser to the Commissioner on the organisation and training of policewomen.[7]

The financial crisis of 1931 was such that savage economy cuts were being widely made and it was feared that the development of the Women's Police Force might be checked. Florence, as the President of the National Council for Women, went into action and, using the great influence she had acquired, arranged to be allowed to address a meeting in the House of Commons on 11 March 1931, to insist upon the Women's Police Force '. . . being increased and revised as an essential part of the Police Force all over the country'.

Her brother, Kenneth, once said to me that Florence was an absolute saint putting up with the most intolerable things and never complaining. He did not elaborate and I did not like to question him, but I think he may have been referring to the Lloyd 'invasion' (Chapter Seventeen). These very odd relations charged into Florence's Cambridge world and became more intrusive as time went on, particularly in the matter of expecting to be invited to the Harvey Road Sunday luncheons. She was endlessly kind to her sisters, Alice and Jessie (Lloyd), when they were lonely, and to Kenneth himself, when he had breakdowns and was very trying. When her brother, Walter, became Regius Professor of Physic and moved to Cambridge, he and his wife were frequent visitors. Walter was a fascinating talker, but the total burden of family must have been considerable.

It is no exaggeration to say that these Harvey Road luncheons became world famous. Like other undergraduate members of the family, I was often invited to what, in those days, was a jolly family party – that was in the early 1920s. Food would rumble up from the kitchen below in a hoist which would then disappear into the floor. My uncle Neville would circulate excellent claret: conversation was always easy and, if Maynard was present, sure to be very amusing. These luncheons were a focal point for the family and remained so, even when they became very much more. Heads of Houses had, for years, been pleased to be invited, but during the Second World War, international statesmen became aware of the quality of their hostess. If Maynard had promised that he would come down from London on a certain Sunday, he would never allow anything to cause him to disappoint his mother. On one occasion, when a Dominion Minister was on a flying visit to London, on important Treasury business, the only day he had free was a Sunday. He had to come down to Harvey Road, for Sunday

60.   Florence Ada Keynes in old age, *c.*1956.

luncheon, to be able to do it.

That the mechanics of such luncheons – indeed, the fact that the whole household could operate smoothly during the war, depended upon Suzanne Rendell. Suzanne came to Harvey Road in 1942 to nurse Neville Keynes, then aged 90, but rendered herself invaluable and much esteemed by the whole family, about whom she came to know more than she would ever tell. As Florence got older, Suzanne became, as it were, her lady-in-waiting, and when royalty called at Harvey Road, as indeed they did, it was her duty to entertain the royal lady-in-waiting, whilst the principals conversed in private.

It was in 1956, at the age of 95, that Aunt Florence came to London for the last time and her daughter, Margaret, brought her to call on us. She was, at last, tired of living and had come to say goodbye. When she left, we felt we had been in the presence of a very great and good woman – a saint.

Chapter Sixteen

DR. ALICE EVANGELINE BROWN
(1846-1947)

The Rev. John Brown wrote of his sorrowful parting from his congregation at Park Chapel, Manchester in 1864, 'I went away with heart torn and bleeding taking my wife and my two young children, one of them a babe scarce two months old'. The babe was Alice. Whereas her father's heart healed quickly, hers was to endure sufferings from which it did not.

Like her elder sister, Florence, she was educated at the Manse School and went on to Newnham College, Cambridge in 1882, but she did not stay more than a year. She had not won an Exhibition like Florence, and it is possible that financial pressures at home did not allow more than one year at Cambridge.

In 1881 there were only 25 women doctors[1] and it would have been in keeping with the family belief in the advancement of the position of women that she should aspire to become one. But she had to content herself with a period in medical training in general practice at Hampstead and then had to go back to Bedford and serve as an assistant mistress at the Manse School, presumably until her mother disposed of the school in 1892, when Alice was twenty-eight. It may have been in those years that events took a course which contributed to turning her into the sad, embittered woman my generation knew. It is said she fell in love with an organist – maybe at Bunyan Meeting – but that his prospects were not considered good enough for her mother to allow the friendship to develop. In the 1880s very few daughters took the bit between their teeth and certainly not those with mothers as strong as Mrs. John Brown. No doubt the organist married some other member of her father's congregation, whilst Alice suffered the pangs which helped to sour her.

61. Dr. Alice Evangeline Brown.

When she was 32, however, she managed to break away. She entered the Royal School of Medicine for Women in 1896. In 1901 she was granted the Triple Qualification jointly by the Royal College of Physicians of Edinburgh and the Faculty, now the Royal College of Physicians and Surgeons of Glasgow. In 1902 she was granted the L.R.C.P. of Brussels.

Her mother and father had moved to Upper Park Road, Hampstead in 1903 and she lived with them for the rest of their lives. This may not have been the way she wished to spend her life. For very many years she held various medical positions under the London County Council, mostly at Infant Welfare centres. Though women were grudgingly accepted by the medical profession, they did not get the more interesting positions. I remember on one occasion when I was staying at Upper Park Road, she came back from her work blackly depressed. She was working in a grim area of London amongst the casual labourers' families – many of them Irish – which gathered round the St Pancras and Camden Town railway goods yards. What depressed her was the excessive birth rate and the hopelessness and fecklessness of the majority of her patients, and she did not seem to draw any satisfaction from her work and only dwelt on the misery of the human lot. Evangeline was a remarkably unsuitable name.

It was about the same time that she and her brother, Kenneth, took me to the Great Empire Exhibition at Wembley. She gazed at some huge, complicated machine and at the crowd admiring it and observed, 'Man looks contemptible beside his works'.

But I must not give the impression that she was a bore or ever boring, very much the reverse. She had the most charming talking voice and great conversational gifts. In 1923 Kenneth had one of his more serious breakdowns and Alice took him to Taormina. They cabled for me to join them them and I remember sitting enthralled whilst Alice talked. She covered a wide range of subjects, always tending to be sardonic and, though personally kind, she never gave public figures the benefit of the doubt or considered any cause worthy.

She also wrote amusing letters. We have only one which she wrote to her sister, Jessie, in 1931. Jessie was busying herself with genealogy and it so happened that Alice had been reading David Ford's diary:

> Our ancestors [she wrote], were so deeply interested in the welfare of their souls, that they quite ignored any worldly details, which would have been great value to their descendants . . .

> Here is a gossipy piece. David Ford relates[2] that he went to Coggeshall over a church quarrel. The minister there, a few weeks previously, had baptised his seventh son and fifteenth child and he was in a very uncomfortable state arising from intoxication. Do you wonder? I think his wife would have had still more excuse, but she is not mentioned. . . .

> If I come on Wednesday there ought not to be too many people. The trains by King's Cross are despicable, so I must use Liverpool Street, which I dislike.

At one time Kenneth, 15 years her junior, used to take her on continental holidays, but later he would take other companions and leave her at home looking after her ageing parents. Finally, crippled by arthritis, she had only his sick and intermittent company. What a tragically wasted life. She must have been attractive, with her bright brown eyes, and she was clever and amusing. Perhaps Mrs. John Brown had no more to answer for than the average parent of unmarried daughters in those days, but sometimes I wonder.

Chapter Seventeen

THE LLOYDS

Albert Hugh Lloyd	**1864-1936**
Jessie Lloyd (born Brown)	**1866-1946**
Muriel Eleanor Haydon Lloyd	**1893-1939**

Florence Ada was a normal name for a girl whose mother's name was Ada, but Alice Evangeline! Mrs. Brown's father, David Everard Ford, was an evangelical, but her husband was not. Had there been a disagreement and, when the third daughter appeared, did John Brown dig in his toes and insist on plain Jessie? All their other children had family second names; so I got a copy of her birth certificate: it read simply, 'Jessie, girl, daughter of John Brown and Ada Haydon Brown, formerly Ford'.

Jessie was educated at the Manse School. She did not, like Florence and Alice, go on to Newnham. She was a very good tennis player. That sounds improbable to those who only knew her in later years when she weighed 17 stone or so, but when young, length of limb no doubt counted. Where and when she met Albert Hugh Lloyd of Manchester, we do not know; presumably, through her Ford uncles who had a business there. They were married in 1892, and their only daughter, Muriel, was born in 1893.

Albert Hugh was a most extraordinary fellow – a little terrier of a man – and, although it was not my intention to write about in-laws, he impinged on the family to such a degree that he must be noticed. His father, Humphrey Lloyd, was a Welshman who came to Manchester in the booming days of the cotton trade and built-up a very fine business. They had a large wholesale warehouse in Church Street with travellers calling on small shops in mining villages from South Wales to the North-East coast. They specialised in miners' shirts and working clothes. These were made up in a factory they had in Wigan and the coarse twill of which they were made was woven at another mill they had at Dukinfield. I remember being shown over this mill when it had just been converted to electric drive, but there was the old beam engine still *in situ*. Beam engines were the first kind of steam engine used in textile mills and this one would, today, be treasured as a gem of industrial archaeology.

Albert Hugh was a very shrewd and successful man of business, but he hated it and, from early days, had wanted to get out and pursue his passion for archaeology.

I must have first been aware of the Lloyds in about 1916. It would have been nice to have had a jolly girl cousin, but Muriel, at the age of 23, wore pince-nez and was, I thought, a cold fish. The Lloyds did not have a home: they had aways lived here and there in furnished houses because they were counting the days till Albert could get out of the business, and Manchester, and descend on Cambridge. That event took place in 1924.

Albert talked with the most insufferabe precision, came out with quite incredible pomposities, yet always wore his hair *en brosse*, which seemed incongruous. He also had extraordinary fads to do with health. (My father, nevertheless, thought he was a good fellow and could get on with him.) Jessie lacked social ease and was a fanatical teetotaller, though was not averse to trifle heavily laced with sherry, whilst Muriel, though academically gifted and a devoted daughter, remained remote and difficult to like. My father estimated that Albert was worth one- or two-hundred thousand pounds (£1.5-£3 million). He had had a good war, since his factories turned out uniforms in addition to working clothing, and he had invested wisely.

62. The Lloyds, *c*.1903.

He arranged a coat of arms for himself, the shield of which embodied three boars' heads – (apposite, we said): the shield duly appeared on their enormous Rolls Royce, which Muriel drove. In those days Rolls Royces were almost exclusively driven by a chauffeur who had been to the special training course at the Rolls Royce Works in Derby. This course Muriel had attended, making, I am sure, studious notes, and, at the end, being perfectly capable of taking a class herself. She then drove the monster, with Albert perched beside her, his hackles up, ready to bark at anybody, whilst Jessie, behind the glass partition, rode vast and solitary, cocooned in an enormous fur coat.

Their descent on Cambridge was in the grand manner. They rented the Master's Lodge at Trinity Hall for six months, whilst Henry Bond and family were abroad. Meanwhile, they bought the lease of St John's House, Grange Road, a large modern affair (now a language college) which they decorated with incredible splendour and stuffed with antiques. They then settled down to entertain Cambridge. There was, however, one difficulty – teetotallism, which rendered their parties rather subdued. However, Albert would, after dinner, take the Heads of Houses and Professors, no less, to his study to examine some Graeco-Roman artefact. It was rumoured that, unknown to Jessie, he had a drink locker concealed in a bookcase.

Long before Albert Lloyd was able to leave Manchester, he was working on his subject, Magna Graecia. As soon as the war of 1914-18 was over, the Lloyds set off by road for Southern Italy and Sicily, where they returned, year after year. Considering the state of the roads on their first visit and the unreliability of motor cars, this was really very brave on the part of Muriel, the sole driver. They met only one steamroller, patching up appalling roads between Calais and Ventmille. This was before the days of the Rolls. Motor tax certificates used then to give the colour and make of car, and Albert was amused when, on one occasion, his hotel bill was made out in the name of Signore Mole Humber. When Italian village crowds remarked upon Jessie's size with uninhibited admiration, translation rested with Muriel. Her Italian was good, but she probably did not translate the finer points, even if, classical scholar as she was, she had grasped them.

Muriel came down from Newnham in 1917 and it was upon her skill and endurance as a driver, and on her knowledge of Italian, that Albert depended. She was a classical scholar of distinction, being a double First and the winner of many prizes. As the Humber was replaced by the Rolls, and Albert got less and less tied to Humphrey Lloyd & Son Ltd., their expeditions lasted longer and their application increased. The combination of an astute man of business and a first-rate classical scholar produced remarkable results. The collection of Greek coins of Italy and Sicily which they built up was, according to *The Times*, 'Unequalled by any other collection in private hands'. It was vested in Muriel from the start, partly because its collection had depended on her scholarship and partly with an eye on death duties. Albert made this vesting clear in his Will, and also specified that the collection should eventually find a home in the British Museum on the condition that the Museum would produce an illustrated *Catalogue of the Lloyd Collection of Greek Coins* within three years, for which they would be paid £2,000 (£46,000). At the time of Muriel's death the collection was on loan to the Ashmolean Museum, Oxford, but in her Will she had confirmed her father's wish that it should go to the British Museum.

Muriel's skill in deciphering medieval documents led her to study Papal records in the Vatican archives relating to the University of Cambridge in the last quarter of the 14th century, and she, and her father, had collaborated to produce a history of Christ's College,[1] Cambridge, when it was known, prior to 1505, as God's House. She also became a governor and treasurer of Homerton College, where her work was said to be outstanding. As far as I know, she was not aware that her great-great-grandfather, David Ford, was a member of the college in 1787 (*see* Chapter Two), for I do not think she had ever studied his diaries.

Albert Lloyd matriculated in 1926, at the age of 62, and was then admitted to Christ's College as a Fellow Commoner Research Student. He became much attached to the college, on the one hand, studying its early history, and, on the other, placing his business experience at its disposal. Not only was his shrewd judgement in business matters recognised, but also his genuine scholarly instincts, and he was encouraged to seek a Ph.D. The gossip was that Muriel wrote his thesis, but I think the subject suggests that it was a joint effort. It was: 'The Place of Coinage in Greek Foreign Trade down to the end of the Fifth Century B.C.'[2] From 1928, when the university made him a Doctor of Philosophy, till he died in 1936, he was able to move in academic circles with, as it were, a handle to his name, thus realising the ambition he had formed so many years earlier as a young man in a Manchester warehouse.

Muriel was not so fortunate. Her collaboration with her father had been her life. She struggled on without him for three years and then, when the 1939-45 War shut her out from the lands they had studied together for so many years, she took her life. This may partly have been a manifestation of our family enemy, 'Ford depressions', for her father had left her considerable private means and the war was no more menacing for her than for everyone else.

I think one must avoid giving too unprepossessing a picture of Jessie. It is true that she was a difficult woman: even my father had had trouble with her when he helped in the sale of the Lloyd warehouse in Manchester, but then Albert must have been an annihilating husband. My sister, Helen, told me that when she was staying at St John's House, Albert came down to breakfast one morning in a foul temper. It happened that Muriel was in the target area. 'You only hurt when you try to please', her father said to her. Jessie had been at close range for many years.

Jessie had many acts of kindness and generosity to her credit. For example, by the time her brother, Walter, was suffering his terminal illness, he had spent all his savings and was in need of money for day-to-day household expenses. Jessie gave him £2,000 (£28,000). After Albert's death she lived a further 13 years. She moved out of St John's House to a very luxurious flat – Manor Court, Pinehurst – and, after Muriel's death, engaged a chauffeur to drive the Rolls. It was true that she worried obsessively about the evils in villages consequent upon the home-brewing of wine, but her various ailments disappeared and she began to enjoy life. She returned, with renewed enthusiasm, to genealogy, and we must be grateful to her, since much of the material on which the genealogical tree at Appendix I of this history depends is drawn from her research.

She also gave much time and thought to the proper disposal of the considerable fortune her husband had left. She recognised his attachment to Christ's and, to commemorate his connection with that college, set up a fund under her Will to be known as 'The A. H. Lloyd Benefaction' for the purpose of endowing a Research Fellowship in history, archaeology or similar subjects. In addition, during her lifetime, there were covenants in favour of the college. The total benefactions amounted to over £60,000 (£738,000).

To commemorate her daughter, she made various gifts to Newnham College. There was a sum of £14,000 (£172,000) to build and equip a Principal's Lodge, and £15,000 (£184,000) for its upkeep. Work could not begin till 1958 and it then took a year to complete. The architect was Louis Osman. It seems that he paid tribute to the Lloyds' devotion to Magna Graecia, for the layout he adopted is reminiscent of Greco-Roman villas in those parts. The single-storey at the back gives magnificent entertaining rooms overlooking the Principal's garden, but not having Roman central heating, nor the slaves to fire it, it is, I have been told, apt to be rather cold in the Cambridge winter.

The incised letters across the entablature are faced with gold leaf and read:

63. The Principal's Lodge, Newnham College, Cambridge, from the garden.

64. Architect's sketch of the Entrance.

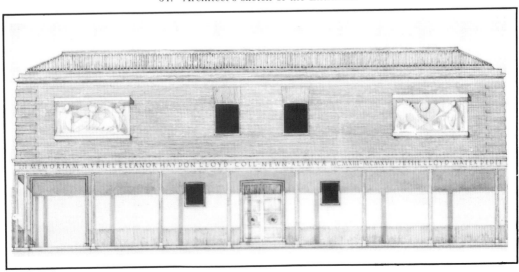

IN MEMORIAM MURIEL ELEANOR HAYDON LLOYD . COLL . NEWN
ALUMNAE . MCMXIII . MCMXVII . JESSIE LLOYD MATER DEDIT

Thus, posterity is not left in doubt as to the origin of the building.

We all made fun of the Lloyds, but one must recognise their genuine devotion to scholarship, their belief in the importance of learning and of the things of the mind, and of the wisdom with which they spent the considerable fortune which Albert had partly inherited, but largely made in many years of uncongenial work in Manchester.

Chapter Eighteen

SIR WALTER LANGDON-BROWN
(1870-1946)

Part I – Introduction by Neville Brown

Walter Langdon-Brown's contribution to medicine was so important that I think only a member of his profession can do justice to his achievements. I have been fortunate, therefore, in persuading Milo Keynes, his great-nephew, a Fellow of the Royal College of Surgeons, to contribute Part II, that is, the main body of this chapter, whilst I, as a layman, can only sketch in some of the background.

Born at the Manse, Bedford in 1870, the year of the Franco-Prussian War, Walter Langdon Brown[1] was educated at Bedford Grammar School. He was later to become a governor, which must have given him great satisfaction. Bedford, with its good schools, was like Cheltenham, a town to which servants of the Crown overseas, largely in India, used to retire. India has always infected its conquerors with its sense of caste, and sons of the minister of a local chapel must have been made aware of theirs at Bedford School. I once heard Walter discussing old school fellows with my father; a name would be mentioned and Walter would say, with a malicious chortle, 'Oh, I expect he is driving a tram in Vancouver'.

Besides being chapel, he was a 'swot'. Not only did he win the School Exhibition of £60 (£2,300) for four years at St John's College, Cambridge, for Natural Science, but also confounded his masters by winning the prize for an English Essay several years running: they believed that good English depended on classical scholarship.

Milo tells, in Part II of this chapter, of his subsequent distinctions and it is evident that Walter had every reason to proceed on his way with confidence, yet he did once sadly say to me, 'The gods punish us for our follies rather than our crimes'. I think he was thinking of his first marriage which was a disaster.

Frances Pressland was a nurse at St Bartholomew's and, poor woman, was wholly incapable of keeping up with him. They used to eat at Pagani's, in those days a very good restaurant in Great Portland Street, where Walter acquired his taste for good food and good wine. At the end of a suitable course, Frances would produce a bag into which their attentive, regular waiter would transfer scraps. Back in Welbeck Street, she would sit on the floor, surrounded, like a witch, by ten or a dozen cats, who sat in a circle round her and would come forward, one at a time, to be given a morsel from the bag. It was an eerie sight and the smell was what one might expect. Alas, gin, as well as cats, sustained Frances, who died in 1931.

It was in those years that Walter read and read, voraciously, as had his father, and with the same wide-ranging taste. As a result he became recognised as the man of the widest culture in his profession. His book of collected essays, *Thus we are Men*,[2] gives one some idea of the way in which he would blend material drawn from the past with ideas far ahead of his time.

Walter, like his grandmother, Jane Elizabeth Down, and his mother, Ada Haydon Ford, was a born teacher, and he had his father's pastoral sense of duty to his flock – in his case, patients and students at St Bartholomew's. This, quite apart from his professional dedication and brilliance, meant that when his students qualified and started up in practice, the consultant to whom they would send their patients was Langdon Brown.

65. Sir Walter Langdon-Brown, Regius Professor of Physic, Cambridge, at a ceremony laying the foundation stone at Bedford School science building in October 1932.

When the War of 1914-18 was over, he was, therefore, able to buy a house in Cavendish Square, which ranked with Harley Street in the eyes of the public and the profession. He bought the lease of No. 31 on the south side of the Square at the east end, which has since been redeveloped and now carries a 20-storey office block.

Walter was deeply interested in the psychology of Stevenson's *The Strange Case of Dr. Jeckyll and Mr. Hyde*[3] and liked to think that Stevenson visualised No. 31 as Dr. Jeckyll's house. It had a pleasant hall and small garden, as described by Stevenson. The garden had been roofed over and made a most impressive consulting room. I have examined the 1875 Ordnance Survey of Cavendish Square and find it difficult, but not impossible, to reconcile the site of No. 31 with Stevenson's description. I think Walter knew that he was playing with an illusion, but he very much enjoyed doing so. This was a family characteristic which came out strongly in Maynard.

Walter Langdon Brown was of a very warm disposition and could be exuberantly affectionate. Being unhappily married and having no children of his own, which he greatly regretted, he delighted in playing the fairy uncle to his niece, Margaret Hill's family of four, which he would entertain lavishly and frequently, taking them to enormous meals at Frascati's where, as at Pagani's, any party of his was well looked after by the waiters. On their birthday they even had a printed menu bearing their name. They were also taken to Hamley's and told they could choose whatever toy they fancied, to Maskylin and Cook's Magic Show, to his weekend house at Crockham Hill in Surrey, and Polly was taken on some of his Italian holidays. He would also join them on their holidays at West Runton in Norfolk where they had a house. Walter was a huge man, and on one occasion broke the springs of the Hill's 'baby' Austin motor car: it was thought remarkable that he could get into it in the first place!

The Hill children were very fond of him, responding as much to the warmth of his affection as to his generosity, particularly Janet (head down in plate 66) who became a doctor and a psychologist, and was later greatly impressed by how far ahead of his time he was in psychosomatic medicine.

I do not know when Freda Hurry became Walter's secretary and then his mistress. She was alive and very attractice with bright black eyes, black (later grey) hair and a pretty, pale complexion. The liaison was a great shock to my father. He, and my sister, encountered them by chance visiting the Autumn Exhibition at the Walker Gallery in Liverpool. Walter, my father's eldest brother, was his idol and he was speechless all the way home. Freda, however, had much to do with Walter's ultimate worldly success and recognition. If one looks at Walter in the family group of 1902 (p. 103) and thinks of the years of hospital wards and of Welbeck Street, one can imagine that a lot needed doing to make him, shall we say, presentable. Freda tidied him and polished him, as well as making him very happy. Like my father, he had a natural *joie de vivre* and, when Frances died in 1931 and he immediately married Freda and came out, as it were, from the shade, his enjoyment of life was evident and infectious.

When he was appointed Regius Professor, there was great rejoicing, and I remember being shown a Seal of Appointment of Elizabeth I (though the office was established in 1540 by Henry VIII). I was taken to dine at Corpus Christi College and I realised then what an asset to any Combination Room Walter could be. He was a most entertaining conversationalist, spicing his remarks with an elegant malice. I think it was on that visit he said to me, 'There is no satisfaction in life equal to the esteem of one's peers'.

I am afraid that becoming Lady Langdon-Brown rather went to Freda's head, for she became very grand and put on airs. She was also very extravagant. Walter did not seem to mind and she had done so much to make his position, that one did not grudge her a touch of *folie de grandeur*. When he died she was lost. She went on a trip to South Africa, probably

66. David, Janet, W.L.B., Maurice, Polly and Margaret at West Runton in 1925.

a present from Jessie, for Walter had died penniless. She came back with some disease which could not be identified and lay for many months in a private ward at St Bartholomew's. She did not survive, but I do not think she wanted to.

Part II by Milo Keynes

Jane Langdon in marrying John Haydon in 1769 gave her surname to the family. In successive generations it reappeared three times, in each case borne by doctors of great distinction.

There was first her grandson, John Langdon Down (1828-96) who, as we saw in Chapter Three, was the first to recognise and describe a variety of mental deficiency in infants, now known as Down's Syndrome. Then there was her great-grandson, Sir Walter Langdon-Brown (1870-1946), and her great-great-grandson, Sir Geoffrey Langdon Keynes (1887-1982).

As Neville Brown tells in Part I of this chapter, Walter Langdon Brown was born in Bedford and did well at Bedford School. Before going to Cambridge in 1889, he spent a year at Owen's College, Manchester, working at biology. At St John's, where he was a foundation scholar, as well as one from Bedford School, he obtained a first-class in parts I and II of the natural sciences tripos in 1892 and 1893, and then spent a year as a Hutchinson research student, during which time he worked at physiology, a subject that he was later to apply so successfully to clinical medicine.

He entered St Bartholomew's Hospital with an entrance scholarship in 1894, and on qualification M.B., B.Chir. in 1896, he became house-physician to the remarkable Dr. Samuel Gee, now only remembered for 'Gee's linctus'. In 1901, he took the M.D. at Cambridge, gaining the Raymond Horton-Smith Prize for his thesis entitled 'Pylephlebitis'. Walter had a wide education in clinical medicine, and after his time with Dr. Gee was appointed senior resident medical officer to the Metropolitan Hospital, becoming after two years assistant physician and pathologist, and in 1906 full physician. Meanwhile at St Bartholomew's Hospital his progress was slow: he was a demonstrator of physiology from 1899 to 1906, combining this with the post of casualty physician in 1900, and demonstrator of practical medicine three years later. In 1906 he became medical registrar and demonstrator of morbid anatomy, until in 1913, at the age of 43, he was made assistant physician, becoming full physician in 1924. He retired from the active staff at Bart's six years later, at the age of 60, and was made Consulting Physician. He was elected a Fellow of the Royal College of Physicians in 1908, Croonian Lecturer in 1918, Harveian Orator on 'The Background of Harvey' in 1936, and served as Senior Censor there from 1931 to 1934.

In 1900 Walter went to Pretoria as senior physician to the Imperial Yeomanry Hospital during the South African War, and in the 1914-18 War he was physician to a territorial force hospital, No. 1 General Hospital, based at Bart's. He was President to no less than four sections of the Royal Society of Medicine; those of Urology, Therapeutics and Pharmacology and the History of Medicine, as well as first President of the Section of Endocrinology. This was in 1946 when he was too immobile to deliver the inaugural address on 'The Birth of Modern Endocrinology'. In 1932 he was delighted to return to Cambridge to be Regius Professor of Physic and Fellow of Corpus Christi College, retiring from the professorship three years later at the retiring age, when he added a hyphen to his name by deed poll on becoming knighted.

Walter Langdon-Brown's introduction to physiology at Cambridge was carried on at Bart's on becoming a physiology demonstrator there. His first contribution to clinical medicine was the interpretation of the signs and symptoms of disease in terms of physiological reactions; at the same time he began to put therapeutics, or the treatment of disease, on a scientific rather than empirical basis. In 1908 the first edition of his *Physiological Principles in Treatment* was published, the last and eighth edition coming out 34 year later in 1942.

At Cambridge, Walter had been particularly influenced by Gaskell whom he described as 'one of the greatest minds that ever adorned British physiology', adding that an account of the sympathetic nervous system written before Gaskell was like writing a description of the circulation before Harvey. *The Role of the Sympathetic Nervous System in Disease* was the subject of his Croonian Lectures in 1918, and this continued his interest in endocrinology from the close connection of the system with the ductless glands. His next book was *The Endocrines in General Medicine* (1927), and later it was claimed that he could be regarded as the founder of modern clinical endocrinology in this country. He was famous for his naming of the pituitary gland as the leader of endocrine orchestra (in his Horsley Memorial Lecture in 1935), but modified this in his last (inaugural) lecture at the Royal Society of Medicine in 1946 by recognising 'that the hypothalamus holds the still more important rank of conductor'.

Langdon-Brown had early on applied his knowledge of the autonomic nervous system and the ductless glands to the elucidation of neurotic behaviour, as well as applying the work of Pavlov on gastric secretion in bridging the gap between the laboratory and the ward. He was a friend of Dr. W. H. R. Rivers, brought to Cambridge by Sir Michael Foster in 1893 to lecture on the physiology of the special senses, who was later to become an authority on war neuroses, a subject that had concerned Walter in the South African War.

The *Dictionary of National Biography* states that Walter was the first English physician to relate the work of psychologists such as Freud, Jung and Adler to the practice of clinical medicine. He was a pioneer in consideration of 'the whole patient' and in psychosomatic medicine.

Lord Horder, who entered St Bartholomew's Hospital at the same time as Walter, told that:

> L-B was fond of cats and one day when a psychasthenic patient came to see him, the cat showed that tiresome feline indecision as to whether it wanted to remain in the room or go outside. It went to the door and mewed. Curly (his Bart's nickname) rose automatically and let it out, continuing his questionnaire with the patient meanwhile. He was just seated when the cat mewed to be let in. When the sequence was repeated the patient became resentful and asked if it were his care or the cat's to which the great consultant was going to attend. 'Both', said Curly, 'you've both got the same disease'.

On another occasion, when a patient having described at length a variety of vague symptoms ended by saying, dramatically, 'And doctor, I never want to get up in the morning', Walter replied, 'Don't worry, I have suffered from that all my life'.

Walter Langdon-Brown was greatly involved in medical education, and was a most influential teacher of clinical medicine. He was described by one of his students as 'a thoughtful, experienced, observant doctor when confronted by a clinical problem, employing his senses, his wits, his imagination and his humanity in its solution . . . It was an inspiring picture . . . At the bedsides of patients, he exemplified his own teaching, combining humanity, philosophy, science and clinical art in a very rare degree'. Lord Horder noted that he 'was massive in his body but, unlike his Johnsonian prototype, the expression of his mind was not rough-hewn nor ponderous, but rather delicate and fine. It was like his gait, which was short-stepping and quick, with body bent forward . . .'.

The collection of his lectures and essays *Thus we are Men* (1938) shows the breadth of his interests and learning, as well as the quality of his writing. The book really examines human nature: he was a humanist at heart. In an obituary notice, he was described as 'a charming host with a great knowledge of good food and good wine, a vast fund of anecdote, and a gift for stimulating conversation. One remembers him sitting in his combined consulting-room and study at Cavendish Square, surrounded by cats, or standing like a rock in the seethe of more mobile persons at some medical meeting. He said many good things, which he enjoyed as much as his hearers'. His inaugural lecture as Regius Professor showed his continuing interest in medical history, and a few months before he died in 1946, *Some Chapters in Cambridge Medical History* appeared, a book that I reviewed for the St Batholomew's Hospital Journal as a junior medical student. The review (hesitatingly shown him), was, in fact, received with kindliness, appreciation and some amusement that I, his great-nephew, had done it. In his last years I used to go and see him and Freda, first when they were living in the Lodge at Corpus during the war and later, in a house off the Madingley Road. It was always a pleasure to do so and not at all intimidating as it so easily might have been. Increasingly, although with an alert mind, he showed the effects of Parkinson's disease with its great difficulty in moving his large body, but there was never any complaint. Always he gave the impression of wanting to know what I thought, and carefully considered any opinion given. The ability to make the young feel of interest and importance is a rare quality and one which, in the next generation, Maynard showed to a high degree.

Chapter Nineteen

JOHN HAROLD BROWN
(1873-1957)

He was a man, take him for all in all,
I shall not look upon his like again.
Hamlet, Act 1 Sc. ii.

Harold was the nicest of the Browns: his mother thought so and so does his son. At the Manse, if a letter had to be posted there would be a row if Walter was asked; Kenneth wouldn't know where the post office was, so Harold had to go, and that was the pattern all through his life. He missed much schooling at Bedford Grammar, having been made to lie on his back for a year as treatment for curvature of the spine. Academically, he was considered the fool of the family so he was sent up to Manchester to join his Ford uncles in business.

As we have seen in Chapter Five, David Everard Ford had been able to get his eldest son, Everard, into Philips's, the great Manchester wholesale warehouse, through the offices of F. V. Lowe, a member of his Richmond Chapel congregation. Everard had risen to be head of the silk fabric department – very important in Victorian days. His younger brother, Palmer, set himself up under the style of P. C. Ford & Co., as an agent for silk goods, no doubt receiving guidance and, possibly, some business from his elder brother. He was joined by Gerard, the youngest of the family. When my father, Harold, aged 17, was sent up to join these uncles in Manchester in 1890, Palmer was 48 and Gerard forty-one.

Concern about the appalling conditions under which the working-classes lived had been steadily growing, particularly amongst Liberal Nonconformists, and Boys' Clubs and Settlements run by young men from public schools and universities were springing up. It was in accord with his background and the times that my father should choose to live at the University Settlement in Ardwick and that, in 1894, he should, together with Goodier Haworth, found the Ninth Company of the Boys' Brigade in Hulme, a notably poor district in Manchester. He became the President of the Manchester Battalion from 1916-21 and I well remember hearing him address 2,000 well-scrubbed, well-disciplined small boys, who packed the Free Trade Hall for a Battalion Church Parade and sang hymns with a verve which exceeded that of the Hallé Choir in the Hallelujah Chorus. I knew a number of Boys' Brigade boys in later life and what excellent citizens they had become.

The family business he had joined was a very small affair. I do not think the Ford brothers, Palmer and Gerard, had the business qualities with which their sister Ada was so well endowed. Gerard lacked decisiveness, but he had a fine Haydon presence and was a good speaker, so found Congregational and public affairs more to his taste.

Before my father joined, Gerard had been very much engaged in the matter of the Manchester Ship Canal. Liverpool had never been an efficient port and railway charges were high. In the 1880s, Manchester, with its immense world-wide export and import trade, was feeling itself strangled, and the Canal for sea-going ships was proposed. A great parliamentary battle followed and, in 1883, Liverpool and the railway interests won, and the Ship Canal Bill was rejected. Manchester did not accept defeat, but mobilised on a grand scale; all sections of the community were involved and it is interesting to note the large part the Nonconformists played. Alderman Southern was a leading spirit; he was a descendant of the Southern who 'had a large business as a builder and wood merchant', of whom Ada Haydon Ford wrote when describing her father's Richmond Hill congregation when the Ford's arrived in Manchester in 1843. After a fierce political struggle with powerful interests on both sides, Manchester was victorious. The Manchester Ship Canal Bill was passed in 1885 and in 1887, after grave financial difficulties had been overcome, the first sod of what was to be one of the greatest engineering achievements of the 19th century was cut.[1]

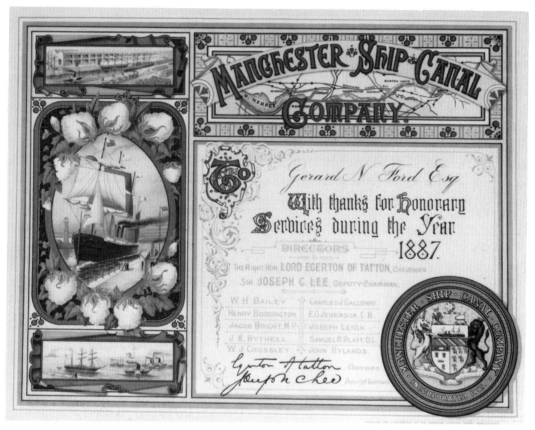

67. Certificate issued to Gerard N. Ford in recognition of his work in Nonconformist circles in support of the building of the Manchester Ship Canal.

Such outside activity on the part of the junior partner of the struggling firm of P. C. Ford & Co. did not help its growth. It had been doing a small home-trade, but Harold developed an export trade with West Africa. Palmer and Gerard had paid him by commission, but when he married in 1903 they made him a partner and his income fell because their earnings were much lower than his.

He had met my mother through his uncle Everard Ford of Philips's. My mother's uncle, Robert Carse, had come over from Belfast as a young man and, like Everard Ford, had worked his way up to be the head of a department in Philips's. When his wife died he asked

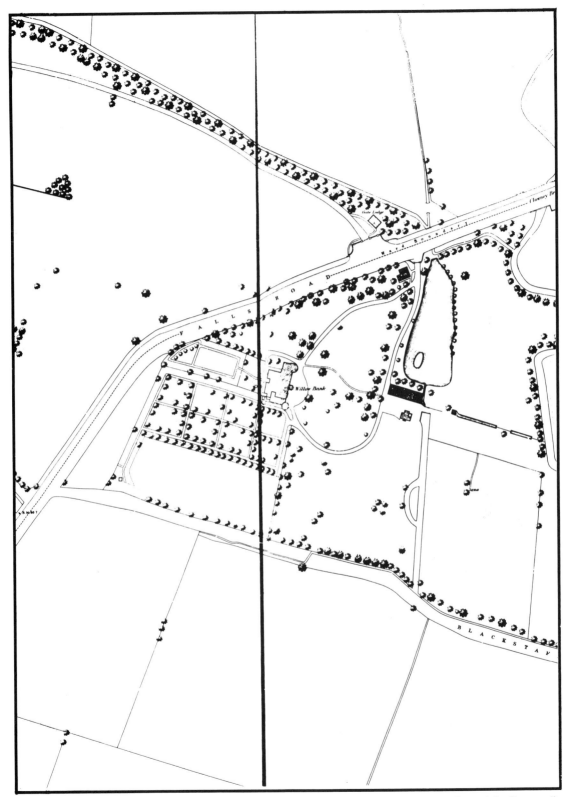

68. Willow Bank, Falls Road, Belfast, from an 1858 Ordnance Survey map (Crown Copyright Reserved).

his niece, Ellen Carse Easdale, to come over and keep house for him. Her father, William Easdale, had been a linen merchant. When the American Civil War (1861-5) cut off supplies of raw cotton there was great distress amongst Lancashire cotton operatives, but in Belfast linen rose sharply in price and trade boomed. At the end of the war, prices collapsed and there were multiple bankruptcies throughout the Belfast linen industry, which brought down William Easdale. He had a large property, Willow Bank, by Clowney Bridge on the Falls Road to the south-west of the city – that is the route by which floods of southern Irish came in, in search of work in the linen and shipbuilding industries which the Ulster-Scots had built up. The Willow Bank area became a Catholic 'ghetto', and is now the site of the Celtic Park, St Louise's School, Our Lady's Hospital and is, intermittently, a 'no-go area' for British troops.

69.   Charles Musgrave Ford.

My father provided all the drive and most of the hard work to develop P. C. Ford & Co., and his uncles, Palmer and Gerard, ended up as passengers. Palmer died in 1913 leaving two sons. For one, a job had to be provided in the business, but the other, Charlie Ford whom my father always spoke of as being a fine fellow, had no intention of going into business. From his photograph, it looks as if he was a throw-back to his grandmother, Jane Elizabeth, and the Haydons. He went to sea and ended up as Commodore of Cunard in command of the *Queen Elizabeth*, and I reproduce an account which he gave on his retirement in 1952. (Appendix IV.)

On one occasion when I was crossing in the *Queen Mary* I made myself known to her commander, Captain Illingworth, as a cousin of Charlie Ford's, and was at once enthusiastically welcomed and put at his table. Panache in the air is limited and the V.I.P. lounge a poor thing as compared with the glory of the Captain's table in a great liner. Maynard crossed many times in the *Queens* under Charlie Ford's command and he once told me that he thought the strain of command of such ships, though not apparent, was, in fact, very great.

Gerard became the Chairman of the Congregational Union in 1911 and accordingly an important figure in that world. It was my father's tremendously hard work which made this possible, but he never jibbed and loyally provided the wherewithal for his uncle's Congregational activities, comfortable life and more besides. Kenneth always said that Gerard was born to be a rake. As a young man he once went to the theatre but felt the pull of the flesh and the devil so strong that he never dared to go again. I remember, though, that there used to be 'Hand Maidens of the Lord'. Their godliness had to be outstanding and their looks above the average, but if you were the Chairman of the Congregational Union, such things had to be strictly platonic and so they remained. Harold encouraged some discreet endowments and the old rake manqué died, still venerable, in 1934.

Harold had made a very good business out of P. C. Ford & Co., and the name was duly changed to Ford & Brown, but owing to the drawings of his uncles, it had never been able to accumulate capital on any considerable scale and was vulnerable when the Japanese entered the West African Market. Though the firm survived till his death in 1957, it was never on a scale commensurate with his personal standing among Manchester merchants. I remember one of them taking me aside and saying, 'We all think the world of your father. He is both shrewd and kindly. You often get one or the other in a man, but rarely both'.

I never had a wrong word with him. I think this is very unusual as between father and son all through adolescence and, in my case, all through the acute boredom of a junior partner in a declining business. He had the great gift of being able to administer a reproof, on the rare occasions on which he did, without leaving a sting. I sometimes think he did not give me as much guidance as he might, but if he had, perhaps our relationship would not have been as happy. It must have been a cruel blow to him when the business, which it had been his life's work to build up, faded to such a degree that in 1936 his son had to seek his fortune elsewhere, but he never breathed a word of reproach or self-pity. He was very distressed when I had to throw my first independent company into voluntary liquidation, but stood by me and in later years, when success came, never showed a trace of jealousy, but only wholehearted satisfaction.

He, himself, found great satisfaction and restoration of self-respect in the success he had on the board of public companies, and also as a governor of John Rylands Library. I heard him make a speech of extraordinary charm which lifted his hearers out of themselves. This gift

70. Ellen Carse and John Harold Brown, c.1939.

clearly came from John Brown who exercised it over his American visitors to Elstow. (They 'felt a strange spell of enchantment' (p. 100).) His son could stop people quarrelling and he could handle a public meeting. On one occasion, he faced angry creditors out for blood at a meeting of a Sheffield steel company. They were demanding that the company should go into immediate liquidation, but he persuaded them to give it another chance. A few years later that company was turning out large quantities of armour plate in the 1939-45 War: it was Sanderson Bros. & Newbould Ltd. The obituary notice which appeared in their 'House Journal' on my father's death in 1957 ran:

In the depression of the early 1930s, his courage and buoyancy had much to do with the recovery of Sanderson Brothers and Newbould Limited, of which he later became Chairman. During the war, he deputised for Lord Rothes as Chairman of Brocklehurst Whiston Amalgamated Ltd., of Macclesfield. He was, for very many years, on the board of Marland and other Rochdale spinning mills. He was Chairman of Humphrey Lloyd & Sons Ltd., of Manchester, and a member of the board of Simpson and Godlee Ltd., till his death.

Harold Brown had a rare combination of gifts to bring to the service of any company of men. His intuitive shrewdness was of a very high order: he could see into the heart of the matter or a man in a flash, yet there was no trace of aggressiveness. Rather there was a kindly warmth and gaiety of spirit for which all men in all walks of life loved him.

Chapter Twenty

EVERARD KENNETH BROWN
(1879-1958)

Everard Kenneth Brown should have been a happy man. He had brains, vigour, and attractive personality and had won great professional success, but he was cursed by 'Ford depressions' and, in his old age, became a pitiable figure.

On 2 December 1793, David Ford wrote, in Long Melford: 'I have this day been shaken over hell, surely the legions of devils are let loose on me'.

In 1937, I remember his great-grandson, Kenneth Brown, in his study in Hampstead, sitting groaning and repeating over and over again, 'Caught, caught like a rat in a trap', and this was not long after one of his most spectacular successes – 'The Mongoose Case', which led to the resignation of Sir John Reith, the head of the BBC.

Kenneth was born seven years after his five brothers and sisters, when his mother was forty-two. His nephew, Maynard Keynes. was nearer to him in age than his brothers. We get a first glimpse of Kenneth launching 'The Lighthouse', the date of which was probably 1888:

> The Manse
> Bedford.
>
> It is proposed to publish monthly a hectographed journal entitled THE LIGHTHOUSE.
> This journal will deal with topics of the day, and form a convenient synopsis of the events of the month. Its politics will be Gladstonian Liberal; it will appear on or about the 15th of every month,
> THE LIGHTHOUSE will draw its information from reliable daily journals but all articles will be in accord with editorial policy.
>
> E. K. Brown, Editor.

(This in remarkably good writing for a nine year old.)

It was followed in 1889 by 'Kenneth's Weekly'. These preceded the family journals to which he was to inspire his young Keynes nephews and niece. In 1893 Kenneth was 14, Maynard, Margaret and Geoffrey, 10, eight and six, respectively. It was natural he should join their family holidays on the Yorkshire coast and that the 'Lealholm and Langstone Gazette' should follow 'Kenneth's Weekly'. We have several numbers but not all are dated and one has to depend on internal evidence. In the 'Lealholm Gazette' of, most probably 1893, we find what one might claim to be the first published work of John Maynard Keynes (see plate 71). Twenty-six years later the same author wrote of the proposed collection of Reparations from Germany under the Treaty of Versailles . . . 'it would represent a policy which, if it were really entertained and deliberately practised, the judgement of men would soon pronounce to be one of the most outrageous accounts of a cruel victor in civilised history'.[1]

It is very probable that on those early Yorkshire holidays, Maynard Keynes was greatly influenced by Kenneth Brown, who at 16 would have absorbed the outlook of his parents and would be passing on the Gladstonian Liberalism which 'Kenneth's Weekly' boldly proclaimed. The 'authentic sources' to which Maynard refers in his 'A Hard Sentence' were no doubt provided by Kenneth.

In the 'Langstone Gazette' of 1895, Kenneth, as well as contributing a learned article on the London and South Western Railway network, contributed an article on 'How to

> 8
>
> ## A Hard Sentence.
>
> This is the sentence of a prisoner, who was tried at the assizes held at Thetford Norfolk Saturday March 20th 1813.
>
> Edward Philley, aged 23, and James Bidwen, aged 18, committed Sept. 8th 1813, by the Rev — and — charged with feloniously stealing out of a shop sundry articles. The sentence was death.
>
> [Obtained from authentic sources by] J. M. Keynes

71. John Maynard Keynes' first published work.

Photograph Groups', which he illustrated with what, I think, is the best photograph of the Keynes children ever taken.

Kenneth had done well scholastically at Bedford Grammar School. He was a hard worker and had a first-class brain. When he left school, he was articled to Purchase & Co., of Bedford, friends of his parents. When he took his final examinations in 1902, he was admitted, with first class honours, to the Roll of Solicitors and was awarded the Daniel Reardon and Clement's Inn Prizes. He was then overtaken by the inherited weakness which was, intermittently, to cripple him through life. He had what was described as a nervous breakdown and the cure prescribed was a long sea voyage, so he was put on a slow boat engaged in the meat trade with Buenos Aires. That attack of 'Ford depression' passed. His parents moved to Hampstead in 1903 and he went with them, and set up in practice at 11 St Pancras Lane in the City, the capital necessary having come from the carefully invested profits from his mother's school. He presented her with a fine trinket box decorated with mother-of-pearl, now in the possession of her great-great-grand-daughter, Griselda Hill.

He was able to engage a clerk by the name of Emil Adolph Mercl, who initiated him into the ways of his profession. In 1909, Kenneth Brown and Mercl (who never qualified) amalgamated with another young firm, Charles and Alfred, later Sir Alfred Baker. The Bakers were to become Kenneth's lifelong partners and friends and the objects of Mercl's lifelong hatred. The new firm had the remarkable title of Kenneth Brown Baker· Baker, the very oddity of which stuck in the mind and invited speculation. They established themselves in Lennox House, Norfolk Street, Strand, and the practice grew and grew.

Kenneth, shy son of the Manse, though of great vigour of mind and body, lacked consistent social confidence, whereas Mercl was magnetic, uninhibited and made an immediate impression on

72. Geoffrey, Maynard and Margaret Keynes.

all who met him. Kenneth once told me of an incident which took place in the late 1930s, but it indicated the pattern which had been set from the start. Mercl, a great party-goer and night-club habitué, met the Duke of Marlborough and made a great impression. Shortly afterwards, the Duke arrived at Essex House, Essex Street, Strand (the whole new building occupied by Kenneth Brown Baker Baker since 1929), for a consultation with Kenneth and Mercl. He was worried about death duties. Kenneth was not immediately impressive on some occasions, but Mercl mesmerized the Duke. 'There are ways and means, your Grace, ways and means. Don't worry, leave it all to us'; and beaming and gleaming, showed the Duke, a much relieved man, out of the front door. He then came back to Kenneth and said, 'What the devil are we going to do about this Kenneth?' He was wholly out of his depth and had no idea how to proceed. It was left to Kenneth to preserve the Marlborough estate. He used to go down to Blenheim and once he came back on the same train with Winston Churchill, who had been working on his *Life of Marlborough*. He looked seedy, down-at-heel and gave the air of being a finished man. Yet, a few years later he was to be the greatest single factor in the defeat of Nazi Germany.

One of Kenneth Brown Baker Baker's famous cases was that of *G.W.K. Limited and Another v. The Dunlop Rubber Company Limited*. G.W.K. Ltd., was a small firm of motor car manufacturers in Maidenhead,[2] which had agreed with the Associated Rubber Manufacturers Ltd., that they would exhibit their cars fitted with that company's 'Bal-lon-ette' tyres at Olympia in October and at the Scottish Motor Show at the Kelvin Hall, Glasgow in November 1924. In return, they were to be supplied with tyres for all their cars at special prices. At Olympia, nothing unusual happened, but in Glasgow, during the night of 20 November, a gang of Dunlop men obtained access to the Kelvin Hall and removed the

'Bal-lon-ette' tyres from the G.W.K. exhibit and replaced them with Dunlop tyres. Dunlop probably calculated that the victims had not got the resources to do more than protest. They did not foresee that G.W.K. would go to Kenneth Brown, whose Nonconformist blood was immediately aroused, and who was ready to risk the costs of taking them to court. He briefed Sir Patrick Hastings, K.C., one of the most famous advocates of the day[3] who appeared before Lord Chief Justice Hewart, on 9 February 1925.[4] G.W.K. Ltd., were awarded £500 (£9,500) and Associated Rubber Manufacturers Ltd., £2,000 (£38,000) and costs. When Dunlop appealed in June they briefed Sir John Simon, K.C., and Mr. Norman Birkett, both very famous advocates, which showed how seriously they viewed their position. Mr. Norman Birkett explained that his clients had a new Board and gave certain assurances which no doubt included financial clauses, so that Kenneth Brown advised his clients to agree to bring the proceedings to an end.

But it was the beginning for Kenneth Brown Baker Baker in the motor trade. That the great firm of Dunlop should have been so thoroughly trounced made a great impression, and all the leading firms, at home and abroad, flocked to the solicitors who could effect such things. I remember that Kenneth had a magnificent Delage which was a present from that firm and, when I visited Detroit in 1934 with a letter of introduction to his clients, the great General Motors Corporation, I was overcome by the welcome I received.

During the 1914-18 War Kenneth was called up and put in charge of the legal affairs of the Northern Command at York, but had on occasion to seek, as it were, compassionate leave to settle quarrels between Mercl and the Bakers which threatened the firm's existence, and were to dog it till the parties concerned retired or died. The strain on Kenneth, of holding together a partnership afflicted by such a cancer, must have been very great and a factor in his depressions. But with Kenneth at its head, the firm prospered and, between the wars, they were perhaps the best known firm of solicitors in London, employing what was in those days the extraordinary total of 160 people. Kenneth was a great lawyer, incredibly thorough and hard working. He once said to me, 'You do everything you can possibly think of in preparing a case, knowing that the other side will do so too: then you do something more and you win'. More cases are lost through poor preparation than through poor pleading, and his briefs were masterpieces. He preferred to fight cases before juries because he said a judge might have got out of bed the wrong side, or have a bee in his bonnet, but not so all 12 good men and true. Allied to Mercl, a man unqualified, of foreign descent, contemptuous of his profession and wholly without scruple, it was not surprising that the firm was sometimes unpopular. To Mercl, no holds were barred: he would do anything whatsoever to win a case. It was said that if you killed a man by dangerous driving, you simply had to go to Mercl, at Kenneth Brown Baker Baker, to get you off. And the more noisome and unsavoury a divorce case, the more likely it was that he would be acting for the winning side.[5]

Kenneth believed that when a client came to him in distress and put himself in his hands, his only duty was to that client. He agreed with Dr. Johnson that: 'A lawyer has no business with the justice or injustice of the cause which he undertakes, unless his client asks his opinion, and then he is bound to give it honestly. The justice or injustice of the cause is to be decided by the judge'. His propensity to become emotionally involved when somebody was being oppressed or bullied did not quite square with this.[6] He used to say, rather sadly, 'The Law is open to all – like the Savoy', and would have welcomed the advent of Legal Aid.

Kenneth Brown's most famous case was, perhaps, *Lambert* v. *Levita*,[7] which the press labelled as that of the 'Talking Mongoose'.

It was as President of the Railway Club (1928-58) that he met Richard Lambert, the author of the standard life of George Hudson, a vigorous 19th-century railway entrepreneur.

Lambert was the editor of *The Listener* and he was also a member of the Council of the British Film Institute.

A certain Lady Levita, the only daughter of a rich Glasgow merchant, was a member of that Council. Her husband, Sir Cecil Levita, K.C.V.O., was a retired Lieutenant-Colonel, with a distinguished war record, and a former chairman of the London County Council. She was something of a Lady Macbeth, for when she quarrelled with Lambert she urged her husband on to a course of action which was to prove disastrous.

On 7 February 1936, Sir Cecil Levita invited Mr. Gladstone Murray, Controller of Programmes for the BBC and Lambert's immediate superior, to lunch and spoke adversely and viciously about Lambert. He said that Lambert believed in a 'talking mongoose', that he had moved house three times because he believed in the evil eye, that he was vindictive to his staff, was somewhat insane and unfit for his post. He further said that if Lambert remained on the Council of the British Film Institute, he would have to go and see his old friend, Mr. Norman, the chairman of the BBC to get him to withdraw the consent of the BBC for Lambert to serve on that Council. Gladstone Murray was shocked that such an attack should be made on Lambert, and thought it was his duty to let him know.

Lambert, fearing not only for his membership of the Council of the Film Institute, but also for his position as editor of *The Listener*, went, in great distress, to Kenneth Brown. He could not engage in expensive litigation, but this did not weigh with Kenneth, where a small man was under threat of a gross injustice. He issued a writ on behalf of Lambert, claiming damages and alleging slander by Sir Cecil Levita. Levita's solicitors were Lewis and Lewis, another famous firm with whom Kenneth Brown Baker Baker had frequent duels, so the lines of battle were drawn. As in the case of *G.W.K. Ltd.*, he briefed the best possible counsel, namely Sir Patrick Hastings, K.C., and Mr. Valentine Holmes.[8] The case was heard before Mr. Justice Swift and a special jury on 4, 5 and 6 November 1936, and the press gave it headlines.

In an effort to prevent Lambert bringing the case to court, Sir Stephen Tallents, Public Relations Officer of the BBC, had interviewed Lambert and recorded his interview in a memorandum. Kenneth Brown had obtained a copy and Sir Patrick Hastings skilfully managed to get round the rules of evidence[9] and produced it in court, with dramatic effect.

Memorandum

I saw Mr. Lambert at 11.10 on the morning of 6 March. I told him I was instructed:

(1) To urge him to take a week's leave, as his doctor, I understood, had advised, and to consider the matter quietly again thereafter.

(2) And to assure him:
(a) That his position with the Corporation was not at present in any way prejudiced or damaged:
But to tell him:
(b) That if he went on with the course which he had indicated the previous morning, there was a serious danger that he might well prejudice his position with the Corporation because:
[1] He could make the Corporation doubt his judgement.
[2] He could seem to be placing his own interest in priority to those of the Corporation.

S. J. Tallents, 6.3.36.

In his summing up, Mr. Justice Swift said: 'It was a dreadful thing, when a man in a public position was affronted and outraged and brought an action demanding redress for the wrong which had been done him, that his employers should be approached behind his back and asked to bring pressure to settle the matter'.

The jury answered every question in favour of Lambert, who was awarded £7,500 (£172,000) and costs (these would have been many hundreds of thousands of pounds in

1986 values). This was the largest amount given in a slander action in those times and the award created a great sensation in the Temple as well as in Court.

Redress for Lambert, and disgrace and the erosion of their fortune for the Levitas, was by no means the end of the matter. The whole tenor of the case and, above all, Sir Stephen Tallents' memorandum was taken by the public to indicate an intolerable state of affairs within the BBC, and on 13 November the Prime Minister, Stanley Baldwin, announced in the House of Commons that a special Board had been appointed to look into the matter and, on 14 November, it became known that the new Charter of the BBC would not be laid before Parliament until its report had been received.

The report appeared on 16 December 1936, in the form of a White Paper – Cmd 5337. It did not add greatly to what had come out in the legal action, but it commented that 'the BBC officials have only themselves to blame for the unfortunate impression caused by the singularly inapt words in the memorandum', and, in the debate in the House of Commons which followed, there were references to 'an amazing hugger-mugger administration', to paternal autocracy and strong criticisms of Sir John Reith. The Government had to announce that arrangements would be made whereby the BBC might draw advice from the Civil Service on staff matters.

73. Everard Kenneth Brown.

A few months later Sir John Reith resigned. Many years later, Malcolm Muggeridge, in a television interview, asked him why he had resigned from the BBC. Sir John Reith paused, blinked and said, 'I felt I was not being fully extended'. Autocrat that he was, I think that he could not stand the implied and explicit criticism of his rule. No doubt, he hoped for untrammelled great office elsewhere, but he never again held it. 'Reith sank dishonoured to the outer dark', as Sir Maurice Bowra was to write.[10] The career of the man who had given the BBC a tradition respected all over the world might have ended differently if Richard Lambert and Kenneth Brown had not both been interested in railway history.

Kenneth's interest in railways went back to his childhood. He gave me a drawing, alas now lost, of the imaginary railway routes round the Manse garden. His interest became legal and historical, focusing on the great legal battles which had to be fought before a line could be built and on its subsequent financial ups and downs. Collecting books on such matters became his principal hobby and his collection, of great antiquarian interest, was one of the most remarkable in the country. When he died, I had the privilege of handing it over to the John Rylands Library, University of Manchester.[11] It was received with great enthusiasm.

Kenneth was popular with his nephews and nieces: as a good bachelor uncle he could be counted upon for generous tips – crinkly Bank of England five pound notes (£65) were usual at Christmas, which he frequently spent with us at Bowdon. He was often in high spirits and we were not of an age to be other than amused by his atrocious puns and witticisms. We simply enjoyed his boisterous gaiety and it was not until later that we heard of his depressions, his psychologist and his electric shock treatment, so frequently repeated as he got older. It appeared in the end greatly to have damaged him.

I saw more of Kenneth than of any of my other relations and feel I owe to him as much as to my father the transmission of family lore and attitudes. It was he who had preserved the diaries of David Ford and David Everard Ford. He gave two BBC broadcasts[12] on David Everard Ford, based on his diary, but his stammer, which was on occasion bad, somewhat marred their delivery.

Though he saw much of his nephews and nieces – Margaret Hill was particularly kind to him in his depression – he himself did not enjoy a normal family life. He lived at 10 Upper Park Road, Hampstead, his parents' house and, until his sister Alice 15 years his senior died in 1941, she was his chief companion, though he did have certain women friends who were not presented to the family.

I do not know who contributed to his obituary to *The Times* of 4 June, 1958, but the appreciation was, I think, exact. It read: 'As a legal consultant he was the embodiment of shrewdness, informed by a wide knowledge of law and a deep insight into human nature. But few realized that behind the professional facade – on occasion formidable – frequently genial – there was a passionate hatred of oppression and injustice, an unusual measure of compassion for the weak and a rare strain of emotional warmth'.

Chapter Twenty-One

JOHN MAYNARD KEYNES
(1883-1946)

Baron Keynes of Tilton, O.M., C.B., F.B.A., F.R.S.

More has probably been written about Keynes and his work than any other man of his times. It is difficult to pick up a serious work of economic, financial or sociological content, or any modern history in which he does not figure. I shall try, therefore, to confine myself to a few personal and family recollections.

When, in 1925, Maynard married Lydia Lopokova many were surprised and Bloomsbury was horrified. Lydia was born in St Petersburg in 1892 and had graduated at the Imperial Ballet School. She was the loveliest of ballet dancers and had danced for Diaghilev for 17 years.

I used to see much of Maynard in 1923-4 but had not seen him and Lydia together till 1934. He was lying on his bed in the Waldorf Astoria, New York, as he was already having trouble with his heart; Lydia came in having been given so many dollars a day to spend in the stores. This she had joyfully done. They were amused by and at ease with each other. I was to see Maynard again during the war years when he was carrying the main burden of this country's desperate financial problems. I doubt whether Maynard would have become the greatest economist of the 20th century nor a statesman of world repute unless Lydia had detached him from Bloomsbury and made him supremely happy. But for her love and care in Washington in 1945, this country might not have been saved by the American Loan. In his *Essays on John Maynard Keynes* and his *Lydia Lopokova*, Milo Keynes has written most charmingly of them both.[1]

I first met Maynard as a 15-year-old schoolboy in January 1920. He had been in Manchester on business and came out to lunch with us at Bowdon, Cheshire. *The Economic Consequences of the Peace* had been published in December 1919 and its impact had been terrific. Maynard's name was on everybody's lips and in every paper one opened. Then he appeared amongst us, brilliant and fascinating: we were spellbound. He told us amusing details about the negotiation of the peace treaty and how travelling to and from Versailles had been difficult. One day he had been leaving Gordon Square and there were few taxis. A chauffeur-driven private car came along: he waved it down, got in and said, 'Victoria, please' and was duly driven to the station.

It so happened that I was the editor of my school magazine and had contributed an article on the Treaty of Versailles. Maynard was so unfrightening that I ventured to show it to him. He looked through it seriously and said, 'Well, Neville, you know your policy is the same as mine', and attached me for life.

It was in January 1920 that *Punch*[2] published a review of *The Economic Consequences of the Peace* in the form of doggerel. It conveyed, however, the reaction of conventional people at that time and, as I have never seen it reproduced, I give some extracts. It started off with:

> There was a superior young person named Keynes
> Who possessed an extensive equipment of brains,
> and being elected a Fellow of King's,
> He taught Economics and similar things.

The versifier then went on to recount how Keynes made his mark at the Treasury, went to Paris to represent the Chancellor, and there too made a great impression but resigned in disgust. We are told that he could not, however, be lightly dismissed as 'Pro-Hun' or 'Pacifist' and the rhymester continues:

> And yet there are faults to be found all the same;
> For example, I doubt if it's playing the game
> For one who is hardly unmuzzled, to guy
> Representative statesmen who cannot reply.
>
> Still we feel, as he zealously damns the Allies
> For grudging the Germans the means to arise,
> That possibly some of the Ultimate Things
> May even be hidden from Fellows of King's.

Punch could be forgiven in 1920 for failing to realise that this Fellow of King's had written a book which was to influence the course of the world's history but, after half a century, there were others who, less excusably, were lacking even in hindsight. In reviewing Robert Skidelsky's biography of Maynard in *The Sunday Times*, John Vincent wrote: 'Had Keynes died in 1925, he would be remembered as a minor don . . .; in other words not remembered at all'. To which I replied in a letter to *The Sunday Times* published on 13 November 1983 as follows:

> It is clear that John Vincent is not aware of Keynes's *Economic Consequences of the Peace*, published in 1919, nor of its influence on world opinion.
>
> It is difficult today to convey an impression of the bitter atmosphere at the end of the war of 1914-1918. It was felt that Germany had wrecked European civilisation, inflicted untold suffering and destruction, and that she must be made to pay for what she had done.
>
> Though in Hitler's war, the doings of the Germans had been infinitely more atrocious, the whole emphasis at the end was not one of vengeance, of reparations, but of rehabilitation, of repairing a broken machine and feeding starving peoples. Hence, instead of a decade of misery followed by the rise of Fascism and another war, Europe was quickly restored.
>
> The starting motor of this great swing in world thinking about what one should do after a war, was Keynes's *Economic Consequences of the Peace*. It had a tremendous impact from the moment it appeared, particularly in America.
>
> Those in authority there, most of them, had read the *Economic Consequences* in their impressionable youth; and instead of reparations and inter-Allied debts dominating the scene, we had UNRRA, the loan Keynes negotiated for Britain, the Marshall Plan and so on, on a scale and with a generosity unequalled in human history.

As family we were all proudly aware that Maynard had, in his *Economic Consequences of the Peace*, written what Virginia Woolf described as a moral book[4] and one which had touched the conscience of the world. When I went up to Cambridge and qualified for membership of the 'Keynes Club', he made me the Honorary Secretary in 1923 and 1924. I still have the list of members amongst whom there are a number of well-known names. I do not know whether a complete list of all the members during the many years that the club continued has ever been compiled. It might show one amongst many of the reasons for the width of his influence on opinion. The club operated on the same basis as the Apostles. Someone read a paper (on occasion Maynard himself), and then lots were drawn as to the order in which members, who were mostly undergraduates in their second and third year, had to get up, go over to the fireplace, face the room and make some contribution to the discussion. If they had none to make they had still got to get up, go over to the fireplace and say so. Maynard's warmth and sparkle had an extraordinary effect upon us all. The shy and fumbling amongst the undergraduates were made to feel that they had said something of real interest which he would take up and elaborate. But woe betide the pretentious.

I had joined my father in the family textile business in Manchester and, in November 1926 Maynard came down at the invitation of the Short Time Commission of the Master Cotton Spinners' Association. The nemesis of surplus capacity had overtaken the huge cotton spinning industry. He had meetings with the masters and with the men, being shown into separate rooms, filled, he said, with exactly the same sort of people except that one lot was notably more intelligent than the other – they were the men. I had to arrange for the typing and duplication of the speech which he made to a large public meeting. He did not manage to put it over well and said to me afterwards, 'The pen, and not speech, is my weapon'.

He knew nothing about Lancashire and asked me about the spinning trade. I remember telling him that whilst the spinning mills which had modernised themselves were going bankrupt, old-fashioned family concerns like those in Royton, Oldham, which had spent nothing on plant, were surviving except when they cut prices against each other out of family pride. 'Montagues and Capulets', he said. I said I had not heard of mills of those names. I forget what he said, but my abiding recollection is of the skill with which he saved my blushes.

The whole textile trade went from bad to worse and, after years of decline, I found myself very depressed and not knowing what to do. About that time I was present at one of my Aunt Florence's famous Sunday family luncheons at Harvey Road, Cambridge. Maynard detained me in the dining-room and explained that he was really very comfortably off and if I wanted help in getting out of the textile trade I had only to let him know. It was not the generosity so much as the extraordinary kindliness and enveloping warmth which remains vivid 50 years on.

When the 1939-45 War started he got hold of me and advised me to convert the personal loan he had made into shares in my company, 'Because if I collected a bomb my executors would have to demand repayment of a loan which might be difficult for you'. It was not a bomb he was thinking of as much as the heart condition which was oppressing him but again, it was his foresight on my behalf which was moving.

During the war, at the Ministry of Aircraft Production, I found myself in charge of photographic supplies for the R.A.F. and of Lease/Lend imports of photographic film-base of which we had no production in this country. When the war was drawing to an end, we were asked to put up plans which would provide employment after the war. I had put up a plan for the production of film-base in this country but could not rouse any interest. Then I happened to be in Cambridge and Maynard asked me to dine at King's. I mentioned my difficulties. He said, 'But this is most important; the balance of trade is going to be one of our most serious problems'. I asked him if I might mention his name and he agreed. I let his view be known and put the name 'Lord Keynes' at the head of the circulation list of all subsequent papers. There was immediate interest, but I felt I had to ask to be relieved of anything further to do with the matter as I was a civil servant (temporary) and the scheme had been conceived by the managing director of Ilford Ltd. He was Wilfrid Dimsdale, my brother-in-law, and government finance might be involved. In the event it was not. Ilford Ltd., and BX Plastics Ltd.,[3] jointly formed Bexford Ltd., which erected a photographic film-base plant at Brantham in Suffolk, later to win the Queen's Award for Exports.

The *Punch* view of Maynard persisted in Establishment circles for many years. He had spent 20 years in attacking Bank of England policies, with all the fervour with which his ancestors had attacked the Church of England and *its* policies, but in 1941 he was elected to the Court of the Bank of England and, as Roy Harrod records,[4] the current joke became 'which will make an honest woman of the other is anyone's guess'. Whichever way round it was, Maynard certainly enjoyed his new respectability. He had put me up for his Club and one day when he was paying his bill in the Coffee Room he said, 'You know, I don't like the design of my notes'.

The last time I saw him was a week before his death when my father and I lunched with him. Recollections of our conversation gave rise to correspondence which appeared in *The Economist* of 3 February 1951. They had published a leader in which they pointed out that his economic teachings in the 1930s had been distorted in a manner which would not have been possible if he had lived. I wrote a letter to *The Economist* supporting that view and sent a copy to my father in Manchester. The next day I got a furious telephone call. It was most improper to publish remarks made at a private family occasion, albeit six years previously: I must telephone *The Economist* and stop the letter. Dutifully I did so, only to find that they apparently regarded my letter as being of importance and begged me to get my father to lift his ban. After some telephoning, a compromise was agreed. I was to make no reference to the family, nor to say that it had been my father who had led the conversation and I was not to sign the letter. So it appeared thus:

> Sir, – I am glad that you write 'Keynes was supremely unfortunate in the moment of his death'. I lunched with him a week before his death. I asked him whether he ought not to take life more easily and how long he thought he could work with the Government.
>
> He replied that there were a number of things that he wanted to see through, amongst them what he called, with justifiable pride, 'my loan'. About the Government he said he did not know. He thought they might at any moment become uncontrollable and do something 'absolutely crackers' (his exact words) when he would have to part company.
>
> Keynes's enemies could wish for no bitterer revenge than that his teachings should have become the hocus-pocus of a so illiberal socialism. – Yours faithfully,
>
>   ONE OF HIS PUPILS
>
> London,   W.1.

When *The Economist* appeared I saw why they had been so insistent. There was also a letter from Hugh Dalton, who had been Chancellor of the Exchequer in Attlee's first Labour Government to which Maynard was referring. It started as follows:

> Sir. – I write to you to supplement, and to correct some false impressions which may be created by your last week's article on Maynard Keynes, successively my teacher, my friend, and my adviser at the Treasury.
>
> Of course, much of his economic thought goes all against the grain of the editorial policy of *The Economist*. He was a very powerful stimulating and humane thinker, whose teaching has certain inspired and sustained the Left in British politics rather than the Right.
>
> You have no warrant for your belief that, had he lived longer, he would have moved your way. I speak with a degree of knowledge shared by very few, . . .
>
>   Yours faithfully,
>
>   HUGH DALTON
>   Ministry of Local Government
>   and Planning,
>
> London, W.1.

I was in my early 30s when his very great book, *The General Theory of Employment, Interest and Money*[5] was published. In it, there were moral questionings, and this time on the economic structure of our society in relation to unemployment and the distribution of wealth. He had come to doubt the classical theory which held that there were in-built mechanisms acting, as might the keel of a yacht, to restore equilibrium. In any case there was a need to supplement them. Many governments had followed what they believed to be his teachings in the 25 years in which the devastation of the war was being made good and there was no unemployment. (Indeed, western Europe imported overseas labour which may have produced situations less easy to right than war damage.) Keynes's ideas were, of course, seized upon by politicians and interpreted to suit party ends. Rival sects sprang up, Keynesians, Monetarists, Neo-Keynesians and others.

74. Maynard and Lydia in Berlin, 1925.

I think it is forgotten that whilst his book appeared in 1936, he, himself, was incapacitated in 1937 by heart trouble and soon, thereafter, indeed, until his death in 1946, was wholly employed as the government's chief financial adviser. Had he enjoyed the longevity of his parents and lived another 20 years, the course of this country's post-war economic and political history would probably have been very different. One should remember that in his *A Tract on Monetary Reform* (1923) we have what may be the best account extant of the injustices to which inflation gives rise and the close connection between public finance and the value of money.

The practical validity of Keynes's *General Theory* may be in doubt but his greatness as a prophet, in the Old Testament sense, is not. Six Harvey Road was not a Manse but it had the values of a Manse and the young Maynard saw much of his maternal grandparents at the Manse in Dame Alice Street, Bedford. Eton, Bloomsbury and the world stage upon which he entered following the publication of the *Economic Consequences of the Peace* could not have been further removed, but throughout his life he remained exceedingly close to his parents and Harvey Road. Was it not to the generations of Dissenting preachers and teachers from whom he was descended, and to their traditions, that he owed his intense urge to better the human lot and his extraordinary power of influencing the minds of men?

Maynard and my father had no features in common, yet one day at Harvey Road he came into the drawing-room from behind the curtained doorway where the light was poor and I could have sworn it was my father. Maynard was a genius, my father was merely able, but they shared the same acute perception and immediate response, and above all, an outgoing warmth and buoyancy. I think that their intuitive gifts came from the Haydons and the warmth from John Brown. Sir Austin Robinson did not know of Jane Elizabeth Down, or the Haydon and the Cornish Langdon ancestry, but he was, I think, on the right track when he wrote:

> If one could picture the Keyneses and the Browns bringing their diverse gifts to endow the infant, one might say that it was the solid Keyneses who brought a precision of thought, a pleasure in detail, a practicality of outlook, perhaps also a pleasure in good living.[6] It was the more brilliant Browns who brought the sparkle and the quick, intuitive leaps of intellect, the almost feminine perception of the essential and inevitable pattern of things, which enabled Maynard Keynes to outpace in his rapidity of thought all those of us whose intellectual movements are more pedestrian. But the infant would himself have been the first to remind us that heredity is no such simple matter. And, indeed, it was the curious conjunction of contrasting qualities which made Maynard Keynes so essentially unlike the common run of mankind. There was, however, one thing in his make-up on which he would sometimes dwell: he was, improbable as it might seem in one of his intellectual gaiety and nimbleness, utterly and completely English. And sometimes, in days of stress, that Englishness would unexpectedly peep out.[7]

It did more than peep out when Hitler's war was upon us. He wrote a letter to *The New Statesman and Nation* on 14 October 1939, which read: '. . . The intelligentsia of the Left were the loudest in demanding that Nazi aggression should be resisted at all costs; when it comes to a showdown, scarce four weeks have passed before they remember that they are pacifists and write defeatist letters to your columns, leaving the defence of freedom to Colonel Blimp and the Old School Tie, for whom three cheers'.

Until Roosevelt's Lease/Lend Aid measures and, later, the American entry into the war, our external financial position was desperate. We were fighting Germany and Italy single-handed and had had to sell our foreign assets to pay for raw materials and warlike supplies. Then, in August 1945, when the dropping of an atomic bomb on Hiroshima terminated the war, Truman, who had replaced Roosevelt, immediately cut off Lease/Lend. This made alternative American assistance imperative, but neither the American administration and public, nor our own, grasped why. The task of obtaining it fell on Keynes and, as he wrote to his mother from Washington in October 1945, 'It is the roughest assignment I have ever had'. Apart from the inherent difficulties of presenting our case to the Americans, he was hampered by ignorance at home, but had magnificent support from Lord Halifax, our Ambassador.

He was successful. There are many accounts of his remarkable performance, notably that of Roy Harrod,[8] and a loan agreement was signed on 6 December. Harrod wrote:

> Keynes was speaking now. The rustle of papers died down. His discourse lasted for three days. It was the pure gold of perfect English prose, describing a situation of vast complexity with the lucidity and good arrangement that only a master mind could have achieved. It was so easy and light and sparkling, that there was never a dull moment. Those most sympathetic and those least sympathetic agreed in thinking that this was the finest exposition to which they had ever listened or were ever likely to listen.

On his return to London he had to convince the Government and the country that the loan was necessary and that he had got it on the best terms available. He made a famous speech in the House of Lords in which he told their lordships:

> Men's sympathies and less calculated impulses are drawn from their memories of comradeship, but their contemporary acts are generally directed towards influencing the future and not towards pensioning the past. At any rate I can safely assure you that this is how the American Administration and the American people think. Nor, I venture to say, should it be becoming in us to respond by showing our medals, all of them, and pleading that the old veteran deserves better . . .

The Lords approved the agreement by 90 votes to eight, but 100 peers abstained. That

75. Lord Keynes and Lord Halifax in Washington, 1945.

he had been up against almost as great difficulties in London as in Washington comes out
in a letter he wrote to Lord Halifax from Tilton[9] on 1 January 1946:

Dear Edward,
I have taken a fortnight off letter writing to attend to bran-pies (it was a great success)[10]
and such matters. But perhaps, though late, you'd like to hear how I found the odd and
disturbing Parliamentary position when I got back.
It was a mixture of ignorance and (on both sides) pure party politics. The ignorance
was all-embracing. So far as the public was concerned, no one had been at any pains to
explain, far less defend, what had been done. And as for the insiders, so dense a fog screen
had been created that such as the Chancellor and the Governor of the Bank had only the
dimmest idea of what we had given away and what we had not. The Chancellor had been
worked up into a great state of indignation about the sterling area which was based (in my
opinion) on entire misapprehension of what we had been doing. The Governor of the Bank

told me frankly that it was from my speech in the House of Lords he learnt for the first time that the loan was *not* tied to purchases in the U.S.

————

However, the ignorance was not the real trouble – I suppose that is normal among the great, and inevitable and indeed quite proper among the public. Both political parties were split on issues which had nothing to do with the technical details; and both sets of party leaders decided that a complete abdication of leadership would be the happiest way out. A section of the Socialists thought they detected too definite a smell of *laissez-faire*, at any rate of anti-planning, in the American conception of international affairs.

————

One final conclusion. My impression is that the *fait accompli* is now being accepted, at any rate in official circles and in the Bank of England, as something which must be loyally and sincerely carried out. I think you can reassure the Americans on this, if the public reception of the programme here leads them to doubt it. Political trouble there will certainly be, for the Cabinet is a poor, weak thing. But I am hopeful that the technicians will now turn their technique in the agreed direction.

————

For me, I think the time has come for me to slip out of the Treasury, if not suddenly, at least steadily. When I return to London from the country, I shall have to reach a clear notion what happens next. Being of a resigning temperament, I shall not last long in this galère in any case; so I had better go when I can go quiet and friendly.

Yours ever,
[copy initialled] M.K.

He did go, quiet and friendly, a little over three months' later. His death was at a juncture in our history which made it one of the most serious losses this country has ever sustained. It was deeply felt by ordinary people all over the country. I remember very well how, though they did not grasp the importance of his achievement, and though they could not fathom the financial dangers ahead, they felt anxious that he would not be there to pilot us through.

Chapter Twenty-Two

MARGARET NEVILLE HILL, C.B.E. (born Keynes) (1885-1970)

David Hill has written of his mother:

> What of the character of the person who achieved so much? In some ways she resembled Maynard. She was no scholar in the bookish sense, but she had his flair for rapid intuitive reasoning and for getting to the heart of the matter, by-passing inessentials. She had his instinct for taking calculated risks and acting without too much circumspection. One very attractive side of her character came from her father; she had inherited his gift of being able to get pleasure and relaxation from games, hobbies, theatre, all manner of pastimes and sharing it with others, particularly children. She was basically serious-minded, but had a streak of comic, slightly mischievous whimsicality which made her such amusing company. She would provoke and tease by a modicum of fabrication and a fair measure of exaggeration when recounting an adventure or experience – the intention was not to deceive but, as she said, to make a good yarn better: there was never a trace of conceit or pretentiousness. Sentimentality and effusiveness embarrassed her. She did not feel at ease with people who paraded their erudition or sophisticated wit; she was at her best with more ordinary people. Her conversation and her writing were never contrived to impress: instead, simplicity and clarity seemed to come effortlessly.

I was deeply interested to read what David had written, because here were characteristics which were so marked in a previous generation. Eccentric and exaggerating to make a point or tell a story – this is 'Ford dramatic' coming down from David Everard Ford – clear in my father and it is remarked upon in Maynard by Virginia Woolf (Chapter Five).

I once heard my father warn Margaret, of whom he was fond, 'If ever you feel like doing something peculiar or dramatic, don't: its David Everard coming out'.

'Rapid intuitive reasoning and getting to the heart of the matter, by-passing inessentials' – that comes out in so many of the family. There is an early example when Jane Elizabeth Ford (born Down) (1809-90) tells her husband, 'Your course is now clear, you must resign'.

Florence Keynes wrote of her aunt, Mary Ford (1835-1913) who was running the Glen Villa branch of her mother's school (*see* Chapter Nine) in 1867, as being wilful, handsome, adored by her girls, a skilled seamstress and a most successful gardener, 'in fact, very clever, she could do anything well in which she was interested'. And now we have David writing of his mother:

> As a girl and young woman Margaret had excelled at a variety of handicrafts, and even taught bookbinding at Wycombe Abbey. Her practical skills were displayed in later years when she personally directed and supervised the reconstruction of more than 50 houses to accommodate her tenants. She had a passion for gardening which was to stay with her for life. She had a hand-loom and wove colourful fabrics, and she had talent as an artist, but it was not till she was 50 that she took up oil painting seriously when, after a few lessons, she reached exhibition standard.

Of course, the ghost of the gifted Mary Ford must remember that, so far as gardening is concerned, she is competing with that of John Keynes, Margaret's grandfather, the Mayor of Salisbury, and one of the most celebrated horticulturists of his day. And there were the skills that went to Neville Keynes superb collections of butterflies and stamps.

But such accomplishments are not what David was thinking of when he refers to his mother as having achieved so much.

Margaret came home from Wycombe Abbey School in 1903 and, in 1907, her mother suggested that she might assist Eglantyne Jebb, who was running a Juvenile Employment Exchange, started by Florence. Eglantyne Jebb was to become famous for founding the Save the Children Fund, and she and Margaret established a very close relationship.[1]

A. V. Hill had joined the Committee of the Juvenile Labour Exchange in 1912 and Margaret married him in 1913 and, by 1919, had a family of four. When they arrived in Bowdon, Cheshire, in 1920, I at 16 was fascinated by her Keynes charm and the sparkle which David describes, and A.V., a most brilliant man, made a great impression on me.

It was when they moved to Hurstbourne, Bishopswood Road, Highgate in the Borough of Hornsey in 1923 that Margaret entered the field in which she was to achieve so much. David writes of his mother's major achievements:

> She took part in starting a new Child Welfare Centre and was also appointed to the Board of Guardians of the Borough. In 1927 she served on Hornsey Council's Maternity and Child Welfare Committee. Then, in 1929, she was elected as an Independent member of the Hornsey Borough Council and served on numerous Council Committees dealing with Welfare, Housing, Nursing and Education. Fifteen years later, in 1944, she was to become an Alderman.

76.   Margaret Neville Hill.

It was in 1933, at the age of 48, that she embarked on her first big work. She founded the Hornsey Housing Trust. This was a public utility company for cheap and convenient housing of old people and underprivileged large families. By 1939 the Trust owned 50 houses, with 250 tenancies. From 1939 onwards she concentrated on the care and accommodation of old and incapacitated men and women. Hill Homes Ltd., which made Margaret famous, was formally established in 1944. In 1967 there were six large residences in Hill Homes, accommodating about 200 old people with an average age of 84, and her reputation had become such that she was able to attract funds from rich private bodies like the Goldsmiths' Company. Recognition of her pioneering work came with the award of a C.B.E. in 1957.

Her work, for some years, had attracted attention outside the confines of Hornsey. In 1941 she played a leading role in the formation of the National Old People's Welfare Council and, in 1943, she had contributed greatly to the work of the Nuffield Survey

Committee on the 'Problems of Ageing and the Care of Old People', on which subject she lectured to the Royal College of Physicians and to the British Association.[2]

In addition to the building operations connected with Hill Homes Ltd., Margaret had, as vice-chairman of the Council House Committee of Hornsey in 1946, been able to have built to her own specification 34 bungalows to house old people, to be known as Keynes Close.

In local government circles, also, Margaret was at the height of her powers at just the right time. Her independent and original approach, her willingness to take risks, to ignore formal procedures, must have irked some of the people she had to deal with. But, in the 30s, she was rarely frustrated in her ambitions. There were enough allies in high places with minds big enough to appreciate her quick intuitive way of proceeding and her dynamic approach.

77. A. V. and Margaret Hill, approaching eighty.

I happened to be having tea at Bishopswood Road soon after the 1945 election which returned a Labour Government with an absolute majority. They all seemed pleased and Margaret asked me what my father thought. I said he was very depressed and anxious. Margaret said, 'Oh, Harold always was a shocking old die-hard'. But I think their views may have become less far apart as time passed, for David has written:

> Soon after the war she found local government less congenial and the Town Hall less rewarding as a base for promoting her schemes. It is true that in 1946 her influence in the Borough Housing Committee had led to the building of Keynes Close, but, by 1948, she came to realise that the Hornsey Borough Council was no longer the council she had known. The local government elections of 1945 had returned a flood of new Labour members to the borough: Margaret, with long, hard experience behind her, wholly untheoretical, found she was out of tune with the new politicised body. In 1948 she resigned from the council. Perhaps, not everyone regretted her going but many did, from the Town Clerk downwards. The M.P. for Hornsey

wrote to say that '. . . you have brought to Local Government a combination of three qualities which so few local authorities have the good fortune to get – idealism, a clear and incisive judgement and, at the same time, an eminently realistic approach to human problems . . .'.

Margaret and A.V.'s hospitality at Hurstbourne became a legend, and was enjoyed by countless relatives and friends for nearly 45 years. If she could help it she would never let a Sunday pass without a gathering of grandchildren. She had amassed a large collection of inexpensive antique china, furniture and curios, Hurstbourne was full of them: it had been a relief from council committees to drop into the little antique shop in Highgate Village on the way home, and, before the war, when the Caledonian Market flourished, she had a wonderful eye for treasures amongst the vast piles of junk displayed there.

A. V. Hill, a Companion of Honour, Fellow of the Royal Society and a Nobel Prize Winner, was not only an outstanding physiologist, but also an excellent speaker, and a man of great modesty and charm. He was a Fellow of both Trinity College and King's College, Cambridge. When he and Margaret were, in the years after the war, representing this country at scientific and other international gatherings, it must have been apparent to many why our standing in the world was so much greater than our power.

Chapter Twenty-Three

SIR GEOFFREY LANGDON KEYNES
(1887-1982)

M.A., M.B., B.Chir., M.D., Cambridge; F.R.C.S., England; F.R.C.P., London; F.R.C.O.G., F.R.C.S., Canada; Honorary LL.D., Edinburgh; Honorary Litt.D., Oxford, Cambridge, Birmingham, Sheffield and Reading; Honorary Fellow, Pembroke College and Darwin College, Cambridge; American Surgical Association; and British Academy, F.B.A.

It was my misfortune to have seen less of Geoffrey than of any of my other cousins. My first recollection of him was of about 1920 when my father took us to London for some special family occasion and Geoffrey seized the opportunity to take blood samples from all of us in order to establish our groups. This seemed to us a peculiar experiment. He also said he was having great trouble in remembering what he had read whilst preparing for the Primary Fellow of the Royal College of Surgeons examination: this also seemed odd. What we did not know was that as a young surgeon with the British armies in France in the 1914-18 War, facing the appalling casualties, he had devised a blood transfusion apparatus which became standard in this country for the next 20 years. Nor did we realise that in four years in France he had lost the student's attitude to purely academic work, though his practical experience was far greater than that of the examiners who might fail him. My last recollection was 60 years later, when at Lammas House, Brinkley, he beat me decisively at croquet and then expounded with great clarity and precision where I had gone wrong. He was over ninety.

Of his remarkable achievements during those 60 years, there are, fortunately, many records, one of which is his own *The Gates of Memory*.[1] There is also a tribute inspired by his son, Milo, published in 1984 in the Annals of the Royal College of Surgeons of England. In addition to a number of appreciations by colleagues, there is a full list of his writings, not only on surgical and medical matters, but also on bibliography and literary subjects.

Thanks to the evangelical vigour of Dr. Arnold, Rugby was the public school which most commended itself to Nonconformists. It was there that Geoffrey met Rupert Brooke and, as a result of a spontaneous impulse, began recording Rupert's poetical and literary output – that is, he took his first step towards bibliography.

Geoffrey won a Foundation Scholarship at Pembroke College, Cambridge, his father's college, and took a first-class in Natural Science in 1909, and then a scholarship to St Bartholomew's Hospital in 1910 and, in 1913, won the Brackenbury Surgical Scholarship.

We thus have the two main facets of his life, in both of which he attained extraordinary distinction. In his presidential address to the Bibliographical Society in 1953, he said, 'I have devoted a lifetime to the craft of surgery, and have gained much additional satisfaction from the craft of bibliography'. He went on to dismiss the idea that he had originality in either field – a wholly unsupportable contention. The Royal College of Surgeons supplement to their Annals, though it covered mainly his achievements in the field of medicine and surgery, also included an article by Nicolas Barker, editor of the *Book Collector* which gives some idea of his remarkable bibliographical works and of his wide literary interests.

After his experience as a surgical specialist with the B.E.F. in France in the 1914-18 War, in which he was Mentioned in Despatches, he returned to St Bartholomew's and also held appointments at Mount Vernon Hospital, the Radium Institute, the L.C.C. Thyroid Clinic; at the Royal College of Surgeons, he was a Hunterian Professor in 1923, 1929 and 1948.

Early in the 1920s he began research on the connection between mastitis and breast cancer, and these were the subject of his Hunterian Lecture in 1923. In 1927 he began to publish reports on the results he was obtaining from the use of radium, and from 1929 he was publicly advocating conservative treatment for cancer of the breast in place of 'the gross mutilation of the patient's body involved' in the conventional American Halstead operation going back to 1898. Writing in 1980, he was able to report, 'At the present time the radical operation is seldom done in Great Britain' and that 'young researchers come to me to find out how I came to have such advanced views 50 years ago'.

During the War of 1939-45, Geoffrey served as Senior Consultant in Surgery to the Royal Air Force. Those dedicated members of the Royal Flying Corps of 1914-18, who had the vision to establish the Royal Air Force as a separate force and to equip it so that it could save us in the 1939-45 War, had not given much thought to the treatment of casualties. After all, losses when aircraft were shot down were, they thought, likely to be total. Geoffrey was horrified to find that little more than old-fashioned scalpels were available. That many casualties would be terribly burnt had not been foreseen. When the Director-General of

78. Geoffrey Keynes, Group Captain R.A.F.V.R. (later Acting Air Vice-Marshal).

Medical Supplies ignored his memorandum urging the setting up of an orthopaedic service and provision for the treatment of burns, he ignored Service conventions and wrote direct to the Air Ministry. But worse was to follow: he got Maynard to introduce him to Sir Archibald Sinclair, the Secretary of State for Air. There followed the dismissal of the D.G.M.S., and Geoffrey became the most unpopular man in the higher ranks of the R.A.F., but he could not be prevented from ending up as an Air-Vice-Marshal: nor do we know how many air crews, rescued from crashed and blazing aircraft, owed restoration to normal life to his aggressive initiative.

In the Royal College of Surgeons' Tribute, Michael Harmer, F.R.C.S.,[2] writes of the years 1946-56, when Geoffrey was between sixty and seventy.

> I considered calling this decade *The Thymic Era* because it was during these years that he made another new name for himself and that at an age when lesser men would have been content to grow cabbages – or even to write their memoirs! Myasthenia gravis, that devastating disease, had hitherto been described by cynically-minded surgeons as a thoroughly medical condition, that is to say a matter for nice diagnosis and precious little else. Although Blalock had done his first thymectomy in 1936, opposition to surgical

treatment had been considerable both in the USA and in Britain. It was in 1942 that GLK first divided the breast-bone to seek out this strange and inaccessible little gland. By the time he ceased doing so he had performed 281 thymectomies, had established the surgical difference between hyperplasia and neoplasms and had established in *The History of Myasthenia Gravis* and in 20 other articles, a definitive and significant advance in the treatment of this fell condition. By any standards this was an astonishing achievement. It was Jack Piercy and Denish Nash who helped him for the most part with these operations. Before the war Piercy had been his colleague at the New End Hospital Endocrine Clinic and had assisted him with many hundreds of thyroidectomies. He is emphatic that, in addition to his meticulous technique, Geoffrey's greatest quality was courage, for myasthenic patients were usually desperately ill and the operation itself was of much hazard. For one thing, there was at that time no positive pressure ventilation (now popularly known as 'being put on the ventilator') and for another there is a particularly vulnerable vein which courses across the anterior surface of the thymus gland and which may produce a near mortal haemorrhage if cut during the splitting of the manubrium sterni. Since this vessel had no nomenclature in the textbooks of anatomy Nash christened it the *Greater Vein of Keynes* and he also described a pleasing little anecdote about the 13th patient in the operative series who had to be registered as 12A until she had been safely discharged from hospital.

How he became Chairman of the National Portrait Gallery, established the William Blake Trust and was knighted in 1955; his extraordinary range of friends and achievements in literary and artistic fields are lucidly recorded in his *The Gates of Memory*. He also tells how he married most happily Margaret Elizabeth Darwin in 1917. She was the granddaughter of the great Charles Darwin and shared, with her sister, Gwen, the distinction of writing best-sellers about Cambridge. Her's was *A House by the River* and Gwen Raverat's, *Period Piece*.

Michael Harmer tells us how, when Geoffrey was introducing his brother-in-law, A. V. Hill to the Abernethian Society at Bart's, he said 'I am so often my brother's brother that it is a pleasure, for once, to be my brother-in-law's brother-in-law'.

There was no reason for Geoffrey to have been jealous of Maynard, but he often seemed to be. His own successes were great enough for him to have no cause, but there was something there which I think must have originated in childhood, though he writes most happily of that and of the tact and understanding of his parents (*see* Chapter Fifteen). Maynard had won a scholarship at Eton, in large measure due to his father's coaching; this was in 1897. In those times, to his mother, the daughter of the Manse, the fact that her first-born had won a place at Eton must have been a matter of intense pride and joy. The younger son was nearly sent to Giggleswick, but he tells us, 'was relieved when the wheel of chance came down on Rugby'.

The feelings generated were to evaporate in later life, but I do not think that the brothers were ever very close. Geoffrey once told me that Maynard did not approve of him – or was it did not like Blake? – my recollection is not very clear, but he then went on to say how much he owed to Lydia, 'who was a perfectly sweet person and brought them together'.

Michael Harmer also tells us how, when a colleague remarked in a friendly way – 'It is sad to hear of Maynard's death' he snapped: 'Sad? *Sad!* It's a tragedy of the greatest magnitude', and turning his back on him, he stalked away.

Chapter Twenty-Four

JOHN NEVILLE BROWN
(1904-   )

Writing about oneself is full of pitfalls, and I would not attempt it except to fill a frame in this gallery. Further, continuous use of the personal pronoun, which is hard to avoid, jars on the reader. I have, therefore, adopted the 18th-century device of writing in the third person.[1] There may also be too much background though I hope this may be of some historic interest since it covers the times of the 1939-45 War which contrast sharply with the times of the Rev. David Everard Ford and the Rev. Dr. John Brown.

1904-37 Bowdon, Cambridge, Manchester. Escape from Textiles

Neville Brown was born in May 1904 in Old Trafford, Manchester. A sickly childhood, starting with diphtheria and dogged by acute hay-fever, meant that he was not fit enough to go away to school, so when his parents moved to Bowdon, Cheshire in 1912, he was sent to a local private school. In 1920, A. V. Hill, his cousin Margaret's husband, was appointed Professor of Physiology at Manchester University. He found that, like many boys of 16, Neville was interested in model engineering, so he gave him an old treadle lathe which was being thrown out of the physiology laboratory at the university, and much general encouragement: but he did more. A somewhat amateur war-time schooling, frequently interrupted by illness had not made Neville an attractive candidate for a Cambridge college. Having passed 'Little-go' (the Cambridge University Entrance Examination) in 1922, he had no college to which to go. It was A.V. who came to the rescue. He had a word with an old Blundell's school friend, Knox-Shaw, the Tutor of Sidney Sussex College and there Neville went and was very happy. Such flagrant nepotism would be out of the question today, but he never felt ashamed, because he remembered Maynard saying that Cambridge was full of loungers who made no contribution whatsoever; he would allow a man to stay up even if he only beagled or played in a jazz band and he would still be able to send down 1,000 out of the 5,000 men then in residence.

It was only many years later that Neville realised what a great man lay behind the charm and modesty of A. V. Hill. In his old age, he had trouble walking, so Florence's lady-in-waiting, Suzanne Rendell, escorted him to Winston Churchill's funeral in 1965. She walked back with Attlee, who told her that A. V. Hill's contribution to the winning of the war with Hitler's Germany had been so great that when he became Prime Minister in 1945 he would have recommended A.V. for any honour he cared to have. But A.V. was perfectly happy with his C.H. already recommended by the Churchill government. Professor Lindemann, Churchill's Scientific Adviser, had quarrelled with Sir Henry Tizard, A. V. Hill and P. M. S. Blackett, all distinguished scientists, and had blocked any greater honour.

For Neville, Cambridge was followed by a silk-weaving mill in Macclesfield where he learnt about the construction of silk fabrics and jacquard looms. He did not realise that he was the sixth generation down from William Everard, the 17th-century silk-weaver in Spitalfields, and that all but one had traded in silk. The West African trade which his father had developed consisted largely of supplying gorgeous silk headsquares and damask fabrics which the Gold Coast and Nigeria bought freely when there were good prices for cocoa. The early traders down the West African coast had been the Dutch on their way to the Dutch East Indies and on their return journey they brought Javanese batik prints which they traded with the Africans. These were very fine indeed and have influenced the taste of that coast ever since. Designing silk headsquares to match was very fascinating though silk was going out and artificial silk was taking over. Neville started in his father's business at £240 (£4,580) a year, which he thought extremely generous, but when cocoa went up to £80 a ton in 1928-29, and great prosperity resulted, he was allowed a share in the profits. He thought himself a rich young man and bought a car and an old Morecambe Bay prawner which he kept at Fleetwood. He knew nothing about sailing and was extremely lucky not to be shipwrecked.

In 1929 there was the Wall Street crash. Cocoa fell to £20 a ton and the West African trade folded up. Father and son did not know that for them it was never to revive, but, for a young man, it was most trying grimly to sit doing nothing year after year. In 1934 his father most generously allowed Neville two months' leave and provided him with a bundle of introductions and money to visit America and to study Roosevelt's 'New Deal'. It was remarkable that important Americans would spare time to receive a callow young Englishman with the apparent interest they showed. He was surprised and grateful.

The 'New Deal' may or may not have helped world recovery, but in West Africa it was the Japanese who benefited. Neville had then married Ursula Dimsdale, a cousin of his brother-in-law, Wilfrid Dimsdale, but had to face the fact that the family business was fading away and that, whilst his father was making a great success of his outside directorships, there was no future for him.

It was Maynard who offered the means of escape. As told in Chapter Twenty-One, he had said that if Neville found the right opportunity, he would be ready to finance him in getting out of the textile trade. Wilfrid Dimsdale was then established in Ilford Ltd., which was a group of English photographic material manufacturers amalgamated by his uncle, Sir Ivor Phillips. Wilfrid thought well of the photographic trade and its future, and introduced Neville to a Yorkshireman by the name of Harrison. He had bought a small factory on the Slough Trading Estate making the Dekko 9.5 mm amateur ciné camera, but wanted to sell out. He held himself out to be a very fine engineer but no businessman: in fact, he was the reverse and Neville found that he had bought a pup. Though the photographic trade looked promising, the little Dekko factory and its product were hopeless and Harrison was quite incapable of designing follow-on products. Unless, therefore, drastic action was taken, Neville realised he would be party to a fraudulent bankruptcy, i.e. in ordering goods knowing that they could not be paid for. So he sacked Harrison and threw the company into voluntary liquidation, losing his whole investment and loans from his wife and friends, and relinquishing his own service agreement in favour of the creditors. He then set off for Dresden and acquired a 35 mm slide projector agency as the future for home projection seemed to lie with the large colour pictures obtainable from 35 mm slides, rather than the flickering black and white images of the 9.5 mm ciné camera. His father, though himself very pressed by reason of the decline of the West African trade, lent him £1,000 (£22,000) with which to start trading. But by the end of the first year £800 had gone.

Neville had noticed that all the Bakelite film developing tanks used by amateur photographers were imported and did not see why they should not be moulded here. He designed what he hoped was a better developing tank and risked the then large sum of £180 (£4,000) for a set of moulds. When the first specimens arrived, he put in a test film and sat twiddling the stirring rod. Suddenly, he realised that he was sweating profusely due to sheer panic because if the film did not come out properly developed, he would be bankrupt and would never be his own master again. But the Nebro/Johnson's Developing Tank was a great success. He, or rather Johnson of Hendon (wholesalers to the photographic trade) sold hundreds of thousands over the years. Once, when talking with a flamboyant character, a manager of De La Rue's plastics division, he explained that he had so arranged his prices that Johnsons made a good profit. The character slapped him on the back and said, 'My boy, I see you've grasped the first principle of business. Always see to it that the people with whom you deal make money by you'.

1937-45 – The Threatened War Comes

This country can rarely have been more miserable or more divided than during the run-up to the Second World War. It was still haunted by the slaughter of the first war and felt guilty[2] about the Treaty of Versailles, yet from 1934 onwards it became increasingly clear that Hitler would make war. Those on the Left were fatuously pacifist and those on the Right in sympathy with Fascism. At first, only Churchill, Eden and a few others saw things for what they were. Neville heard a prosperous businessman say that he did not care if Czechoslovakia was chewed up into little pieces, but he also heard a Sheffield bus driver saying: 'Say wat yer likes, this 'ere b. . . . . 'itler's got to be stopped'.

Meanwhile, Neville and Ursula were warned by her relations that if they did not pipe down in expressing their dislike of Franco they would lose their friends. When gas masks came to be issued to the civilian population, memories of the first war, in which Ursula had lost both her brothers, came flooding back to her with such force that she broke down and refused to try on a gas mask. But when war did come, and the air-raid sirens sounded and bombs fell, Neville would go down to a shelter whilst she would sleep soundly in her bed through all but the heaviest air-raids and wake up in the morning saying, 'Well, I am one up on Hitler again'.

Whilst marketing his Dresden-made 35 mm slide projector, Neville had been introduced to A. C. W. Aldis. He was a mathematician who had resigned his fellowship at Trinity Hall to join his brother in a small lens-making works in Birmingham. It was he who had designed and produced the famous Aldis Daylight Signalling Lamp familiar to the Services and the Mercantile Marine.

A few days after war was declared, he appeared in Neville's office and asked him to join him in Birmingham. He said he needed help in carrying the load which the enormous demand from the Services for the Aldis Lamp was going to impose. Neville left a good man to look after what remained of his business and, before September 1939 was out, had settled in Birmingham. The factory was fun but he found that A. C. W. Aldis was a most confirmed centraliser who was incapable of delegating anything. He was thus under-employed and filled in time in designing, together with the chief draughtsman, an Aldis 35 mm colour-slide projector for production after the war. As there was clearly going to be no change in the Aldis organisation, Neville began to think about joining the R.N.V.R. and took up the study of navigation and was allowed time off to attend occasional classes.

Aldis had also allowed Neville leave in May 1940 to go to France on business on behalf of his father. Paris shocked him: London was grimly and completely blacked-out whilst in Paris life seemed to be going on much as usual and their black-out was sketchy in the extreme. They were simply not taking the war seriously. Some collective instinct for survival seemed to have told them that they would not defend Verdun or anywhere else; another slaughter of one and a half million young men they could not survive; anything else they could.

Little did Neville think that, before that month of May was out, he would again be in France, or rather in the shallows off the beaches of Dunkirk. This was because he happened to be attending one of Captain O. M. Watts' lectures when the appeal for volunteers came through from the Admiral in Command of London for men to man small boats to evacuate the British Expeditionary Force from the Dunkirk beaches.

Some time after he got back from Dunkirk, he wrote an account of the experience and sent a copy to a friend in America. In February 1941 America had not come into the war, but in many quarters there was strong support for this country, particularly after the collapse of France, when we fought on alone. But he was surprised to receive a whole-page spread from an American local newspaper, headed:

AWAKE! CITIZENS OF WELLESLEY

Again we say: All Possible Aid to Britain is
America's Strongest Defense.

Urge support of the Lease-Land Bill.

Remember, our opponents are urging the defeat
of his measure so we must hasten to save
America by saving Britain.

There then followed a reproduction of what Neville had written, headed:

ENGLISH YACHTSMAN TELLS GRAPHIC STORY OF EVACUATION FROM DUNKIRK

(*see* Appendix V). This was sent to the newspaper by Richard W. Hale, of Hale and Dorr, the well-known legal firm of State Street, Boston, Mass.

Dunkirk made Neville reconsider joining the Navy. He had seen many, many thousands of men without a weapon amongst them and when Alfred Ewing, of his father's Sheffield steel company, asked him to stand-by for a job in a new steel company he was planning, he parted amicably from Aldis and moved back to London. The steel job did not materialise but the Ministry of Aircraft Production (M.A.P.) wanted someone with photographic and business experience to look after the production of cameras, film and photographic paper for the R.A.F. Photographic supplies were the responsibility of the Directorate of Instrument Production, a Directorate which privately regarded itself as the élite of the Ministry, which was itself the élite of the Supply Ministries, and there Neville spent the war under inspiring leadership.

One would have expected that the Germans would have dominated the field of aerial photography, but they remained stuck with the old Zeiss survey cameras which were wholly unsuitable for the conditions which developed, whereas, through the work of a few brilliant individuals, we had developed techniques which were to make aerial photography of comparable importance to that of the breaking of the Enigma Code in the matter of saving lives and winning the war. Neville was far too close to the production problems, nor was it his business, to know what his department's customers, the R.A.F., were doing with the supplies channelled to them, but some realisation of the dedication of the R.A.F. photographic reconnaissance pilots filtered back. Constance Babbington Smith, the Chief W.A.A.F. Photographic Interpretation Officer, has given a first-class account[3] of the work of that unit, which, coupled with Professor R. V. Jones's writings,[4] throws much light on the very great importance of photographic reconnaissance. To give one example only – the maximum number of flying bombs which landed in London in one day was 100, but the Germans had plans and supplies for two thousand. It was photographic reconnaissance over the Pas de Calais which enabled Bomber Command to be directed to the destruction of the launching sites and the salvation of London.

Since the R.A.F. demands on the photographic industry were so much bigger than those of all the other services put together, the manufacturers developed a habit of referring the other services to Neville's branch at M.A.P. in order to slot their requirements in with the vast R.A.F. programmes and he became, without any authority whatsoever, a sort of *de facto* controller of the industry.

There was no production of film-base in this country. Film-base is the material on which emulsions are deposited to make photographic film and it all came from America and had to be paid for in dollars of which our supplies were nearly exhausted. Roosevelt saved the situation for this country, then fighting Germany and Italy single-handed, by his enactment of the Lease-Lend Bill. Neville had to schedule the requirements on the film-base for the R.A.F., X-ray film and the other services which were eligible for Lease-Lend; whilst the Board of Trade looked after ciné film-base for the cinemas and minute supplies of roll films, all of which had to be paid for in dollars.

The American forces arriving in this country were, at first, inadequately provisioned, and we had to supply them with all kinds of stores. When preparations for the invasion of Europe were being made, the demands of the American forces swamped Kodak in Rochester, N.Y. and the supplies of X-ray base, on which we depended, tailed off and our stocks fell dangerously low. After the British had got as far as Antwerp, but before the mouth of the Scheldt had been cleared of Germans, the Army map-making people, whose requirements Neville had unofficially been piloting through Kodak, said that that stocks of map-making film-base had been found at the Gevaert factory near Antwerp. Would we send over experts to advise? Ilford Ltd. (then bigger producers of X-ray film than Kodak of Harrow), used to draw their X-ray film-base from Gevaert, so Neville asked Wilfrid Dimsdale, who was the production director of Ilford Ltd., if he would go to Antwerp with him to see if Gevaert had stocks of X-ray film-base. They were asked whether they would go in uniform. The Germans might re-take Antwerp and, if they were taken prisoner, they would be better in uniform, but time was pressing so they went as they were. On arrival they were shown into the office of a Brigadier in Brussels. He looked surprised and said, 'Who are you?'

'We are from M.A.P., sir'.

'But I only asked for you a few days ago'.

(The Ministry of Aircraft Production prided itself on speedy action.) He didn't know what to make of them: if they had been in Squadron-Leader's uniforms he could have placed them; so he played safe. 'Well, I had better put you in the . . .', and mentioned the hotel reserved for officers of field rank and above. 'You are going to Antwerp: well, I suppose you had better have my car'. So they arrived at the Gevaert factory in some state. Wilfrid knew the people there and they spent a long time explaining how they had to work for the Germans. Neville and Wilfrid could almost see them thinking of how they would explain, if the Germans re-captured Antwerp, that they had to receive these English civilians when they arrived with such military backing. They were able to report to the army that there was indeed some topographical film-base used for map-making. But they were also able to arrange that large stocks of X-ray film base, which Gevaert held, should be flown home and these saved the U.K. from a serious shortage of X-ray film during the last months of the war.

Antwerp was under fire from the first of the V2 rockets. Neville and Wilfrid were down by the Scheldt when, suddenly, without any warning, there was the most tremendous explosion and a huge fountain of water sprang up in the river. There was decided tension in the mess where they lunched. V2's were new to everybody and the fact that they arrived without warning was trying.

Back in London, many found the V1 flying bombs and V2 rockets more trying than ordinary air-raids. All were desperately tired, but knew the war was won, and found the effort of bracing themselves for more almost too much.

1945-59 Post War
In July 1945 when Attlee had a landslide victory and Churchill was dismissed, the war with Germany was only just over and Japan had not yet been forced to surrender. The fact

that the first Labour Government with an overall majority came into power at that particular time had important consequences.

A high proportion of that majority were academics wedded to the idea of a detailed direction of the economy, together with various other enthusiasts, none of whom had ever 'had to pay the wages on Friday'.[5] Materially, the cupboard was bare, but industry had formed an extraordinary habit of obedience and there was the immense government administrative machine in place with powers which could never have been accepted in peace. These war-time powers were maintained, indeed expanded, but whilst starving, devastated Europe made the most astonishing recovery, we still had food rationing in 1952 when they had forgotten all about it.

Such were the conditions under which Neville had to try to get business going again. He had to build an office in a cellar, largely with his own hands, using aluminium sheets no longer required for aircraft, and had for a warehouse to make do with an air-raid shelter in Holloway.

79. John Neville Brown, c.1954.

One day, A. C. W. Aldis suddenly appeared. He came into Neville's aluminium-lined cellar office, opened a suitcase, and brought out the Aldis 35-mm slide projector Neville had outlined in his drawing-office five years earlier. He had made 250 and wanted Neville to sell them.

Through the Aldis agency and the Developing Tanks, Neville got on his feet and was able to build an organisation. The amateur photographer loves gadgets and, with a starved market, it was easy to design these and have them made for sale under the NEBRO trade mark, but continental agencies of importance, such as that of Ferrania films and German cameras, were also acquired. The post-war cellar was vacated in 1950 and a move made to a building in Newman Street, W.1 and a sizeable warehouse in Clapham in place of the Holloway air-raid shelter.

From 1945 till 1959, Neville did absolutely nothing and had no interests outside business. Holidays were a matter of a few days now and again. The business grew and prospered and he was employing a staff of eighty. It was in 1956 that Neville and his wife Ursula parted. In those days partners of respectable firms of solicitors frowned on collusive divorces but usually had members of their staff who could arrange such matters without exposing the firm's clients to the risk of blackmail. Ursula and Neville's aunt Florence had become good friends and Florence subsequently said to Neville, 'You were quite right to get divorced'. He always felt that there was some element of reproof in this commendation, but

Florence was as wise as she was kindly and Neville and Ursula remained good friends for Ursula's remaining 20 years.

Why did Neville retire at the early age of fifty-five? There were a number of reasons. The more people one employs, the more headaches one faces and, unless one has a paternalistic sense of duty, one longs to be relieved of such things. Another factor was the appearance of the Japanese. Neville had seen what they could do to the channels of trade in textiles and did not want to endure the same thing in the photographic trade. Also, there was a General Election coming in 1959 in which he feared that Labour, after a spell of opposition, would get back. He was wrong because that did not happen until 1964, but he was right in fearing what Labour would do. He had built up his business before Corporation Tax, living thin, and ploughing everything back. Of course, he did not foresee the specific taxes which were imposed five years later when Balogh was appointed adviser to Prime Minister Wilson and Kaldor to Chancellor Callaghan, but he knew enough of Labour Party thinking to know that it was their intention to reduce the share of private business in the economy. There was no unemployment so they would not be inhibited by the damage which might be done to small and growing firms.

Twenty years later, the climate became wholly different. A tax structure designed to cripple private business has been modified beyond recognition, but one could not foresee that change in thinking and fiscal policy, and in any case, it would not have come within Nevile's active business life. When, therefore, an interested buyer came along in 1959, he sold. He had given shares to his leading staff which they sold favourably, and those who did not retire got service agreements with the new owners.

Neville had bought the lease of 77 Newman Street in 1950, and some years later the lease of No. 76. When he sold Neville Brown & Co. Ltd., he kept the leases and, after allowing the new owners of the business time to turn round, both the old buildings were demolished. Built in 1820 as private houses they were of no special merit. Neville knew nothing about property development but had a good agent – R. Wilks of Davis & Co., and put up an office building of 5-6,000 square feet on the site of the two old houses. It stood empty for some anxious years, but it was eventually let to British Rail's advertising department and subsequently sold, most satisfactorily but, alas, before the real property boom set in.

After 1959 . . . Freedom

Neville was now free to do the many things in which he was interested. The first of these was to take up yacht cruising and that, indeed, became his main interest for the next 15 years. The oversight of the designing, building and equipping of cruising yachts is fascinating, particularly if one has got single-handed cruising in mind. It was in those years that Sir Francis Chichester was showing that an 18-tonner, if suitably equipped and rigged, was easier to sail single-handed than smaller cruising yachts and Blondie Hasler was pioneering automatic wind-vane steering. Neville had a nine-ton yawl, *Amadea I*, built by Whisstock's of Woodbridge in 1959, followed by *Amadea II*, another yawl of 18-tons in 1964, both designed by C. R. Holman. Based on the East Coast, he cruised in Holland, down Channel, Brittany, Ireland and Scotland. It gave one great flexibility to have a vessel which could carry a crew of four in considerable comfort for sea-passages but which could also be sailed single-handed in sheltered waters. Nothing out of the ordinary was achieved though a claim was made to have been the last yachtsman to have circumnavigated Roman Britain. Its northern frontier was the Wall of Antonius believed to be the line followed by the Forth-Clyde Canal. Built in 1803, the eastern entrance from the Firth of Forth had silted up and entrance was only possible by kind permission of the Grangemouth dock operators. Also the swinging road bridges which allowed the passage of masted vessels produced traffic blocks many miles long on the main roads of central Scotland. *Amadea I* passed through in

1962 and at the end of that year the canal was closed for good. It was not expected to have the claim contested by a fellow yachtsman, but possibly by an archaeologist.

Ireland was delightful; *Amadea II* was laid-up for the winters of 1965 and 1966 at Crosshaven in Cork Harbour. This was before relations with the Irish had been soured by renewed trouble in Ulster. They would cast political flies over visitors, but Neville made it a strict rule never to rise, and enjoyed all the charm of their hospitality. The Royal Cork Yacht Club (which, though situated in a Republic, proudly retains the 'Royal') organised a grand meet and cruise in company, inviting the Cruising Club of America, our Royal Cruising Club and the Cruising Club of Ireland to take part. Fabulous American yachts crossed the Atlantic to attend and, excellently organised, it was a great success. A member of the Royal Cork Yacht Club said afterwards, 'We thought that we would get on well with the Americans but that we would find the British sticky. In fact, we found that we could not make contact with the Americans but found the British congenial'.

80. *Amadea II* in Killeany Bay, County Galway, 2 June 1966.

Elizabeth I complained that though she had to spend excessive sums of money on Ireland 'yet we receive nought else but news of fresh losses and calamities'.[6] Why did she, Cromwell, William III and subsequent rulers of England trouble to occupy that beautiful but wet island inhabited by a turbulent people? If one proceeds about the Channel Approaches under sail the answer is clear. The prevailing winds are westerly, which means that it can be a hard slog to windward from Torbay or Plymouth to Land's End, only to find that a Frenchman from Brest has had a beam wind from the start and holds the weather gage all the way to Cork. Cork and Bantry are magnificent natural harbours and, if France or Spain ever held them, England, with its tiny population encircled by the great Catholic powers, would have been in a desperate situation.

In 1796 the French did, indeed, manage to get a full-scale invasion fleet to the mouth of Bantry Bay, but a most unusual easterly gale stopped them beating-up the long narrow bay to land Wolf Tone at Bantry Town. It also enabled the English fleet to arrive in time to deal with the would-be invaders. This was a highly dangerous moment in our history. We were in still greater danger in 1939-45 with the Germans encircling us from Norway to Brest. We had resigned the use of Cork and Bantry to the neutral Republic of Ireland before the war and the English Channel and St George's Channel were closed to us. But James I had planted Presbyterian-Scots in Ulster over 300 years ago in order to have a secure foothold in Ireland and, thanks to their descendants, it was possible to build 26 airfields in Northern Ireland. From these, Coastal Command of the Royal Air Force could range far out into the Atlantic and, in conjunction with the Fleet Air Arm, make the approaches to the North Channel too hot for German submarines. They accounted for twenty-nine.[7] It was through the North Channel alone that supplies of food and war-like materials reached us, but even more important, it was through the North Channel alone that the American forces which were to liberate Europe poured in. Without the loyalty of Ulster the outcome of the war might have been different.

Another interest was in Colchester. An Essex seedsman, Kenneth Ireland, a man of unusual flair and ability, bought control of an old firm of ironmongers in a rambling shop in Colchester High Street. A most valuable site was being used to house wheelbarrows, galvanised sheeting and the like. He noticed that a furniture shop and a ladies' dress shop were similarly not exploiting to the full the valuable sites they occupied. They were family businesses and he persuaded them to join with him in building a fine new store on the ironmonger's site, sell the other sites to Tesco and the like, and establish a sort of miniature Peter Jones in Colchester. It was a brilliant conception and Neville went in with him financially, became a non-executive director, and remained on the board of this venture, Williams & Griffin Ltd., for 20 years.

During the 1960s, new universities were appearing all over the country and it was decided to establish Essex University near Colchester. There was great enthusiasm and many Colchester firms, as well as private individuals, contributed financially through seven-year Covenants. Neville thought that there should be a Keynes Visiting Professorship. His cousin, Professor Richard Keynes, kindly agreed to help by becoming a Trustee and Professor James Meade, by agreeing to act as arbitrator, if necessary. A variety of economists from all over the world held the chair, but Neville was a little disappointed in that they were all mathematicians and it seemed to him that their inaugural lectures, though ingenious academic exercises, had very little to do with the real world where things were not as tidy as mathematical equations.

A venture, undertaken at about the same time as Williams & Griffin, was in a different trade. A sailing friend, John Hobbins, had a small business, or rather a way of life, which consisted of running an old motor barge up and down the East coast with cargoes of sand and gravel. He showed Neville his balance sheet: the sums were tiny, but all were in their proper proportion. So, when he wanted to add to his fleet, Neville gave him mortgages secured on the vessels he bought. John Hobbins had a friend, Michael Uren, a civil engineer, who gave up his job to join him in a new venture they had thought up. It appeared wildly ambitious. They proposed to build a 2,000-ton suction dredger to dredge sand and gravel for concrete from the banks off the Essex coast, as land-based pits were becoming exhausted and environmental considerations were limiting further development. They made such a good impression on the Crown Commissioners that they got one of the first licences to dredge sea aggregates off the East Anglian coast . Neville took up shares in their company and made loans but they got important sums from the Industrial and Commercial Finance Corporation, and wonderful support from Barclays Bank. In spite of much talk to the contrary, it has never been impossible, in this country, for men of real ability to attract capital and get on their feet.

Twenty years on the board of Civil & Marine as a non-executive director were very happy and most interesting and Neville watched it grow, from virtually nothing, to an exceedingly prosperous business with a fleet of modern dredgers and valuable shore establishments on both sides of the London river and in Dunkirk.

There were other small companies in which he took an interest, but they did not flourish like the store or the dredgers, and there were some narrow escapes.

It was his swan-song in merchanting – this time money – which, perhaps, amused him most of all. In 1968, Roy Jenkins, as Labour Chancellor of the Exchequer, copied certain continental countries in an effort to check imports without breaking tariff agreements. He imposed upon importers the requirement to pay an 'Import Deposit' equal to half the value of the goods. Customs and Excise then gave a receipt which was a promise to repay the deposit in 180 days, drawn not necessarily in favour of the importer, but in favour of whoever had paid the deposit on his behalf. The banks were asked not to make advances against these Customs' receipts, but of course, the big importers, dealing in millions, found ways round. It was the small man, whose problems Neville knew very well from his own experience, who would be in difficulties. He therefore started advertising as an Import Deposit Broker. He paid the import deposit in the name of whoever would buy the receipt. These were mostly money-brokers, but also many private individuals contacted through advertising. There was a bank manager in Stanmore who sent him an unending stream of rich Indian women, and a bicycle dealer in Halifax who invested heavily.

Neville started this operation from his Highgate flat, but soon had to take on a small staff and then rented a few rooms above a greengrocer's shop in Junction Road, N.19, which was not exactly an address to give financial confidence. It happened that at that time he was a 'name' at Lloyds and his agents, who had a fine office in Fenchurch Street, very kindly allowed him to use it as an accommodation address from which a courier could collect mail.

However, he had a problem when the Halifax dealer in bicycles wanted to come up and see him. The chairman of his Lloyds' agents entered into the spirit of things and, as he happened to be away on the appointed day, he very kindly lent him his magnificent office. The bicycle dealer was received by the most courtly variety of City commissionaire and shown up to the top floor, where he was welcomed by a gorgeous secretary and shown into a most impressive office, where Neville was sitting behind a huge Louis XV table with not a paper on it. When he recovered his composure, there was a pleasant conversation in which Neville explained that, like many City firms, they did their paperwork in the suburbs. He went back to Yorkshire, suitably impressed, and continued to pester Neville with offers of money to invest for him, long after Import Deposits had been wound up.

When people ask Neville what he has been, he replies: a merchant; if they ask him what he dealt in, he says 'all sorts of things, but much the nicest was money, because no customer ever sent it back saying "it didn't work"'.

1971- . . . Suffolk

When A. V. Hill brought Neville down from Manchester to Cambridge in his sidecar in 1920 it was a case of love at first sight for East Anglia with its ancient towns, villages and willowy rivers, and his affections never wavered.

He got to know Woodbridge, on the River Deben, through having boats built there and in 1971, when the time came to leave London, he came upon an old mill house upon the

81.   Kettleburgh Mill and House, *c*.1910.

82.   Watermill House, 1973.

upper Deben at Kettleburgh. The mill had been of great antiquity (there is a Conveyance dated 1637), but had ben pulled down in 1934, and only the mill house, with its early 19th-century facade, remained. There were derelict cottages and a medieval pound for stray animals on the approach road, and a disused gravel pit: the whole area of about ten acres, on both sides of the river, was jungle.

But the proportions of the mill house were good, it faced south, trees could be thinned, jungle cleared, and one could be sure that floods would not be damaging, or the site would have been abandoned centuries ago. Neville bought the mill house and policies in 1971 and, in 1973, added the round-ended wing where the mill itself had been. The 15th-century miller, who saw the possibilities of the site, was right.

Neville has been heard to say that he has enjoyed each decade of his life more than the one before. Now, well into his ninth, in good health with the right wife and a house on one of the best of the East Anglian rivers, he does not recant.

Chapter Twenty-Five

HELEN EASDALE DIMSDALE, F.R.C.P. (born Brown) (1907-1977)

I remember that as a small boy I used to bully my young sister and once reduced her to tears. Later, such a thing seemed quite incredible, for behind her there lurked a hundred and more years of formidable women, Hannah Haydon, Jane Down and Ada Haydon Ford. Hannah was reputed to have a remarkably sharp tongue and all were strong characters with shrewd minds of their own and great ambition, in their case, for their large families.

Helen was educated at first at a local dame's school, Culcheth Hall, and then at Hayes Court, Kent, where she played lacrosse for the Southern Schools. Her intentions appeared early. She took one look at the social life of suburban Bowdon, Cheshire, and decided it was not for her: Cambridge, Medicine and London would be her sphere. Having saved up £20 (£380) she spent it, much to my astonishment, on a very impressive chemistry outfit with which to perform her experiments. Whereas, during vacations, I would work for a few hours in the morning, she would retire to her room and work solidly all day and every day. But she was not unduly serious.

When she went up to Girton in 1925, the West African trade was

83. Helen Easdale Dimsdale.

booming and she was given a yellow Austin Seven in which to get in and out of Cambridge. Very few undergraduates indeed had cars in 1925. This did not stop her working hard, but it aided, together with encouragement from Betty Dimsdale, an active social life. She also played tennis for her college. She wrote an article for her college magazine in which she said it was possible to train undergraduates to become nice pets and was surprised to be

told, on showing it to her Aunt Florence, that it was flippant and not in very good taste –
though Florence was never unkind or censorious. She had a similar surprise at home. The
arrival of a roast leg of mutton for Sunday luncheon being greeted with looks of approval,
Helen said, 'This family is clearly united in the love of the Lamb'. A somewhat pained
silence followed this sally – not that our parents were at all devout.

Her regular attendance at lectures, aided by the 'Yellow Peril', and above all, her
concentrated hard work during the vacations resulted in First Class honours in the Natural
Sciences tripos in 1929. She then went to University College Hospital for clinical studies
and qualified with the Conjoint diploma in 1933. She had married Wilfrid Dimsdale in
1930 and her son, Nicholas, was born in 1935. She did not pass her M.B. B.Chir. till 1937.

As many of our family are doctors, it is interesting that Helen should have married into
a family with ancient and distinguished origins in that profession.

Dr. Edward Jenner, F.R.S. (1749-1823) had discovered vaccination for the prevention of
smallpox and was invited by Katharine[1] the Great of Russia (1729-1796) to go to St
Petersburg to vaccinate herself and her son, the Grand Duke Paul. Jenner excused himself
but said that he had a colleague, a certain Dr. Thomas Dimsdale (1712-1800) in whom he
had complete confidence and who would be ready to attend her. Dr. Dimsdale had written
several books on vaccination. When Dr. Dimsdale had his first audience in 1768, he
explained that since vaccination had only just been discovered, it was not yet known to be
wholly safe.[2]

A Quaker, he apparently had their gift of inspiring confidence and the Empress asked
him to proceed, adding that she would order relays of horses to be stationed so that he
could be over the Polish frontier before the result was known, because if her reaction, or
that of the Grand Duke, was too serious her subjects would tear him to pieces. There were
no complications and he paid a second visit to St Petersburg. He must have been something
of a courtier, for Katharine rewarded him liberally, ennobled him and recommended him
to Frederick the Great of Prussia, who received him at Sans-Souci and honoured him with
presents. He also went on to Vienna and was received by the Emperor Joseph I.

The Dimsdales still enjoy, by Royal Warrant, the title Katharine conferred, the present
holder being the 11th baron.

To return to Helen. On qualifying, she held appointments at Windsor and University
College Hospital, and Elizabeth Garrett Anderson Hospital, where she was medical
registrar from 1938 to 1939. She was regarded by her colleagues as a most attractive and
vivid person, as well as an extremely competent doctor.

Influenced no doubt by her uncle, Sir Walter Langdon-Brown, she pursued a training in
neurology and neuropathology at Maida Vale, the London, and Chase Farm Hospitals. In
1942, she was appointed neuropathologist for Maida Vale Hospital for Nervous Diseases,
and assistant physician in 1946. She became neurologist to the Royal Free Hospital and
tutor in Medicine in 1952 and in 1944 she acted as first assistant in the Department of
Neurology at the London Hospital. It is of note that, both at this hospital, and at Maida
Vale Hospital, she worked closely with Russell Brain (later Lord Brain), who had married
Stella, grand-daughter of Dr. John Langdon Down, brother of Jane Down, Helen's great-
grandmother.

Her gifts as a teacher had become apparent early for in later years her son, Nicholas was
told by Sir George Pickering, who became Regius Professor of Medicine and, later, Master
of Pembroke College, Oxford, that she was the best student he had ever encountered in
giving an exposition of a patient's case to a medical audience. These gifts in teaching led to
appointments as an examiner, in which capacity she acted for the Diploma of Psychological
Medicine at Durham and also for the F.R.C.S. in medical ophthalmology.

Her immense hard work and dedication to her profession were obvious, but I was very interested to read that her colleagues referred particularly to her skill in diagnosis and to her gift of pithy comment in informal discussion. She also had a wit which would bite. When she and Wilfrid were discussing what to give a rather dim friend, Helen said, 'She doesn't need a book; she already has one'.

Her appointment to the consulting staff at Maida Vale had made her the first woman to hold a clinical neurology consultancy in the country and, when she was elected a Fellow of the Royal College of Physicians in 1949, she was in those days one of the relatively few women Fellows. She served on the Council from 1961-3, chairing some of its committees. It was in 1967 that she followed her great-great-grandfather, John Everard, in being admitted, as he was in 1757, to the Freedom of the City of London – again, a company in which there were few women.

She was greatly esteemed by her colleagues since she was Chairman of the Planning Committee in the 1950s and of the Medical Committee 1963-5 at the Royal Free Hospital, and Honorary Treasurer of the Association of British Neurologists 1961-6.

In 1955 the Royal Free Hospital suffered an epidemic of a little-understood infectious disease; there were 300 cases. Two psychologists, Dr. McEvedy and Dr. Beard, asked to see the case notes and the Medical Committee of the hospital agreed, in spite of strong protests from Helen. After the meeting, she said to a colleague, Dr. A. M. Ramsay, 'You will live to rue the day when you were party to that decision'. She had sensed what her colleagues had not, that the two psychologsts knew little about infectious disease and, further, that they might use the data to the detriment of the hospital. In fact, they did: when their observations were published, the view that there was a considerable element of hysteria in the epidemic spread throughout the profession and was seized upon by the press. After many years of research, Dr. A. M. Ramsay, who was a consultant in infectious diseases, established that the disease was, in fact, viral myalgic encephalomyelitis and that physical and psychological problems could be associated with it. Helen herself was infected and her colleague, Dr. Margaret MacPherson of Elizabeth Garrett Anderson Hospital, said 'She was never the same again', though this was not immediately apparent.

I used to see a lot of her in the early 1960s. Her sparkle was terrific, and she spent money on clothes as a matter of deliberate policy and to great effect, setting off her grandmother Brown's fine pale skin and David Everard Ford's brilliant brown eyes. But, more important, I had the opportunity of seeing her in action professionally and owe my life to her startlingly quick grasp and decisive action. In 1963, I had cancer of the colon which, owing to a negative x-ray result, had not been diagnosed and I was in fact *in extremis*. Helen took one look at me, brushed everybody and everything aside, brought in Sir John Richardson and had Naunton Morgan (later Sir Clifford, and a Bart's man) operating on me almost before I knew what was happening. Her subsequent bedside visit was a model. She came in very smartly dressed, smiling and cheerful, stayed a very short time and left the patient feeling that all was right with the world, himself included.

She and Wilfrid lived in Harley Street and would spend weekends sailing. Once, when Wilfrid fell overboard in the Solent, she got him back aboard, single-handed, which, as yachtsmen will know, can be no easy task. They were to choose West Mersea, Essex, when they came to retire. There was good sailing there and Wilfrid knew it well from his connection with Ilford Ltd., and the film-base plant at Brantham. Unfortunately, in Helen's active years her way of life had not allowed the keeping of dogs, for she was devoted to animals. She regarded them as a part of our common, undivided creation and as between an ailing cat or a patient there was no difference in her approach. She gave good marks to West Mersea because, though the medical service was poor, there was an outstanding vet.

Helen had consulting rooms in Welbeck Street but, curiously, she did not develop any considerable private practice. She was not interested in making money, but interested only in the profession of medicine and her standing in it in competition with the best men of her day. She was a frequent contributor to medical journals (as can be seen from her contemporary *Who's Who* entry), and to Sir John Richardson's *Practice of Medicine* in 1956.

In sum total, her activities were, however, too great: she never let up and her dedication to her profession became increasingly obsessive. She would undertake tasks which she should not, such as treating Wilfrid when he had a breakdown. I think Dr. MacPherson was right about the 'Royal Free Disease' and Helen: tragically, she had to seek early retirement.

Dame Josephine Barnes, a colleague who knew her well, wrote of her, 'I remember her as a very splendid and delightful person. It was a great sadness that she retired prematurely because she lost so much of the might-have-been achievements of her later years, but her contributions, not only to medicine and neurology, but also to the cause of women in medicine were very considerable'.

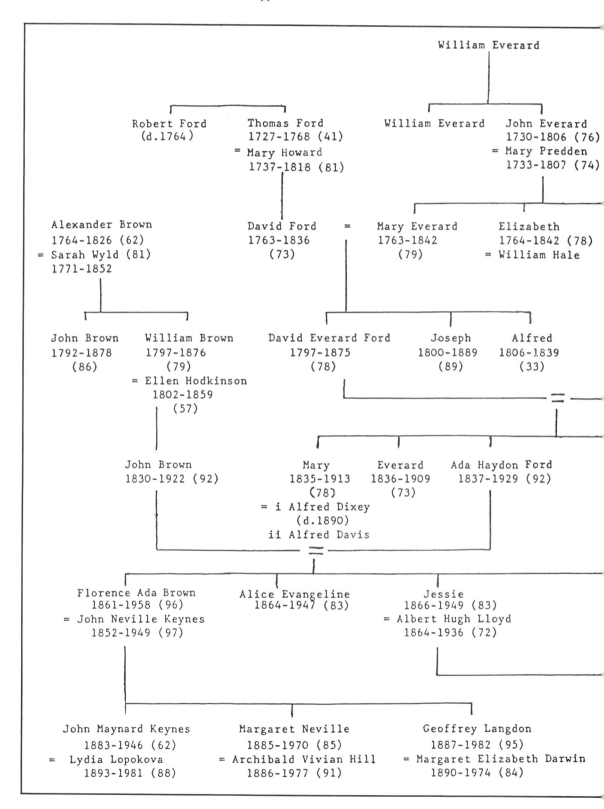

William Everard

Robert Ford
(d.1764)

Thomas Ford
1727-1768 (41)
= Mary Howard
1737-1818 (81)

William Everard

John Everard
1730-1806 (76)
= Mary Predden
1733-1807 (74)

Alexander Brown
1764-1826 (62)
= Sarah Wyld (81)
1771-1852

David Ford
1763-1836
(73)

=

Mary Everard
1763-1842
(79)

Elizabeth
1764-1842 (78)
= William Hale

John Brown
1792-1878
(86)

William Brown
1797-1876
(79)
= Ellen Hodkinson
1802-1859
(57)

David Everard Ford
1797-1875
(78)

Joseph
1800-1889
(89)

Alfred
1806-1839
(33)

=

John Brown
1830-1922 (92)

Mary
1835-1913
(78)
= i Alfred Dixey
(d.1890)
ii Alfred Davis

Everard
1836-1909
(73)

Ada Haydon Ford
1837-1929 (92)

=

Florence Ada Brown
1861-1958 (96)
= John Neville Keynes
1852-1949 (97)

Alice Evangeline
1864-1947 (83)

Jessie
1866-1949 (83)
= Albert Hugh Lloyd
1864-1936 (72)

John Maynard Keynes
1883-1946 (62)
= Lydia Lopokova
1893-1981 (88)

Margaret Neville
1885-1970 (85)
= Archibald Vivian Hill
1886-1977 (91)

Geoffrey Langdon
1887-1982 (95)
= Margaret Elizabeth Darwin
1890-1974 (84)

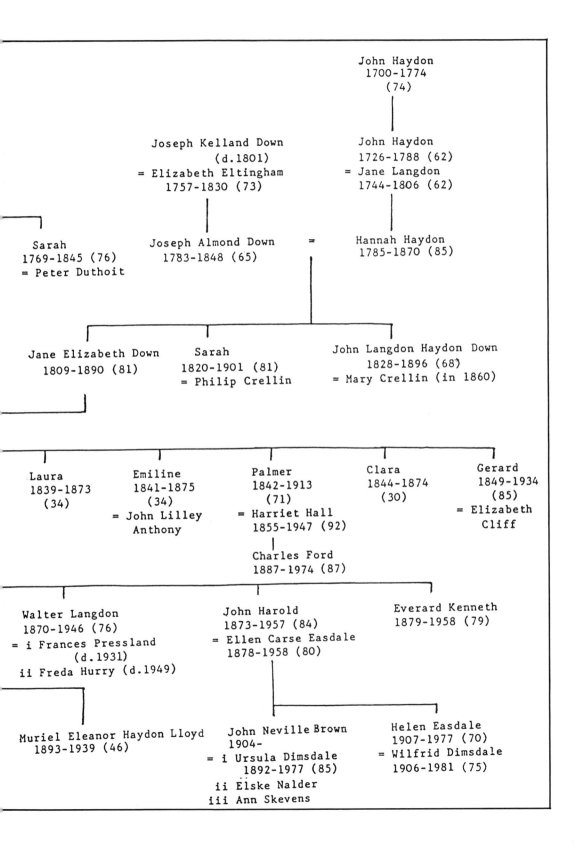

John Haydon
1700-1774
(74)

Joseph Kelland Down
(d.1801)
= Elizabeth Eltingham
1757-1830 (73)

John Haydon
1726-1788 (62)
= Jane Langdon
1744-1806 (62)

Sarah
1769-1845 (76)
= Peter Duthoit

Joseph Almond Down
1783-1848 (65)

=

Hannah Haydon
1785-1870 (85)

Jane Elizabeth Down
1809-1890 (81)

Sarah
1820-1901 (81)
= Philip Crellin

John Langdon Haydon Down
1828-1896 (68)
= Mary Crellin (in 1860)

Laura
1839-1873
(34)

Emiline
1841-1875
(34)
= John Lilley
Anthony

Palmer
1842-1913
(71)
= Harriet Hall
1855-1947 (92)

Clara
1844-1874
(30)

Gerard
1849-1934
(85)
= Elizabeth
Cliff

Charles Ford
1887-1974 (87)

Walter Langdon
1870-1946 (76)
= i Frances Pressland
(d.1931)
ii Freda Hurry (d.1949)

John Harold
1873-1957 (84)
= Ellen Carse Easdale
1878-1958 (80)

Everard Kenneth
1879-1958 (79)

Muriel Eleanor Haydon Lloyd
1893-1939 (46)

John Neville Brown
1904-
= i Ursula Dimsdale
1892-1977 (85)
ii Elske Nalder
iii Ann Skevens

Helen Easdale
1907-1977 (70)
= Wilfrid Dimsdale
1906-1981 (75)

SUCCESSORS

Descendants of A. V. and M. N. Hill (born Keynes)

Polly Hill, Ph.D.
Newnham College, Cambridge 1933-6. Fellow Clare Hall, 1965-
Field anthropologist in West Africa and south India for over thirteen years. Research Fellow University of Ghana, 1954-65.
Smuts Reader in Commonwealth Studies, Cambridge, 1973-9.
Six books published by the Cambridge University Press include *The Migrant Cocoa Farmers of Southern Ghana* (1963).
Born 1914; married Kenneth Humphreys (1916-85).

   Susannah Maynard, born 1956; married Alastair Burn 1979.
      William Alexander, born 1987.

David Keynes Hill, Sc.D., F.R.S. Physiologist.
Trinity College, Cambridge (Fellow 1940-8).
London University, Royal Postgraduate Medical School 1949-82.
Professor of Biophysics.
Born 1915; married Stella Mary Humphrey 1949.

   Harriet Mary Minton (step-daughter), born 1945.

   Abigail Leslie Keynes, born 1950; married Angus Marland 1983.
      James, born 1983.

   Arden Margaret Keynes, born 1953; married Joe Bentley 1977.
      Davina, born 1977.
      Oliver, born 1980.

   Katharine Scarlett Keynes, born 1954.

Janet Rumney Humphrey (born Hill), M.R.C.S., L.R.C.P., M.R.C.Psych.
Member of British Psycho-analytical Society.
Born 1918; married John Herbert Humphrey (1915-87).

   Simon John Everard, born 1941; married Gwen Garrod 1976.
      Tom, born 1977.
      Alice, born 1979.

   Nicholas Keynes, born 1943; married Caroline Waddington
   1967 (marriage dissolved).

Sarah Maynard, born 1945; married David Matthews 1970
(marriage dissolved).
Ben, born 1972.

Andrea Vanessa, born 1948; married Mark Leonard 1968.
Emily, born 1972.
Hannah, born 1974.
Lucy, born 1978.

Charlotte Miranda, born 1954, married Mark McCarthy 1984.
Piero, born 1985.

Maurice Neville Hill (1919-66), Ph.D., F.R.S.
Fellow of King's College, Cambridge. Oceanographer.
Born 1919; married Philippa Pass 1944.

Mark Oliver, born 1945; married Denise Callwood 1978.
Katharine Olivia, born 1981.
Maximillian Rodney, born 1984.

Julia Margaret, born 1947; married Jeffrey Woodward Riley 1971.
James Maurice, born 1977.
Philippa Clare, born 1979.
Thomas Adam, born 1981.

Alison Maynard, born 1949; married Charles Andrew Chivers 1980.
Thomas Maurice, born 1980.
Sarah Jane, born 1982.

James David, born 1953, married Anne Stewart 1987.

Griselda Katharine, born 1956.

Descendants of Geoffrey and Margaret Keynes (born Darwin)

Richard Darwin Keynes, C.B.E., Sc.D., F.R.S. Physiologist.
Fellow of Trinity College, Cambridge 1948-52; Fellow of Peterhouse 1952-60; Fellow of
Churchill College since 1961.
Professor of Physiology in Cambridge University 1973-86.
Publications include *The Beagle Record*, Cambridge University Press (1979) and *Charles
Darwin's Beagle Diaries*, Cambridge University Press (1988).
Born 1919; married Anne Pinsent Adrian 1945.

Adrian Maynard Keynes (1946-74); married Rosemary Mackinley Young 1971.

Robert Geoffrey, born 1974

Randal Hume Keynes, born 1948.

Roger John Keynes, born 1951; married Hilary Lister 1975, marriage dissolved 1983.
  Oliver Adrian, born 1978.
  Laura Margaret, born 1979.

Simon Douglas Keynes, born 1952.

Quentin George Keynes
Traveller, photographer and lecturer. Born 1921.
A collector of travel books.

William Milo Keynes, M.D., F.R.C.S.
Trinity College, Cambridge; St Bartholomew's Hospital, London; Harvard Medical School.
Clinical anatomist, surgeon and writer.
University posts at Cambridge, St Bartholomew's Hospital, The London Hospital, Harvard
University and Oxford.
Formerly Reader in Surgery and honorary consultant surgeon at Radcliffe Infirmary,
Oxford. Born 1924.
Publications include *Essays on John Maynard Keynes*, Cambridge University Press (1975),
Lydia Lopokova, Weidenfeld & Nicolson (1983).

Stephen John Keynes, M.A., King's College, Cambridge; Merchant Banker; Director of:
The English Trust Group plc; Sun Life Assurance plc; formerly Director of: Charterhouse
Finance Corporation Ltd.; Arbuthnot Latham Holdings plc. Member of Board: Independent
Broadcasting Authority, 1969-74. Chairman of Trustees: Whitechapel Art Gallery; English
Chamber Theatre; William Blake Trust.
Born 1927; married Mary Knatchbull-Hugessen 1955.

Gregory Robert Edward Keynes, born 1956.

Elizabeth Harriet Keynes, born 1957.
  Jordan Joe Railton Fack, born 1983.
  Maximilian Fack, born 1988.

Toby William Keynes, born 1959.

Martha Paganel Keynes, born 1961; married Paul Newton 1984.
  Ella Claire, born 1986.
  Nancy Mary, born 1988.

Zachary Edmund Keynes, born 1962.

Descendant of W. H. and H. E. Dimsdale (born Brown)

Nicholas Hampden Dimsdale, M.A., King's College, Cambridge.
Fellow of the Queen's College, Oxford, since 1961.

Economic Adviser Department of Economic Affairs 1964-6.
Estates Bursar of The Queen's College, Oxford, since 1977.
Managing Editor of *Oxford Economic Papers* since 1979.
Born 1935; married Verna Lorraine Moore 1968.

Appendix III

RELATIVE COSTS OF LIVING

David Everard Ford, when still a student, set out to have a chapel built in the Hertfordshire village of Wood End. He personally collected £225. That was in 1820: we should be interested to know the approximate equivalent in 1986. I, accordingly, asked my nephew Nicholas Dimsdale, a Fellow of Queen's College, Oxford, what records were available which would enable a reasonable comparison to be made and he kindly went into the matter in some depth and provided me with a cost of living index stretching over the last two hundred years.

Obviously, index numbers need to be treated with great caution in comparing standards of living stretching over two centuries. The ordinary middle-class family now spends a considerable proportion of its income on goods and services which did not exist, or to which they did not aspire, in 1850. One has only to think of what is spent on motor cars, foreign holidays, telephone, central heating, television and hi-fi equipment. One has also to allow for what is taken away in rates and taxes and what is given back in health, housing and pensions. And one has, I think, above all, to remember the importance to the middle-classes of cheap labour, from cab drivers to governesses, which was readily available to them up to 1914.

Retail Price Index

The index number for each year is relative to 1913 = 100. For convenience a factor is then given. If the price in any year is multiplied by that factor, the 1986 approximate equivalent is obtained.

Year	Index	Factor	Year	Index	Factor
1713	55	60	1885	89	37
1780	67	50	1890	87	38
1785	77	43	1895	81	41
1790	80	41	1900	89	37
1795	100	33	1905	90	37
1800	144	23	1910	94	35
1805	140	23	1915	121	27
1810	153	22	1920	244	14
1815	135	25	1925	173	19
1820	124	27	1930	155	21
1825	129	26	1935	140	24
1830	105	32	1940	179	19
1835	94	35	1945	226	15
1840	118	28	1950	283	12
1845	99	34	1955	371	8.9
1850	89	37	1960	420	7.9
1855	112	30	1965	503	6.6
1860	111	30	1970	628	5.3
1865	111	30	1975	1159	2.7
1870	108	31	1980	2267	1.5
1875	109	30	1985	3208	1.0
1880	103	32	1986	3317	1.0

It is interesting to note that though there were slight fluctuations, the value of money was about the same in 1913 as it was on the passing of the Reform Bill in 1832. In the second half of this century, however, the value of money in 1986 fell to only one-seventh of what it had been in 1945.

In the long period in the 19th century in which the value of money was stable, there was little change in manners and morals: those obtaining in 1913 were not notably different from those of 1832. Though there are very many reasons for the extraordinary change in manners and morals between 1945-86, one is tempted to correlate them to some degree with the great fall in the value of money. If Aunt Mary was hospitable and generous, her views were likely to influence her nephews and nieces more than if she was a poor relation, which would have been her fate if, as was often the case, her fortune had been invested in War Loan and the like.

Nicholas Dimsdale gives as sources for the Retail Price Index:

1713 and 1780-1850. – Henry Phelps Brown and Sheila V. Hopkins, *Price of Whole Composite Commodity from Seven Centuries of the Prices of Consumables compared with Builders' Wage Rates*, reprinted in *A Perspective of Wages and Prices* by H. Phelps Brown and S. V. Hopkins, Methuen, London (1981).

1850-5. – G. H. Wood, *Real Wages and the Standard of Comfort since 1850*. Journal of the Royal Statistical Society 1909, reprinted in *Essays in Economic History*, vol. III, edited by E. M. C. Wilson, London (1962).

1855-1965. – C. H. Feinstein, Index of Relative Prices from Table 65 in *Statistical Tables of National Income, Expenditure and Output of the U.K. 1855-1965*, Cambridge University Press, Cambridge (1976).

1965-83. – Economic Trends 1948-81 Annual Supplement for 1983 – H.M. Stationary Office 1981-3 (July 1984).

1985-6. – National Institute Economic Review (August 1987, Table 7).

Appendix IV

CHARLES MUSGRAVE FORD (1887-1974)

I reproduce, by kind permission of the Editor of the *News of the World*, an article which appeared in July 1952 on Charles Ford's retirement from The Cunard White Star Line:

47 Years of Memories at Sea
by Commodore C. M. Ford, C.B.E.

I can't tell you that the salt spray was in my blood, for I didn't come from a sea-faring family. My father had a business in Manchester, and the gloom of his office just didn't appeal to me. At the age of sixteen I decided on the wide open spaces. My parents did all they could to stop me, but when they saw I was determined they sat back and declared that I would soon get over it. How wrong they were.

Looking back now after a lifetime in the Merchant Navy – with moments of excitement, anxiety, thrills and maybe some hardships – I can only say I'd like to do it all over again. Maybe I've been lucky to have become the Commodore of the Cunard White Star Line; I started at the bottom. As a green apprentice I sailed to Australia and then to Japan, where in the year 1905, in Tokyo Bay, I saw the Mikado review his Fleet after the Russo-Japanese war. Better this, I thought, than a stuffy office and a half-day on Saturdays.

The year 1911 saw me the proud possessor of a Master's Certificate and the year 1912 brought a highlight, for then I began my long association with the Cunard White Star, and the climb to join their band of captains.

But first came the 1914 war, and a quick transfer to the battleship Jupiter. Getting supplies through to our Russian allies was our job. I'm not likely to forget those days up in the White Sea. I've never known anything tougher. With the temperature 26 degrees below, twenty to thirty ships, carrying arms and equipment were trapped in the ice round Archangel Bar and we had to get them out. We managed it somehow. I was sent off with three blue-jackets to man a land observation post on top of a hill at Alexandrovsk, where for a fortnight or so a tent was our only shelter. We were all right as long as we remained frozen, but when we came back to the ship and thawed out our troubles started. For that bit of work I got my first medal: the Order of St Anne, 3rd Class, from the Tsar of Russia.

Typical of the Service, I went from the White Sea to the Red – the coldest to the hottest – and it wasn't long before I got my first command – a Q boat (armed decoy ship) used to trap German submarines. Those were among my happiest days of the First World War – sailing round the Mediterranean looking for trouble. One beautiful morning we had an hour's private battle with a U-boat which was glad to break off the battle and put into Beirut. When Lord Allenby's troops marched in they found the sub abandoned, and my crew and I got £400 (£11,500) prize money.

With joyful acclaim the war ended, and back I went to Cunard for those carefree days when the world went gay. Trips round the world were really something then. I went round the globe three times in the *Franconia*, still a young man, enjoying the world, my work, and the great freedom which the sea gives. Next came the Atlantic run, and the years when war loomed once more, until it crashed upon us in 1939 while I was at sea in my first Cunard command – the *Antonia*. We were a week ahead of the *Athenia*, one of the first victims of the war, torpedoed with hundreds of women and children aboard on their way to Canada. I got safely into Montreal, where our ships again put on their war paint of grey.

October 1939, and I was given command of an armed yacht patrolling the Clyde defences. Captain of a similar craft was an old shipmate, Commodore Illingworth, whom I was later to follow as captain of the *Queen Elizabeth*.

In 1941 I was in S.S. *Erato* of Hull as commodore of a convoy. Outward to Gibraltar, the Admiralty radioed that 12 submarines were following my convoy – pretty tough for the $7\frac{1}{2}$-knot fellows. Three hours later the battle began. I saw four ships go down, and there was little one could do about it. Then, at midnight, the *Erato* got one in the engine-room. Seven minutes later she was under the sea. I was the last to leave – but not on account of any heroics. I fell down the coal bunker while groping my way to the boats. Not a very dignified thing for a commodore.

It was in April 1944, that my dreams came true: I walked on to the bridge of the *Queen Elizabeth*, master of the greatest ship in the world. How many times have I crossed the Atlantic? More than I care to remember. I had to admit that to His Majesty when he honoured me with the C.B.E. in 1946. Many thousands of British and American troops will remember the *Queens*. We carried 15,000 soldiers at a time, plus a crew of 900 and a staff of 275, in all weathers, and not once could the German Navy stop us. We were never escorted on the journey, relying on our speed and zig-zag course to get us through. Only once can I remember an underwater explosion which shook the ship. 'Are we torpedoed?' asked an officer. It crossed my mind that it was going to be difficult if we found ourselves with a football crowd in the water all at the same time.

It was an unforgettable moment when V-Day came, and we steamed into New York with the first returning American Division on board. The city went mad. All craft in the bay blew their whistles or sirens, and millions of hands waved from skyscrapers. I was a proud man when I was handed the American Legion of Merit.

As I write, a photograph on my desk reminds me of the one man who caused me to break a strict rule that no passenger must be allowed on the bridge of the *Queen Elizabeth*. You can guess who it was – Mr. Churchill. There was no keeping him off. We carried them all: royal dukes and duchesses, movie stars and politicians, prize-fighters and bishops; the great and the small from all walks of life. The *Queen Elizabeth* and the *Queen Mary* are not record-breaking ships. Speed alone was never the object. Our watchword was safety first, and safety always. We transported people in comfort and safety across the Atlantic as rapidly as conditions permitted. Strangely enough, my last home-coming in command of the *Queen Elizabeth* was my fastest and smoothest: we averaged more than 28 knots in a journey of four and a half days, which she might have known was to be our last together: she was always the perfect lady.

Appendix V

Dunkirk, May 1940

Neville Brown's account of the evacuation of the British Expeditionary Force.
(As printed in *The Townsman* of Wellesley, Massachusetts of 20 February 1941.)

On Thursday, May 30th 1940, a class of yachtsmen was assembled in Albemarle Street waiting for Captain Watts to begin his lecture on Navigation. He came in and told us that he had just received an appeal from the Admiral at London for volunteers, men who could handle small boats and that it was for a dangerous job. We were not told what the job was, but we all knew.

Captain Watts told us that he had to telephone the Admiral at 3.30 saying how many men would be going. I do not think many of us enjoyed that half hour. Some decided that as they had been accepted for the Navy and were shortly to go to Hove, they were not called upon to volunteer for this job. Several older men like myself with wives and businesses talked it over. We did not want to go, but we could find no answer to two points:

(1) Nothing but small boats would get the B.E.F. off;

(2) We knew how to handle small boats and there were not enough people in the country who did when it was a matter of getting off up to half a million men in a few days.

At 3.30 most of us got into taxis and set off for the P.L.A. offices. London looked very lovely that afternoon.

At the P.L.A. offices we were asked to give the names of our next of kin and the Admiral came in and told us what we were wanted for and that it was a job for stout hearts as we should be under shell fire. We didn't like the prospect.

We were told to reassemble at 6 p.m. I went back to my office in Berners Street, telephoned my wife in Birmingham, sent my Manager out to buy a woollen shirt, a small bottle of brandy and some chocolate, whilst I had a good meal.

Back at the P.L.A. offices we were put into Motor Coaches and sent off to Tilbury. There seemed a certain unreality about the bustle of Whitechapel Road considering what was going on not so far away. I had never been through Dockland before and was appalled at the closely packed houses wedged in between the Docks. Magnificent ships towered over the squalid streets in which hundreds of children were playing. What would happen when the docks were bombed? One put the thought out of one's mind.

At Tilbury we had to 'sign on' as Merchant Seamen. We were told that we had to sign on for a month. We protested: we had been asked to volunteer for two days and we explained that we had businesses and jobs and could not be away for up to a month. No shorter engagement existed and we were faced with crying off or signing on for a month. We signed, but a couple of lawyers walked through the barrier on to the quay pretending that they had signed.

On the quay we were given tin hats and put into ships' lifeboats taken from ships which happened to be in the Port of London. We were put four men to a boat, it having been decided by brief questioning who was 'charge hand', who was 'engine room hand' and who was 'deck hand'. The only practical difference was whether we eventually received a Money Order for £3, £2 10s., or £2. I found myself in a boat with an adventurous ship's officer in civilian dress who had absented himself from his ship in London Docks, a stockbroker whose telephone message to his wife had been to cancel a bridge party and an ex-submarine rating

84. Members of the British Expeditionary Force waiting to be rescued from the beaches of Dunkirk. Many of them re-entered France through Normandy four years later in triumph.

85. Some of those who were not rescued on their way to five years in German prisoner-of-war camps.

retired eight years previously. We were all in poor physical condition, the ship's officer because he had been enjoying his time in port in the conventional way, the stockbroker and I because we were 'office soft' and the ex-submarine rating because of age, bad teeth and tinned food.

The ships' boats were marshalled in lines of about eight or ten and to such lines were made fast to a Tug. By this time it was dark and we set off down the river. The boats sheered about wildly and about 2 a.m. there was some excitement when 'Johnny the Greek' let out piercing yells, 'Help, help, we're sinking'. Johnny the Greek was a curious person. We had noticed him first at the P.L.A. offices. He had a goatee beard, an eye glass and an exquisite levantine manner which didn't quite go with his broad Canadian accent. Who or what he was I do not know except that he was on the Stock Exchange. When he appeared at the Motor Coach he had a yachting cap, a beautifully cut yachting coat lined with scarlet serge, sea boots, field glasses and two enormous suit cases. The rest of us were in office clothes.

At 2.30 a.m. we anchored and the boat crews tried to get a little sleep but it was bitterly cold and I don't think anyone succeeded. At dawn we started off again and at 7.30 reached Southend. Johnny the Greek, quite unconscious of the fool he had made of himself the night before, annoyed us all with transatlantic witticisms and loud demands for 'corfee'. He had never been told that on such expeditions, there is no conversation before breakfast. At Southend, orange boxes full of bread, tinned beef, tinned milk and sardines were handed down to the boats from the pier. Everyone was complaining of the cold. Thin summer suits were feeling very thin. Johnny the Greek opened his enormous suitcases: they were full of pair after pair of thick woollen vests and long woollen pants which he handed to anyone who asked for them. We forgave him everything.

We reached Ramsgate at about 2 p.m. There we were split up into smaller units. Instead of 16 to 20 boats to a tug we were put in two rows of three to a tug or drifter. A Naval Petty Officer on a tug handed out life belts: there were not enough to go around. I happened to be face to face with Johnny the Greek when he pushed forward and grabbed one: the expression on his face was not pleasant. The P.O. finding that we had not enough belts, took off his own and handed it to the nearest man. No one said any more about not having a life belt.

We set off for Dunkirk at about 3 p.m. There was a fair southerly breeze which set up a short sea against the ebb. We had had to bail our ship's boat about every half hour or so. Now we had to bail more or less continuously. That, combined with the short motion of the boat, was very tiring. The tow ropes kept parting and when getting picked up after one such break, the drifter hit us and carried away our tiller. We got very wet.

Our group of boats was under the command of a Naval sub-lieutenant and a midshipman. The sub-lieutenant was a foolish and aggressive lad. The midshipman, aged I suppose, about 14 or 15, jumped from boat to boat whilst we were being towed rather too fast through that short sea, a feat requiring uncommon skill and nerve. He arrived in our boat and found we were bailing all the time. He took off his belt and got down into the bilge to give us a hand. Then he told us the plan of action, said he was off *Hood* and thought this expedition was for him the experience of a lifetime, but that us, volunteers, well, we just took the biscuit. The effect on us was remarkable. We, grown men, feeling wet and cold and miserable had new heart and energy put into us by the praise and encouragement of this child wearing the King's uniform. I do not know the child's name: I wish I did for I should like to recognise it in the Honours List 20 years hence.[1]

The Channel was like Oxford Street, one incessant stream of traffic. Destroyer after Destroyer, British and French, Cross-Channel Boats, Pleasure Steamers, Motor Launches, Fishing Boats, all with their decks crammed with curiously lethargic soldiers. We wanted to cheer: they did not. Then there were the Hospital Ships, brilliantly white with large red crosses on their sides and not a soul on deck, though one saw the occasional nurse through a gangway. There was a curious calm and beauty about these ships but one did not like to think of what was below deck. One could see them from miles away. So apparently could the German Bombers. They got two.

The first thing we saw of the French coast was enormous columns of black smoke – miles of them up and down channel as far as one could see. As we drew nearer, we could see the whole coast blazing.

We had got there too early; we were not supposed to arrive till 10 p.m. when it would have been dark. Actually, our flotilla of about a dozen tugs or drifters each with its strings of ships' boats in tow arrived at 8 p.m. in good light. Then we saw curious black puffs in the sky high over Dunkirk. Every Londoner now knows what they are: then, we did not know it was an A.A. barrage, till high over the top of it we saw a swarm of German Bombers. They were coming for us. We put on our tin hats and crouched in the bilge wondering what would happen. There must have been about 40 or 50 of them. Then, suddenly, we saw about a dozen Spitfires coming up from behind us at an amazing pace. Thanking God and the R.A.F. we peeped up and saw what has since come to be known as a 'dog fight'. One would not have described it as that. It looked more like wolves after sheep. The Spitfires broke up the German formation and chased them round and round the skies. If they

86. Because of her draught, the vessel in the foreground was out too deep for the men to reach her. They had to be picked up by small boats and ferried out.

missed, they made a tight turn and came round and had another shot. A few German bombers got through and bombed our flotilla. At times we couldn't see the ships for huge columns of water. I thought half our lot must be sunk and a few seconds later was surprised to realise that a broken steam pipe on one of the drifters was the only damage. We got a bomb, we said, within 100 yards of us, but I think it was more like 500. A huge column of water towered up beside us and the shock transmitted through the water seemed as if it would knock the bottom out of our boat. The ex-submarine rating started wiping the seats with a rag saying that we must have the boat ship-shape for the boys to come aboard. The rest of us did some bailing and soon we all felt better. We had the satisfaction of seeing a

Spitfire go after the German who had bombed us and shoot him down. He fell, at first like a playing card, and then a stone.

As we got near the harbour, it was interesting to check the accuracy of the News Bulletins. We did not know whether we were being lied to or not. We had been told that a cruiser, three destroyers and two transports had been lost. There they were, either alongside the jetty or sticking up out of the water.

We went past the harbour entrance to the beaches farther up Channel. Our drifter cast us off, remaining herself, in relatively deeper water about half a mile from the shore, whilst we were to be towed in to the beach by a motor boat in charge of the aggressive sub-lieutenant. He made a complete mess of things, doing a lot of shouting and getting a tow rope foul of his propeller. We left him and rowed towards the beach. Our plan had been to have two men on the oars, one to pull in the troops and one to look after the tow rope when the motor boat came to tow us back. We soon found that two dead-beat men could not keep head on to the surf a ship's boat designed to carry 54 persons, and all four of us took an oar. Some of the other crews did not find out in time and several boats broached to and capsized on the beach.

We could not find any troops and found that we were going aground several hundred yards from the shore. We rowed back to the drifter for fresh orders. A Glasgow slum boy dressed as a naval rating appeared from nowhere and came with us to another point higher up the beach. The four of us kept the boat head-on, getting in as close as we could, whilst he yelled at the troops on the beach in unceasing and violent Clydebank. Nine of them waded out, up to their necks in water, and he hauled them aboard. Then we found their weight was putting us aground too far out for men to wade. We rowed back to the drifter, having some trouble with the tide, and put them on board. It was still very dark but the drifter had orders to be out before dawn and the skipper was anxious to be off. Half our boats had not returned but we had picked up a number of boats which did not belong to us. We cruised up and down for an hour, the naval officer in charge not giving the order to sail till he was satisfied he could get no further boats in. Overhead was a German plane. Whenever we moved, he machine gunned us as our wake showed up in the intensely phosphorescent water. His bullets rattled on the deck-house and our gunner and a nearby destroyer blazed at him when his gun flashed. If the Germans had had any number of men trained in night flying and had had the chance to learn about flares from the R.A.F., no ship should have been able to live. The only flares were those dropped by the R.A.F. outside the town where they were co-operating with the Allied rear-guard.

At that time, most of us had not even been through an air raid and the roar of that blazing seaside front, the scream of the German shells and the planes overhead, were very shaking.

> *And gentlemen in England now a-bed*
> *Shall think themselves accursed they were not here*

Those are after-dinner sentiments of ten years later.

At about 3 a.m. we started nosing our way down the channel. At about 3.30 there was a terrific crash and the drifter heeled over on her starboard beam. She did not sink, but stayed at about 60 degrees having run on to a submerged wreck. Luckily we had two large boats in tow. Some of us got off in one on to a passing coaster and others on to a destroyer whose Commander ran the stem of his ship alongside the drifter chancing whatever obstruction it was on which she was impaled.

I got on to the coaster. Her hold was full of silent, sodden troops. Her commander was R.N.V.R., a yachtsman I should think, who had probably never before navigated anything bigger than a motor boat. Her crew were all sorts but they had got 300-400 of the B.E.F. aboard.

At dawn we saw a tug and two Thames barges anchored just clear of the channel.

Dis. 1.

CERTIFICATE OF DISCHARGE

FOR A SEAMAN DISCHARGED BEFORE A SUPERINTENDENT OR A CONSULAR OFFICER.

ISSUED BY THE
BOARD OF TRADE.   No. **39**

Name of Ship and Official Number, Port of Registry and Gross Tonnage.	Horse Power.	Description of Voyage or Employment.
H.M.S. Pembroke IV		J. 124.

Name of Seaman.	Year of Birth.	Place of Birth.
J. Neville Brown	36	Manchester

Rank or Rating.	No. of R.N.R. Commission or Corpl.	No. of Cert. (if any).
Deck Hand.		

Date of Engagement.	Place of Engagement	Copy of Report of Character.*	
		For Ability	For General Conduct
30. 5. 40	Tilbury	VERY B 105 GOOD	VERY B 105 GOOD
Date of Discharge.	Place of Discharge.		
2. 6. 40.	Dock St London		

I certify that the above particulars are correct and that the above named Seaman was discharged accordingly.

Dated this .... day of 19

AUTHENTICATED BY

sd/ .... Coates ....

.... J. B. James ....
Signature of Superintendent or Consular Officer

* If the Seaman does not require a Certificate of his character, enter " Endorsement not required " in the space provided for the copy of the Report.

Signature of Seaman .... J. Neville Brown ....

NOTE.—Any person who forges or fraudulently alters any Certificate or Report, or copy of a Report, or who makes use of any Certificate or Report, or copy of a Report, which is forged or altered or does not belong to him, shall for each such offence be deemed guilty of a misdemeanour, and may be fined or imprisoned.

N.B.—Should this Certificate come into the possession of any person to whom it does not belong, it should be handed to the Superintendent of the nearest Mercantile Marine Office, or be transmitted to the Registrar-General of Shipping and Seamen, Tower Hill, London, E.C.3.

87. Certificate of Discharge, June 1940.

Suddenly, there was a flash and flame, seeming to rise from the middle of one of the barges, spread from stem to stern in a second. In 30 seconds the whole group was a mass of flame. We looked for a plane but there was none. It must have been a magnetic mine which our plane of the night before had been laying. In the distance we saw another larger ship blazing. As it got light, we came to a bend in the channel and I saw we were not following it but were holding our course straight on to the banks. I watched for about a minute and then started up the ladder to the bridge. I told the skipper he was going on to the banks, that I knew the channel, having come up it in daylight the night before. He fumbled with his charts and gazed at me not taking in what I was saying. I repeated it and got him to put the wheel over. A few seconds later we touched, but her head was back to the channel and we scraped clear into it. The ship's officer from my boat was then on the bridge too, having seen what I had seen. He took the wheel for the next half hour much to the consternation of one of the sailors who kept saying to every officer, 'There's a civilian at the wheel, Sir'. I took him aside and told him it was a ship's officer and unblushingly added that Dunkirk was one of his regular ports and he knew it like his own street. We then made ourselves scarce, but not before the R.N.V.R. captain had told me that he had not been in his bunk for four days and nights and did not know what he was doing. The Admiralty had told him to go over a bank, but it was miles farther down the channel. Far from resenting our interference, he was extraordinarily generous about it.

All the way back to Ramsgate there were German planes about, but the R.A.F. plus the destroyers, simply spitting fire, gave them so much to think about that they left us alone. I have never believed in invasion after seeing British Destroyers plus the R.A.F. in action.

The troops on board were dead with fatigue. They were not defeated men, but they were resentful; resentful that they had been sent to face the Germans armed only with their rifles and a Bren or Lewis gun here and there. The Germans, they said, had every conceivable weapon which they used with great skill. They had tommy guns, mortars of all sorts and sizes and the same in field guns. The Germans would arrive, and have a systematic barrage going almost at once. The B.E.F. had been bombed from dawn to dusk, day after day, but they had never been bombed out of a position though they had been shelled out. They never saw a British plane till they got to Dunkirk.

It was then that I realised that this war would be won or lost in the factories. Everywhere seemed stiff with brave, under-armed men.

Theoretically, one was supposed to sign off at the same port as that at which one had signed on. I had no intention of wasting a day going to Tilbury, so half fearing that I might be arrested as a deserter, I wrote from Birmingham where I had returned to my job. By return I got a letter saying that I could sign off at my local Post Office. It happened to be a suburban Newsagents, I hardly knew where, but I went round at once. They had just received a Money Order for me and a form for me to sign. That the Admiralty improvises with such brilliant attention to detail, possibly explains how they performed the miracle of getting off 325,000 men from one jetty and a beach under the nose of the German Army and Air Force.

NOTES TO CHAPTERS

Introduction

1. Thompson, Dr. David M., *Nonconformity in the Nineteenth Century*, Routledge & Kegan Paul Ltd. (1972) (abridged). We owe to another Dr. David Thompson, a former Master of Sidney Sussex College, an outstanding analysis of Keynes' influence on our times in his *Europe since Napoleon*, Longmans (1957).

Chapter 1 John Everard

1. Ford, David Everard, *Autobiography*, ms., p. 20. In Will of Peter Duthoit's dated 1818, he left legacies amounting to £14,590 (£484,000) but, unfortunately, he later went bankrupt.
2. Ibid., p. 17.
3. Ibid., p. 20.
4. Ibid., p. 17.
5. Mrs. D. was Mrs. Duthoit, Mary's youngest sister, Sarah.
6. Ford, David Everard, *Autobiography*, ms., p. 114.
7. Hale, William, *Dangerous Tendency of the London Female Penitentiary*, privately printed Address (1809).

Chapter 2 David Ford

1. Ford, David Everard, *Autobiography*, ms., p. 8. Ford is a common place name and it is probable that our Fords originated in the village of Ford on the river Arun about ten miles west of Broadwater (Worthing).
2. Ibid., p. 8.
3. Ibid., p. 8.
4. The birth of an illegitimate child to David Ford's widowed mother.
5. Ford, David Everard, *Autobiography*, ms., p. 11.
6. Ibid., p. 11.
7. Ibid., p. 13.
8. At the back of Vol. I of David Ford's diary he wrote a list of King's Head Society students at their Homerton Academy.
9. Simms, T. H., *Official History of Homerton College 1695-1978*, Trustees of Homerton College (1979).
10. A calf-bound collection of argumentative pamphlets starting with *A report presented to the King's Head Society to inquire into the circumstances connected with the resignation of a Probationary Student at Homerton Academy 1813*, with David Ford's handwritten notes added to a later dispute. This collection has been lodged with Homerton College, Cambridge.
11. James, Robert Rhodes, *Albert, Prince Consort*, Hamish Hamilton (1983).
12. Simms, T. H., *Official History of Homerton College 1695-1978*.
13. Ford, David Everard, *Autobiography*, ms., p. 14.
14. Ibid.
15. Parker, Sir William B., *History of Long Melford* (1873).
16. *Cary's Great Roads*, 10th edn. (1826), published by Command of His Majesty's Postmaster-General. This is a combination of a railway timetable and an A.A. book for the stage-coach network at its zenith, immediately before the railways took over.
17. Ford, David Everard, *Autobiography*, ms., p. 7.
18. 'Vain-Hope' is a ferryman in the *Pilgrim's Progress* (end of Part I) who ferried an unworthy character across the river who was only to be refused entry to the Celestial City.

Chapter 3 Haydons and Downs

1. Letter to Lady Langdon-Brown, 8 June 1914.
2. Ford, David Everard, Diary (Vol. 5), 13 April 1853.

Chapter 4 David Everard Ford – Long Melford
1. *National Dictionary of Biography* (vol. XIX), edn. (1889).
2. Ford, David Everard, *Autobiography*, ms., p. 48.
3. Ibid., p. 46.
4. Ibid., p. 46.
5. Inflation had amounted to about 38 per cent. since 1793. A golden guinea should have been worth 29 shillings in 1816; therefore, allowing for dealers' profits, D.E.F.'s recollection was correct.
6. Ford, David Everard, *Autobiography*, ms., p. 70.
7. The Southwold Chapel was built in 1748 and is still active.
8. Ford, David Everard, *Autobiography*, ms., p. 48.

Chapter 5 David Everard Ford – Lymington
1. This was a risk he ran. Even as late as 1867, on the eve of Gladstone's reforms, one, James Brighton Grant, a Dissenter and owner of the Deben Brewery, Kettleburgh, Suffolk, was imprisoned and bankrupted for refusing to pay Church Rates.
2. The London-Southampton line.
3. *Essays on John Maynard Keynes*, Milo Keynes, Cambridge University Press, 1975, p. 3.
4. Absorbed by Lloyds Bank plc.

Chapter 6 David Everard Ford – Manchester
1. *Financial Times*, Stockport Supplement (1983).
2. In the next 10 years, that is during the active years of David Everard Ford's ministry, the population was to increase by 116,000 to 358,000.
3. Love & Barton, *Manchester as it Is* (1839).
4. The Agnews became well-known as art dealers in Manchester and moved to London and are now an internationally famous firm.
5. 'Nowhere out of the metropolis is solid capital supposed to be so large as in Manchester. She is wont to say of her rival sister upon the Mersey, that she is able to buy up the whole town of Liverpool, and keep it on hand'. *Manchester Guardian*, 27 August (1838).

Chapter 7 David Everard Ford – Success
1. In David Everard Ford's diary, an entry for 28 January 1851 reads, 'My Mary leaves Taunton for Torpoint tomorrow'. And in the Census of 31 March 1851, she is shown as a visitor at her aunt's house in Torpoint (*see* page 13).
2. Keynes, Florence Ada, *Gathering up the Threads*, Heffer (1950).
3. Ada had not been without her conquests in that quarter. We have a Valentine, dated 25 April 1854, reading 'Fare thee well my dear Ada, a long farewell. Ever in all sincerity and affection. John Lee'. (He was a Lee of the Tootal Broadhurst Lee family.)

Chapter 9 David Everard Ford – Supply Preacher
1. *Wheeler's Manchester Chronicle*, 29 May (1830).
2. She was 42 when she married A. A. Dixey (who had previously married two sisters, having to marry the second in Switzerland by reason of the English ban on the marriage to a deceased wife's sister). He died in 1890, and she then 68 married A. Davis and lived to be eighty-seven.

Chapter 10 John Brown – Manchester
1. 'The arrival in 1850 of so erudite, dynamic and eloquent a personality in the dull and introverted world of Anglo-Jewry created something of a sensation. Here was a man of western scholarship, fluent oratory and rabbinical *semikhah* of undoubted authenticity'. – Bill Williams, *The Making of Manchester Jewry*, p. 186.

Chapter 11 John Brown – Bedford
1. Held by the County Record Office, Bedford.
2. The following list includes not only the tours described in the *Recollections* but also those in a list drawn

up by Mrs. Brown of their foreign holidays. Evidently Mr. Thomas Cook and the Swiss hoteliers were collaborating closely by 1870:
1868 The Rhine and Italy; 1869 Switzerland; 1870 Germany; 1871 Germany; 1874/6/7/80/3/6 Switzerland; 1895 Egypt and Palestine; 1896 Hellenic Cruise; 1908 The Nile; 1909 Mediterranean.
3. Keynes, Florence Ada, *Gathering up the Threads*, Heffer (1955).
4.The 1986 price for such land in Jersey was about £2,500 per vergee, or £5,600 per acre. (E. F. Weston, St Brelade, Jersey.)

Chapter 13 John Brown – The American Connection
1. *Acts of the Apostles*, Chap. XVII, v. 21.
2. It was a philosophy most markedly passed down to his son, Walter Langdon and his grandson, Maynard Keynes.

Chapter 15 Florence Ada Keynes
1. Keynes, Florence Ada, *By-Ways of Cambridge History*, Cambridge University Press (1947).
2. In 1882 new Statutes were passed which gave general permission to Fellows of Colleges to retain their Fellowship after marriage. But they were passed just too late to allow Neville Keynes to retain his Fellowship at Pembroke. It had been the convention for letters of resignation to be wrapped round a piece of wedding cake.
3. Raverat, Gwen, *Period Piece*, Faber & Faber (1951).
4. Keynes, Milo, *Essays on John Maynard Keynes*, edited by Milo Keynes, Cambridge University Press (1975).
5. It was not till 1875 that the Married Women's Property Act came into force and not till 1919 that women got the vote under the Sex Disqualification (Removal) Act.
6. The first woman to become a Mayor was Elizabeth Garrett Anderson in 1908, but that was for Aldeburgh, Suffolk.
7. The papers of the National Council of Women regarding the formation of the Women's Police Force are lodged with the Police Federation at Surbiton, Surrey.

Chapter 16 Dr. Alice Evangeline Brown
1. Scott, Jean M., *Women and the G.M.C.*, British Medical Journal, Vol. 289 (December 1984).
2. Recorded in his Diary – 24 March 1797.

Chapter 17 The Lloyds
1. Lloyd, A. H., *The Early History of Christ's College*, Cambridge University Press (1934).
2. Preserved in the Manuscript Reading Room (Ph.D.261) at the University Library, Cambridge.

Chapter 18 Sir Walter Langdon-Brown
1. Langdon Brown did not hyphenate his name till 1935.
2. Langdon-Brown, Sir Walter, *Thus we are Men*, Kegan Paul (1938).
3. It was the subject of his Cavendish Lecture in 1937 and is reprinted in his *Thus we are Men* (1938).

Chapter 19 John Harold Brown
1. Grant, Roderick, *The Great Canal*, Gordon & Cremonesi (1978).

Chapter 20 Everard Kenneth Brown
1. Keynes, John Maynard, *Economic Consequences of the Peace*, Macmillan (1919).
2. A specimen of one of their 1921 models is on exhibition at the Montagu Museum of Old Cars at Beaulieu.
3. Kenneth Brown frequently employed Sir Patrick Hastings and got to know him well. Patrick Hastings told him that when he was a young man, struggling at the Bar, he used to walk from his lodgings to the Law Courts, but then became worried because he thought the cost of shoe leather would exceed his bus fare.

4. The case came before K.B. Division 9 February 1926. *The Times Law Reports*, Vol. xlii, 26 March 1926. The Appeal was dismissed by the Court of Appeal (Bankes, Scrutton and Atkin, L.JJ.) 7 June 1926. *The Times Law Reports*, Vol. xlii, 2 July 1926.

5. Kenneth Brown Baker Baker is now the major City firm of Turner Kenneth Brown with 38 partners and over 250 staff and a substantial company and commercial practice. The ghost of Mercl has long been laid.

6. 'It is no part of an advocate's duty to feel sympathy for his client, indeed, such a feeling is rather a disadvantage than otherwise'. Hastings, Sir Patrick, *Cases in Court*, Heinemann (1949).

7. *The Times Law Reports*, of 5, 6 and 7 November 1936.

8. When Kenneth first began to brief Valentine Holmes and they were working together on some papers, Kenneth quoted from the Bible. Holmes capped his quotation and Kenneth said, 'I see you too were well brought-up'. Valentine Holmes replied, 'Carr's Lane, Birmingham'. This is one of the most celebrated Congregational chapels, established in 1784, with many great men to its credit.

9. Hastings, Sir Patrick, *Cases in Court*, Heinemann (1949).

10. Charmey, John, *Duff Cooper*, Weidenfeld & Nicolson (1986), p. 141.

11. The most notable items were listed in the Rylands Library Bulletin of March 1959.

12. 30 January and 6 February 1938.

Chapter 21 John Maynard Keynes

1. Keynes, Milo, *Essays on John Maynard Keynes*, Cambridge University Press (1975) and *Lydia Lopokova*, Weidenfeld and Nicolson (1983).

2. The weekly magazine *Punch* was then seen by most literate members of the public. It was on every railway bookstall, in every dentist's waiting room and in every upper-middle-class house.

3. BX Plastics Ltd., was also to provide Margaret Roberts (Mrs. Thatcher) with her first job as a junior chemist. Wilfrid Dimsdale told me that one of the directors had to carpet her and tell her it would be well if she would give more time to chemistry and less to politics.

4. Harrod, R. F., *Life of John Maynard Keynes*, Macmillan (1951).

5. Keynes, John Maynard, *The General Theory of Employment, Interest and Money*, Macmillan (1936).

6. Dr. Neville Keynes kept a well-stocked cellar at Harvey Road. David Hill remembers an occasion when he saw it unlocked and an expert engaged in re-corking all wines over a certain age.

7. Robinson, A. G., *The Economic Journal*, vol. LVII, No. 225 (March 1947).

8. Harrod, R. F., *John R. F. Maynard Keynes*, Macmillan (1951) p. 602.

9. *Collected Writings, John Maynard Keynes*, vol. XXIV, *Royal Economic Society* (1979). Harrod also quotes from this letter, but his selection is different and he does not indicate where he cut (p. 618, *Life of John Maynard Keynes*).

10. Dipping for small presents embedded in a bran tub was a regular feature of the Christmas party Maynard and Lydia gave for their farm workers at Tilton.

Chapter 22 Margaret Neville Hill

1. Wilson, Francesca M., *Rebel Daughter of a Country House – The Life of Eglantyne Jebb – Founder of the Save the Children Fund*, George Allen & Unwin Ltd. (1967).

2. Hill, Margaret N., *An Approach to Old Age and its Problems*, Oliver & Boyd Ltd. (1961).

Chapter 23 Sir Geoffrey Langdon Keynes

1. Keynes, Sir Geoffrey, *The Gates of Memory*, Clarendon Press, Oxford (1981).

2. Michael Harmer's father was also an F.R.C.S., and was a Bedfordian, and a friend of my father's.

Chapter 24 John Neville Brown

1. A good example of writing of oneself in the third person is to be found in *Lord Hervey's Memoirs of the Reign of George II*, Batsford (1952).

2. 'One of the Nazi skills was to play upon British guilt feelings about the terms imposed upon Germany by the 1919 Peace Treaty at Versailles, for which Maynard Keynes bore considerable responsibility'. James, Robert Rhodes, *Anthony Eden*, Weidenfeld & Nicolson (1986), p. 119.

3. Babbington-Smith, Constance, *Evidence in Camera*, Chatto & Windus (1958).

4. Jones, Prof. R. V., *Most Secret War*, Hamish Hamilton (1978).
5. A remark of Lord Robens, a Lancashire Trade Union Leader, who became Chairman of the National Coal Board.
6. Kee, Robert, *Ireland*, Weidenfeld & Nicolson (1980).
7. Smith, D. J., *Action Stations 7*, Patrick Stephens (1983).

Chapter 25 Helen Easdale Dimsdale
1. I use the spelling used by the Dimsdales. The Empress was of Prussian birth.
2. Katharine boasted about the vaccinations in her correspondence with Voltaire.

Appendix V – Dunkirk
1. He was of H.M.S. *Hood* which was lost wih all hands in action with the German battleship *Bismarck* on 24 May 1941.

Index

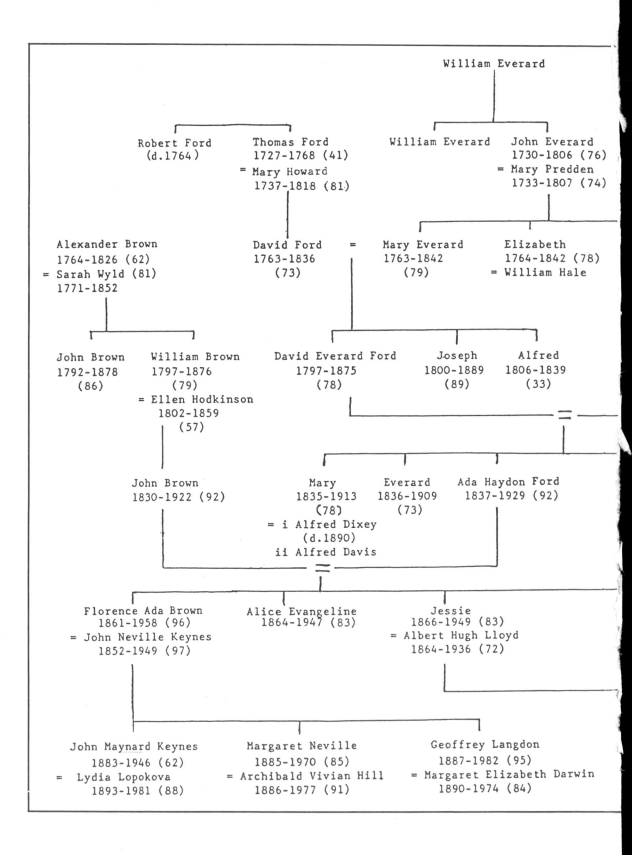